# STAY

## SURVIVAL SKILLS YOU NEED

# ALIVE!

FROM THE AUTHOR OF *BUILD THE PERFECT SURVIVAL KIT*

## John D. McCann

Published by

Krause Publications, a division of F+W, A Content + eCommerce Company
700 East State Street · Iola, WI 54990-0001
715-445-2214 · 888-457-2873
www.krausebooks.com

To order books or other products call toll-free 1-800-258-0929
or visit us online at www.krausebooks.com

ISBN-13: 978-1-4402-1830-9
ISBN-10: 1-4402-1830-7

Cover Design by Paul Birling
Designed by Paul Birling
Edited by Corrina Peterson

Printed in USA

# Dedication

I dedicate this book to my beautiful wife Denise, who is not only my best friend and business partner, but is the only woman I have known that will live in the wilderness with me for a week with little equipment and supplies. She is well skilled in the ways of survival and, as a former home economics teacher in Switzerland, not only knows how to survive in the wilderness, but in an urban environment as well. She is skilled at gardening, preserving food and knitting, and makes the best bread I have ever had. She is a jewel and I would prefer her as a companion in a survival situation over many men!

# About the Author

**J**ohn D. McCann has spent years learning and teaching survival skills, and is the author of the bestselling book, *Build the Perfect Survival Kit,* the only book in publication which handles the subject of survival kits exclusively. He is the founder of Survival Resources, a specialized firm offering custom survival kits that John designs and builds; survival kit components, so you can build your own kits; and survival skills courses. Not only does John teach at his own school, he is often a guest instructor at events like Dirttime in California and the Pathfinder Gathering in Ohio.

John has been featured in articles in the *New York Times* and other publications, and appeared on national television as a guest on the Martha Stewart Show, demonstrating how to make a survival kit. He has written articles for various magazines, including *Field & Stream, Wilderness Way* magazine (where he has been featured on the cover), and Self Reliance Illustrated.

John considers himself a professional student of survival and dislikes the term "expert." He continues in his endeavors to learn about survival and offer products and training that could help save your life. He truly believes that a survival kit and proper training can make the difference in a survival situation. His motto has always been, "Be prepared to survive."

## Photo Credits

This book contains a lot of color photos. Most were taken by the author, unless he appears in the photo, and those were taken by his wife Denise McCann. However, there were some other photos used and those photos have been credited. If no credit appears below the photo, it was taken by the author or his wife.

## Graphics

All custom color graphics by Robert Lyttle.

## Notices

It should be understood that a survival situation can be dangerous, even fatal. Although every effort was made to provide accurate and useable information, the use of this information will not guarantee your survival. Even with the proper equipment and training, people have perished as a result of conditions or circumstances beyond their control. Neither the author nor publisher claims that the information provided here will guarantee your survival in a survival situation, nor do they assume any responsibility for the use or misuse of information contained in this book.

# Table of Contents

Dedication ..................................................3

About the Author ..........................................4

Photo Credits, Graphics & Notices ......................4

Acknowledgments..........................................6

Foreword by Dave Canterbury...........................7

Chapter 1: Introduction .................................8

Chapter 2: The Survivor Mentality.....................14

Chapter 3: The Indispensable Survival Kit.............22

Chapter 4: Knives & Tools for Survival ...............36

Chapter 5: Fire & Light - Survival Assets.............60

Chapter 6: Shelter & Protection from the Elements ....90

Chapter 7: Water Collection & Purification............116

Chapter 8: Signaling for Help .........................140

Chapter 9: Navigate Your Way Back.....................160

Chapter 10: Food to Sustain Energy....................196

Chapter 11: Wilderness Hazards & Safety ..............230

Chapter 12: Final Thoughts & Resources................248

# Acknowledgments

I would first like to acknowledge my father, William E. McCann, who taught me as a child the ways of the wilderness. As a Gold Palm Eagle Scout, he was not only my true mentor, but taught me to appreciate the outdoors. When I was a child we couldn't afford fancy vacations, so we always went camping in the Catskills or the Adirondacks. My father was a true outdoorsman in every manner of the word. He hunted, fished and could survive in the woods with what appeared to be little effort. A tool & die maker by trade, at home he was an avid gardener, food preserver and meat raiser (we always had rabbits and chickens), and an all around carpenter, plumber, electrician and mechanic. He always taught me to be self sufficient and own the skills. He used to say, "Skills will get you through the hard times." I miss him much.

Next, I would like to acknowledge Alan Halcon, who is not only a good friend but also the record holder for the fastest coal with a hand drill – two seconds. Since I started this book, he has been available to help with photos, build shelters, make suggestions and, as a trained "Combat Lifesaver," was very helpful in the medical portion of the chapter on Wilderness Hazards and Safety. We have spent a lot of time in the bush together and he is like a brother. I cherish his friendship.

Robert Lyttle deserves credit for the outstanding job he did on all the graphics and diagrams he made for this book. Not only is he a friend and great at graphics, but he has the ability to understand what I want (when most don't). I truly believe he can look into my mind and see what I want. I thank him for his ability, talent and friendship.

I thank Christopher Nyerges and Dude McLean for their friendship and their expertise. They are true friends and are always available to discuss my thoughts in regard to survival. Not only does Christopher teach and write about survival and self reliance, but he truly lives it in both his philosophy and everyday life, and has since the 1970s. I have much respect for him.

A quick thanks goes out to Steve and Susan Gregersen for photos contributed and Susan's knowledge in regard to layering clothing for survival.

Last, but certainly not least, I would like acknowledge my good friend Roy Peters, who both introduced me to and built my first Native American flute. He was always there with words of wisdom, praise and manual labor when we were building the field camp for our school. His friendship means much and I hold him in high regard.

# Foreword

*Stay Alive! Survival Skills You Need* is a breakthrough in common sense survivability for the person looking to gain basic knowledge of what to do, what to carry and what to know if a wilderness emergency situation arises. This book will give any person, whether new to the outdoors or more experienced, the base knowledge needed to get out of a bad situation and effect rescue through either self rescue techniques or a search and rescue scenario.

Many books on the market today are complicated and preach the need to own vast amounts of primitive skills, assuming that we are not intelligent enough to bring a proper kit with us when we recreate in the wild. John's book does a great job of cutting through the crap and giving the necessary information on both a minimal kit and using it to survive.

I knew after reading John's first book, *Build the Perfect Survival Kit,* that he actually gets it! I have always believed that if people understand basic concepts and the multiple uses of a few basic items they can greatly affect the outcome of a bad situation. This book does a great job of explaining, in simple, understandable terms, the basic skills necessary and simple items that can be carried in a small package to make a bad situation a whole lot better!

This book along with *Build the Perfect Survival Kit* make a great base library of knowledge that can be used by anyone, of any experience level, to understand the basics of what it takes to Smooth It! - Not Rough It! if lost or stranded for a few days in the wilderness.

Lastly, I will say that too many survival books are simply cut and paste toilet paper, taken from age-old military manuals that catered to soldiers, that emphasize the use of issue-type items for emergency use. *Stay Alive! Survival Skills You Need* is packed with information on common everyday items that civilians have access to and can use to build a great kit, and how to use those items to keep them alive!

Dave Canterbury

Dave Canterbury is the Co-Host of "Dual Survival" on
the Discovery Channel, the owner of the Pathfinder School, and
co-owner of Self Reliance Illustrated Magazine.

*Chapter 1*

# Introduction

There are many good survival books out there, so why write another? I have found that although many provide good information on survival, not all actually explain the basics in depth. They assume that the basics are already known, when often they are not. Many people are new at this and need to learn the basics. I also have found that many of these books are what I call "why to" books. In other words, they tell you why to do something, but don't always tell you how to do it. So instead of providing you with just "why to" information, I have tried to explain the "how to" in regard to using a survival kit to survive.

There are various examples, but the following two illustrate my point. Many survival books teach that a shelter is important in a survival situation and tell you why. However, not all books tell you how to make a shelter. I have read many times that a signal mirror is the most underrated piece of survival gear, and why that is so, but never how to use it effectively. In this book, I make a concerted effort to explain how to use the equipment you choose for your survival kit. Hopefully, I have been successful in that endeavor.

I have talked to various experienced survival practitioners who voice the opinion that if you don't have the experience with survival techniques, then you shouldn't be out there. I totally disagree with this position. There are many people involved in outdoor activities who have never taken the time to become survival aficionados or experts. They want to enjoy outdoor activities without making it their life. Of course these people need to learn the basics of how to survive. It is therefore my desire that this book will help provide that information.

## What it's not, and what it is

This book is not about primitive skills, wilderness living or long term survival in the wilderness. This book is not about advanced survival techniques or skills.

This book *is* about teaching you how to survive a short term survival situation with the aid of a survival kit and the skills to use the kit effectively. These situations occur all the time:

- A hiker on a routine afternoon jaunt takes a wrong turn and gets lost and can't find his way back to a known trail. The weather turns bad and protection from the elements becomes an immediate concern.

- A hunter gets so wrapped up in following a blood trail that, before he realizes it, he has become disoriented in regard to his location and it is getting dark. He may have to spend a night in the woods.

- Or, during a canoe trip in the late fall the weather turns bad. The canoe capsizes and suddenly the person is wet and very cold. They get to shore, but in order to avoid the threat of hypothermia they need warmth and shelter immediately.

- While exploring a wilderness area, a hiker becomes lost, and it may take days before they are either located or find thier way out.

There are many more scenarios, but you see why it is important to prepare for the unexpected. Because in the end it will be your skills and what you have with you in a survival kit or on your person that might determine if you survive!

In my first book, *Build the Perfect Survival Kit*, I explained how to make a survival kit through proper planning, selection of components and packaging, so you have a completed

This person is well prepared to survive. A hat and personal flotation device is worn and the equipment is tied into the canoe. Always expect the best but plan for the worst.

kit that fits your specific needs. If you haven't read that book I highly suggest that you get it. In conjunction with this book, the two will take you from understanding and designing a survival kit to effectively using that kit in a survival situation.

In this book, I will not go into depth about various survival kit components as I did in the first. However, I will reiterate the various component groups as they relate to the skills presented here. Also, some new items will be discussed which were not addressed in my first book.

## The comfort of a kit

As you know, a survival kit gives you a comfort zone if you have it on you when you need it. You know that you have the basics with you to survive. You don't have to wonder if you will be able to start a fire because you have selected components for your kit that will provide you with the means to initiate fire in various circumstances. You have the basics to navigate, signal, construct a shelter and obtain water and food. However, your kit is only the first step, so don't let it become a false sense of security. You must be knowledgeable in the use of the components you have selected. You must have the skills to take those components and effectively utilize them.

There are quite a few people I know who never carried a knife as an everyday ritual, until they met me. They are always surprised how often they use a knife in everyday life once they start carrying one. I always explain how a tool, such as a knife, carried on your person is an important element of an overall survival kit. By using the tool often, they become familiar and therefore comfortable with it. This leads to being better prepared to use that component when an emergency occurs.

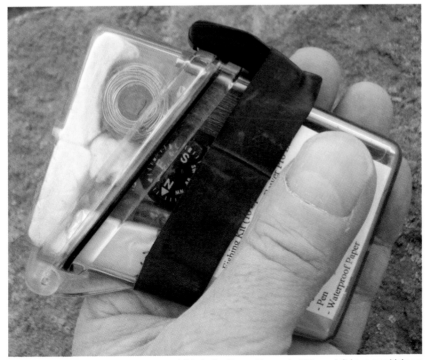

A small survival kit on you when you need it is better than a big survival kit you left in your vehicle or at home.

But what about the other components in your kit? They aren't often used unless you practice with them before you need them. This book will give you the opportunity to learn how to use the individual items you've selected. Hopefully you will use outdoor activities such as hiking, fishing, hunting, camping, canoeing or kayaking to practice in an outdoor environment with the items you choose for your kit. If you don't normally get involved with these type of activities, then you can still practice "backyard survival."

What is "backyard survival" you ask? This is when you go out into your backyard with your kit and use your selected components to perform the functions for which they were selected. Know you can start a fire with the various fire starting items you chose. Don't assume you can, but actually do it. Navigate with your compass of choice and see if you can do so and remain on a straight line for a distance. Practice with a signal mirror until you can hit a designated target quickly and accurately.

As you become acquainted with your individual components and feel comfortable in their use, your overall comfort factor will also be elevated. As stated earlier, a survival kit by itself provides a basic comfort factor, but that comfort factor grows exponentially as you learn to use your individual items to perform actual survival tasks.

The other advantage of "backyard survival" is that if a component fails, or does not suit your needs, you find out in your backyard, not in a survival situation. If the rain gear you selected does not protect you from the rain, you can go in the house and try something else another day. If your fire starting tools don't perform as you had hoped, you can go inside and order something that works better for you. The bottom line is you are not in a survival situation. You have the ability to re-think your kit and modify it for your specific needs. You don't get a second chance when an emergency occurs.

Students learn fire starting at a basic survival course. Advanced skills are good to know, *after* you've mastered the basics.

## Learning the skills to survive

Let's further examine the skills of survival. This book will attempt to provide you with the technical skills to use your selected components. You will learn the most effective manner to use specific items. The benefits of most survival tools remain unrealized until you know how they can help you perform specific tasks when needed. However, a book is no substitution for hands-on training.

One of the best ways to learn survival skills is by attending a survival course. This is where you will learn the subtleties. Many of my students have told me that it is not always the concept they learn, but more important, the nuances of an actual technique that make the process easier to perform.

There are many fine survival schools out there and I have listed some in the back of this book. Don't listen to the hype of some that the only way to learn survival skills is to attend a lengthy week-long course. If that is your desire, and you can afford the time and money, I see nothing wrong with it. But, there are many schools that run one- or two-day seminars or weekend courses. A good friend of mine, Christopher Nyerges, has been running short seminars and courses in California since the late 70s and many of his students come back time and again. They can learn a little at a time and methodically build their skill base. I once had a student that had attended a seven-day course tell me that it was so intensive that by the fifth day he had already forgotten what he had done on the first.

Many people can't take a week's vacation to learn skills, but still have the desire to learn. I have always believed that something is better than nothing, and it is the same with learning. Some skills are better than no skills. Learning a little at a time when you have available time is more important than the plan to someday attend an extended training program. Again, the choice is yours, but get all the training you can afford. It will be money well spent.

Lastly, in regard to looking for training, make sure the program teaches the basics. The basic skills will get you through a short duration survival situation. The advanced skills are good to know, and should eventually be learned, but after you have mastered the basics. The ability to make cordage from plants or spoons from wood are good primitive skills to have, but if you get thrown into a hypothermic situation, fire and shelter are the priority.

Remember, the tools for survival are there if you bring them. But the skills take time and practice. You can't wait until you need those skills to develop them, it will be too late. Both your survival kits and survival skills must constantly be updated. Neither can just be put away for a rainy day. Your kit should be up to date with items that work. Your skills, like a knife, must be sharp in order to work effectively when needed!

Both the unknown and darkness can trigger fear when stranded in the wilderness.

*Chapter 2*

# The Survivor Mentality

I t has become a survival axiom that your most important survival tool is your mind. I agree of course, but would add that your mind must be working properly in order to be an asset. Unfortunately, the onset of a survival situation throws the mind out of balance. The mind controls the body and the body reacts. The psychological situation often triggers a physiological reaction. It is like the feeling you might get in your stomach if you heard a pilot announce "brace for impact." Not a good feeling, but one you can't control.

It is important to understand what causes these feelings so that they can be dealt with in a reasonable manner. Panic is not an asset for those who want to survive. In order to prevent panic, we must understand fear.

## Fear factors

Man has many fears, and many of them, including some you might not even be aware you have, rear their ugly head at the onset of a survival situation. An understanding of the fears associated with a survival situation might allow you to control them when you are lost, stranded or otherwise thrust into unexpected situation.

### Embarrassment

This may be hard to believe, but research shows that this is often the first fear that occurs. This is especially true for those who think of themselves as experienced outdoors people, such as hunters, through-hikers, adventurers, campers, etc. In their mind, they have a reputation to maintain and are fearful of being ridiculed for allowing themselves to get into the situation they are in. The embarrassment of their situation becomes an actual fear.

### The unknown

Being afraid of the unknown is normal. The mind starts asking questions. What will happen to me? Will I be found? What will happen if I can't get out of here? Will I ever see my family again? What is that noise? Where am I? These are all questions people ask themselves, and dwelling on them intensifies the fear.

### Death

A survival situation often causes people to consider the possibility of death, and it can be a strong feeling. This type of thinking can paralyze a person and prevent them from acting in a rational manner, which, of course, thwarts efforts to deal with the matter at hand.

### Discomfort

This a normal fear for many people, especially those who are not very experienced in the wilderness. They are afraid of being on the ground or in the dirt, drinking dirty water, being bitten by bugs, getting muddy, etc. Although only minor discomforts for some, they become extreme fears for others. I once had a student at our survival school who was asked to crawl into a survival shelter that had been built by the class. When he refused, I asked if he was claustrophobic, and he said "No... I'm gross-a-phobic." Finally, after the class kidded him about it, he got in and as soon as the photo was taken he came out like a hornet. We assumed the fear of embarrassment overpowered his fear of discomfort.

### Being alone

Even many outdoorsman have never really been alone. Some never even realize it until it happens. All of a sudden they are alone, really alone, for the first time in their life and it is frightening. Again, the fear can capture the imagination and trigger other fears. In the movie "Cast Away," Tom Hanks, stranded on an island, became so desperate for a friend that he drew a face on a volleyball and named it "Wilson." After four years, while trying to sail back to civilization on a raft he constructed, Wilson falls from the raft and Chuck (the character played by Hanks) can't retrieve him. Who can forget the sadness that overcame Chuck, as he screamed "WILSON!!!" To Chuck, the friend was real and kept him from being alone.

### Darkness

Many people have a fear of the dark even when they are not in a survival situation. But couple this fear with being in an unknown location, where sometimes turning on a light is not an option, and the fear can become overpowering.

Many people have a fear of wild animals.

## Animals

The fear of wild animals is real for a lot of people. People who are not used to being in the outdoors often have never seen nor heard the sounds of a wild animal. The first time can be frightening.

I once had a student, an executive from New York City, at a basic course who had never heard coyotes at night. The second night of the course the coyotes were not only very active in regard to their howling, but several seemed to get into an altercation, as it became quite loud and ugly sounding. The next morning I asked the student how he had slept. He said he had been awakened by the sounds of the coyotes, and it sounded like they were so close that he thought they might attack, so he got out of his tent and hid behind it. This seemed irrational to me, and when I asked what that would solve - putting himself outside of the tent instead of inside - he said, "I don't know, I was just so scared I didn't know what to do." It just shows what fear can do to an otherwise rational, intelligent person.

## Physical Symptoms Of Fear

| | | |
|---|---|---|
| Quickening pulse | Pounding heart beat | Sweating/perspiration |
| Trembling or shaking | Shortness of breath | Dry mouth or throat |
| Difficulty swallowing | Nausea, vomiting, diarrhea | Dizziness, faintness |
| Higher-pitched voice | Dilated pupils | |

## Ignorance

The fear of ignorance happens most often in people who have little training in survival. When the situation occurs, they know they are in trouble and fear that they won't know how to help themselves. Even though many do survive, the onset of the fear can keep them from doing something... anything, to help their situation. Many people will realize that they have more ability than they think, and get to the business of surviving.

## Punishment

This fear more often occurs with children and the elderly. They are afraid that they will be punished for whatever led to their situation: being lost, wandering away, not being where they were supposed to be, etc. This is why children will often hide when they are lost. The fear of punishment for their actions, although irrational from a larger perspective, is real in their mind.

## How to control your fears

As we established earlier, in order to prevent panic, we must understand fear. We now know some of the fears that affect people in a survival situation. But that is not enough. Mark Twain once said, "Courage is resistance to fear, mastery of fear, not absence of fear." We must learn how we can control those fears, so panic does not have a chance to control us.

When fear strikes, we know we must act immediately. Don't run from it, but recognize and admit it. To prevent the physical symptoms of fear from setting in, there are several things you can do:

**1.** People tend to hold their breath when frightened, so breathe, breathe, breathe! Breathing prevents hyperventilation. Take slow, deep breaths to establish a regular breathing pattern, which will help you relax.

**2.** People also have a tendency to freeze when frightened. The breathing helps you to relax, which helps prevent you from becoming tense. Tense muscles can add to anxiety by reinforcing fear.

**3.** Move! When people freeze in the middle of a threatening situation it results in inaction. To break this natural instinct, move. Doing something will lessen the dread of the fear and help you restore confidence in yourself. Staying busy also keeps your mind busy and away from the negative aspects of the situation that reinforce the fear.

**4.** Another way to limit fear is by being prepared to survive! I have always been an advocate of carrying the basic essentials for survival with me whenever I leave the safety of my immediate surroundings, or what I call the "safety zone." I always wear, or have with me, proper clothing for a change of weather. Many times when I am hiking it starts to rain. While continuing on my way wearing the rain gear I keep with me, I pass others in a soaked t-shirt and jeans. I have seen these same unprepared hikers on a hot sunny day without any signs of having water with them.

Preparedness also includes knowledge and training in regard to handling a survival situation. I have "beat a dead horse to death" over the years advocating the necessity of practicing with your survival kit and learning the skills of survival. Being properly equipped is not enough; knowing how to use the equipment is also critical. In John Leach's book *Survival Psychology*, he states, "Familiarity with the use and handling of survival equipment is also essential during training. Unfamiliarity with equipment stops people from using it. Victims have been recovered from life rafts with a survival box (containing flares, rations, first-aid kit and so on) unopened and the necessary contents unused." Carry the essentials to survive and be comfortable with their use.

Lastly, stay physically fit. The combination of preparation, knowledge and fitness for survival develops confidence in yourself and your ability to face your fears in a survival situation.

## Additional survival stresses

We have already established that the major stress of a survival situation is fear. But there are others and we should address them. These other stresses can, and will, affect your emotional state, so being aware of them will help you better identify and deal with them.

### Pain

Oftentimes an injury is involved in, or related to, a survival situation. An injury can result in the stress of dealing with pain. Although pain is a hard thing to ignore or get away from, it can be managed or tolerated, and must be. When possible, don't allow pain to keep you from performing necessary activities to survive, unless this will cause further injury.

Oftentimes, the effort expended performing survival tasks can minimize or reduce your thoughts about the pain. You must still survive, and this takes action. In the Marine Corps, they used to say, "Pain is just fear leaving the body." It may sound stupid, but it allows your mind to accept the feeling of pain, deal with it, and continue with your mission. So try to deal with pain as much as possible and concentrate on the business of survival. Most people have much more tolerance and reserves than they realize.

### Cold and heat

Both cold and heat can stress the body, and quickly. We will discuss both hypothermia and hyperthermia in the Shelter & Protection chapter, but let's touch on the stresses these two killers can provoke.

Cold can lower your ability to perform, and thus your efficiency in a survival situation. Your body becomes numb because the cold lowers the blood flow to the extremities. It can numb not only your body, but your mind. Extreme cold can numb the mind and all you can think about

The numbness caused by cold, like weakness by heat, can be a major source of stress in a survival situation.

Photo by Susan Gregersen.

is getting warm again. This numbness of both mind and body is a serious and major stress and must be dealt with immediately.

As numbness is the major stress of being cold, weakness is the major stress of being hot. The stress of heat increases dehydration. When you become dehydrated, you begin to feel weak and fatigued. Your blood volume decreases when your body lacks the required amount of water. This leads to less nutrients and oxygen being delivered to the cells, resulting in weakness and fatigue.

### Thirst and dehydration

One of the most critical problems facing a survivor is a lack of water and the accompanying problems of thirst and dehydration. Like fear and pain, thirst can be tolerated if you have determination and remain calm and purposeful. However, in order to avoid dehydration you must drink water. When the body's water balance is not maintained, thirst and discomfort result. As previously stated, dehydration decreases the body's efficiency or ability to function, and can also cause irrational behavior. In order to mitigate this stress, stay hydrated to avoid thirst and dehydration.

### Hunger

Although many people believe that starvation is a major hazard of a survival situation, it is far from the truth. How many times have you heard a hungry person, probably because they missed lunch, state they were starving? Most people have enough extra pounds on them to get them through plenty of days with no food. But the mind can see it differently, so the stress of hunger can be real, although not life threatening. Because of this, hunger is one of the easier stresses to deal with if you keep a positive mental attitude.

### Depression

Depression, often caused by boredom and loneliness, can be another major stress. A survival situation can produce long periods of sadness or other negative feelings and these can lead to depression. Just being alone and waiting for rescue can allow depression to creep up on you. Depression can be a difficult problem because it can complicate a wide range of psychological responses. An example would be fatigue leading to a feeling of depression. Depression might increase the feeling of fatigue, which could lead to deeper depression.

The best way to deal with depression is to stay busy, adapt to your situation and maintain a positive mental attitude.

Depression can be a serious stress during a survival situation and must be dealt with by staying busy and maintaining a positive mental attitude.

## Fatigue

In a survival situation, your body is under the constant strain of diminished energy levels. You get less sleep and food which can lead to fatigue. Even moderate fatigue can reduce efficiency and make your more susceptible to hypothermia, poor judgment and injuries. You must be constantly aware of the dangers of over-exertion. As a result of other stresses, you may already be experiencing strain and reduced efficiency. Even though considerable exertion might be required in a survival situation, you must avoid complete exhaustion.

Rest is a basic solution to recover from fatigue. Short rest breaks during extended stress periods can improve the overall output of energy. Fatigue can be reduced by working smarter. Adjust your pace and remember that economy of effort is most important.

## The will to survive

The will to survive has been defined as the desire to live despite seemingly insurmountable mental and/or physical obstacles. Even though you might have the tools (a survival kit) and the training, it might not be enough in a survival situation. You must have the will to survive.

The human mind has the amazing ability to overcome stress and hardship even when there appears to be little chance of surviving. This is when the will comes into play. That mental attitude can bridge the gap between realizing the severity of your situation and understanding it is not going away, and resolving to endure without quitting, no matter what.

Consider the story of Aron Ralston who amputated his own arm with a pocketknife. Ralston, a 27 year old Aspen mountaineer was trapped when a boulder weighing 800-1,000 pounds pinned his arm for five days in a remote desert canyon in eastern Utah. With no water and little hope of survival, Ralston cut through his own arm below the elbow, applying a tourniquet and administering first aid before rigging anchors and fixing a rope to rappel to the bottom of a canyon to meet his rescuers. Ralston told rescuers that he realized he would not survive unless he took drastic action, as he had run out of water days before.

Another incident involves a Colorado fisherman, Bill Jeracki, who cut off his leg at the knee when two boulders fell on his leg while angling alone in a remote canyon stream. Trapped and yelling for hours, he finally made the decision to sever the limb after the weather took a turn for the worse and he became concerned for his survival. He used hemostats from his fishing kit to close the severed artery and vein, then crawled a half mile back to his truck and drove to find help.

What can explain the actions of these men? The will to survive. The will to survive is not automatic, and can be swept away by panic and fear if you let it, but the will to live can be the key difference between surviving and becoming a victim.

Another key asset is optimism. You must maintain a positive, optimistic outlook on your circumstances. If necessary, hope and faith can help. Both prayer and meditation can help, but how a survivor maintains optimism is not as important as having it.

## Minimizing panic

One of the essentials in a survival situation is to minimize panic. You must remain calm and think. Do whatever it takes to persuade yourself to avoid panic and stay calm. This is the basis for accepting your situation and preparing to make the best of it.

An often used acronym in the survival community is S.T.O.P., and in my opinion is worth reiterating. This acronym helps you to remember the steps to take when you are involved with an emergency situation. The steps are as follows:

### Sit

You can prevent running around like a chicken with its head chopped off if you just sit down. Take a deep breath and use this time to initiate the thinking process and minimize your urge to run.

If available, take a drink of water and organize your thoughts.

### Think

Think about immediate problems or dangers, not those that are unreal. If the weather looks bad, you need shelter. Asses your choices and determine what you have with you to help your situation. Where is your survival kit? How can you use it to make your situation better? Knowing you are prepared by being equipped and having the required skills can give you confidence and reduce your fears and stresses. Confidence reduces your chances of doing something stupid.

### Observe

Observe your surroundings and be aware of any dangers. Also determine what resources might be available. Look for basics like water, a safe place for a shelter or campsite, a place to signal for help from. What are the current conditions in regard to remaining daylight, temperature, precipitation, etc.?

### Plan

Now that you and your mind are organized and you are thinking in a rational manner, start to develop a plan. Determine your best course of action with available resources and time. Then make some immediate decisions and get going. If you are going to stay, which is often the best choice for at least the first night, select a campsite and shelter location. Start constructing a shelter; gather water, resources to start a fire and any food you can find; set up any signaling if available; and try to maintain a good spirit. Stay busy on positive efforts.

During your survival ordeal, it is important to maintain your physical as well as mental well-being. Take care of yourself and your equipment. Try to keep your clothing in as good a shape as possible, as it is your first line of defense. Don't be one of these people who show up on the news with clothing torn or missing, cut, bruised and out of their mind. Remember your skills and have faith. Only the strong survive!

*Chapter 3*

# The Indispensable Survival Kit

I knew an old guy who used to tell his students that your chances of surviving are directly proportionate to how much knowledge you carry in your head and not how many gadgets you carry in your survival kit. Of course you can survive without a survival kit - sometimes - if you are an experienced outdoors person who has dedicated your life to mastering the primitive survival skills. Unfortunately, many people who travel in the outdoors, or become involved in a survival situation, have not been so dedicated.

I have already addressed the importance of learning survival skills, and if you were not interested in skills you would not have purchased this book. But even skill does not always guarantee your survival. Almost every book written by an experienced survival expert advocates carrying a survival kit. Personal survival kits are the foundation for basic survival. They are your first line of defense. If you always maintain and carry a personal survival kit, you will always have the basic components for survival. The important thing to remember is "always carry it with you." If you don't have your survival kit with you when you need it, you're already at a disadvantage. If, after reading this chapter, you desire more detailed information in regard to designing and building a survival kit, please refer to my first book, *Build the Perfect Survival Kit*.

## Commercial kits

There are many types of commercial survival kits available on the market today. Some of these kits are well made and provide the basics, some are sufficient, and most are lacking in serious survival components. Although many of these kits provide the basics, the quality of the components must fit the selling price of the kit. I'm not opposed to commercial survival kits, but there are three reasons I prefer self-made kits:

**1.** Oftentimes a commercial kit does not provide the highest quality components. Items are not always selected because they are the best for your survival, but because they fit a pre-determined budget. I have always felt that you should spend as much as you can afford on the individual components for your personal survival kit. After all, you might depend on your kit for survival, and what is your life worth? This is no place to be frugal.

**2.** Design your kit on an item-by-item basis. This way, you are familiar with the individual components. By packaging your own kit, you not only know what each item is (after all, you selected them), but in an emergency you know where each item is located in your kit. When you buy a kit that is pre-packaged, the kit is often tightly packaged to fit in the selected container. You lose the flexibility of choosing a container that allows space for extra items you might want to add. If you do purchase a pre-packaged kit, be sure you become familiar with it before you need it.

**3.** Making your own personal survival kit is not difficult. You can determine what you want your kit to accomplish and design it around those requirements. You can chose your own container, determine the specific components and customize it for your particular needs. It can be

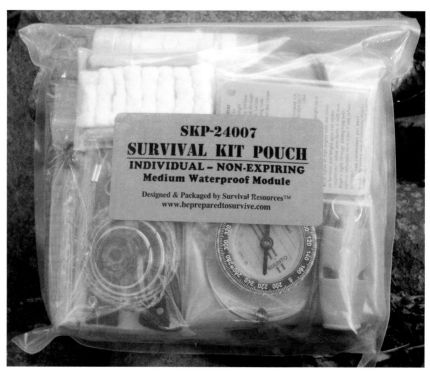

If you buy a commercial survival kit, get one that provides high quality components designed for real survival.
(Photo courtesy of Survival Resources)

the perfect survival kit for you, not one designed by a person who has no idea what your personal needs are. Only you know what is right for you.

## The basic functions

I am often asked how a person knows if they have all the required items in their survival kit. Have they forgotten anything that is essential? I always ask them what type of activities might they have to perform if they get in an emergency or survival situation. Although the components are obviously important, don't try to remember the actual component groups by name, but remember those important tasks you must perform. These tasks will remind you of the component groups. As we all know, a fire is an important aspect of survival. Therefore, you should have a means in which to start a fire.

When putting together a personal survival kit, keep in mind the basics. The basics identify specific functions that will have to be performed in order to endure a survival situation. By understanding the functions that must be performed, you gain insight into the type of items, or components, that should be in your kit in order to accomplish those goals. The items in a survival kit should allow you to perform the following functions:

- Build a fire using more than one technique.
- Construct a shelter in various environments.
- Signal for help using more than one technique.
- Gather and purify drinking water and gather food.
- Navigate back to civilization.
- Carry out basic first aid.

Your survival kit should be made up of components selected for the specific purposes outlined above. The component selection process considers not only the use of a component, but also the size. Obviously, if you are going to build a mini kit for a pocket, you would need to select components that not only fulfill the required purpose, but are small enough to fit into the desired container.

## Component groups

Once we know the types of activities we must perform in a survival situation, we need to select components to provide us with a means to perform those tasks. In order to complete the predetermined tasks, the following are the desired component groups for a survival kit, no matter the size:

| | |
|---|---|
| Fire and Light | Shelter & Personal Protection |
| Signaling | Navigation |
| Water & Food Collection | Medical |
| Knives & Tools | Multi-Purpose Items |

As you can see, if you have selected at least one component for each of the groups above, you should be able to perform the necessary activities possibly required in a survival situation. In some cases, I recommend more than one item from a component group. In the case of fire, an important task, I like to have at least three ways to start a fire. Signaling might require a whistle and a signal mirror. You never know what the situation may require, so having more than one item from a group provides you with more options when you need them.

# The Four Ps of Building a Survival Kit

**1. PLAN IT:** This is an important phase of building a survival kit. Sometimes people just start collecting different things in hopes that they will end up with a viable survival kit. This often results in kits not having some necessary components. Before starting a survival kit, plan what you want it to be and what you want it to do for you. Will it be a personal-carry mini-kit consisting of only the basic components, or a full blown large kit with plenty of redundancy? Know what you want the kit to accomplish. Will the kit supplement a larger kit, or be your only line of defense? Spend some time on this phase and answer your questions truthfully. Only you know what you will expect from your kit, so don't let yourself down by hoping for the best. Make it the best you can right from the planning stage.

**2. PICK IT:** Take some time to determine the appropriate components that will both fit the size of the kit you desire and perform the necessary functions. Remember, size matters. Don't fill half the space of your selected container with one component and then wonder how you will get the rest of the components in there. Some items can serve dual purpose and meet the requirements of more than one heading. An example would be snare wire (from the Water & Food Collection heading) which can be used to obtain food, repair broken items, make a fishing pole, etc. Choose items that you are comfortable with. If one fire starter works better for you than another, and size permits, select the component that works best for you. Trade-offs will occur, but are necessary to address the size vs. usefulness dilemma.

**3. PAY FOR IT:** Determine a budget for your kit. This will help you avoid ending up with one very expensive component, like a good quality knife, with remaining items of lesser caliber, not sufficient for the task required. Distribute your available funds to acquire components of somewhat equal quality. As your budget increases, you can trade lesser-quality items for better ones. But initially, don't overlook component groups because they don't fit a budget. All component groups are important, so address them all even if you need to reduce the budget for each item.

**4. PACK IT:** Finally, package your kit. For me, this is the fun part, and involves getting all the components you selected into the container you selected. Sometimes it works, sometimes it doesn't. This goes back to selecting the right size items to fit in the container.

Once you have packed your kit, you're done and ready to carry it with you. Remember to practice with it before you need it!

## Seasonal & environmental factors

Keep in mind that survival kits can also be based on seasonal or environmental factors. Of course, we cannot always forecast the environment where a survival situation may occur. That is why the basics always remain the same. However, certain additional items may be chosen for the season or environment that you plan to be in.

Obviously, the type of shelter and clothes chosen for a summer hike will differ from those chosen for winter activities, such as skiing or snowmobiling. This would be a seasonal factor. The items chosen for a desert environment will differ from those chosen for a mountain wilderness or jungle environment. An example would be choosing a machete as a tool for a jungle or tropical environment, whereas an ice ax and folding snow shovel would be necessary for a snow environment. A good knife and folding saw would be appropriate for a wilderness area. Keep these variables in mind when designing your personal survival kit.

## Sizing a kit to your needs

Personal survival kits can be broken down further into mini and small kits (which can be carried on your person), medium kits (which can be carried in a fanny or small backpack), and large kits (which can be carried in a large backpack, vehicle, boat, plane, etc.). The size of the kit depends on what you are doing and how much you are willing to carry. Sometimes a combination of kits can be utilized, such as a mini kit in your pocket, a medium kit in your pack, with a large kit in your vehicle. Even though I am an advocate of carrying items that are multi-purpose, I also believe in redundancy.

Items chosen for a survival kit to be used in a wilderness area of the Adirondacks might differ from those for a desert, tropical, or mountainous area.

## EDC: Every-day carry

Before we discuss the various sized survival kits, let's discuss our real first line of defense: you and what you carry on you. This is normally referred to as "EDC," or every-day carry. These are the items that you carry on your person every day. Not occasionally, but every day! They can be carried in your pockets, on a key ring or other ways. I carry the same items in my pockets every day, no matter what I am doing. Therefore I always have the same items with me and I don't have to think about it.

The author's front pocket EDC.

My left front pocket always has a small BIC lighter, an ARC-AAA flashlight, and the key ring for my truck keys, which also contains a tube with a $20.00 bill, a Leatherman Micra tool, a Micron II micro-light, and a mini-flash drive encrypted with color copies of all my important licenses, passport, and documents.

My right front pocket contains a Zippo lighter, a space pen and a very small Victorinox two-bladed knife. It also contains a split ring that holds a mini folding saw, two Ferrocerium rods, two strikers for the Ferro rods,

Thirty-five feet of parachute cord on right rear pocket pallet.

another Micron II micro light, a Fox 40 whistle, a small aluminum capsule with fire starters and a socket for a bow and drill.

My left rear pocket holds my wallet, which also contains a one-hand fire starter and tinder, a Fresnel magnifier, some Band-Aids, a mini zip-lock bag of steel wool and a flat floatable compass. I wear a tactical nylon belt that has a zippered compartment in the back that holds a cable saw.

My right rear pocket always contains a small notebook, a bandana with toilet paper wrapped inside and a Kydex pallet that is wound with 35 feet of parachute cord.

The left side of my belt holds a pouch which contains a Gerber Multi-Tool and a Victorinox Farmer. The right side of my belt holds a fixed blade knife and my Blackberry. I always carry a small neck knife that has a Kydex sheath which holds braided fishing line, fishing tackle, a compass and a firestarter (this will be shown in the "Knife & Tool" chapter). I also carry a Benchmade Griptilian folder.

As you can see, I probably carry more than most, but I have been doing it for as long as I can remember, so it is normal for me. I unload and load my pockets the same every day. I am always my first line of defense.

## Supplemental kits

A couple of years ago I realized that even though I carry the essential elements of a survival kit every day, with redundancy, there were still certain items from component groups that I was not carrying if I did not actually carry one of my mini survival kits. Because of that, I started building what I call mini supplemental kits. These kits can be very small as they only need to carry the additional items from component groups not carried on your person. I include a small emergency water bag with purification tablets, snare wire, magnetized needles, butterfly bandages, antibiotic ointment, a backup compass and, again, some backup tinder. This kit fits almost anywhere and when I go into the field I grab and stick it in a jacket pocket.

A mini supplemental kit supports your EDC.

Another supplemental kit I normally have with me when I go into the field is a brimmed hat that also has a fishing kit, braided fishing line and a firestarter built in, and a button compass cord lock on the chin strap. The hatband has been braided from parachute cord. I showed this hat in my first book and one of the most often asked questions was how to make the parachute cord hatband. So I have posted a tutorial on how to construct your own parachute cord hatband at www.SurvivalResources.com under Articles & Tips - *Modifying Your Own Gear, Making a Parachute Cord Hatband.*

## Mini survival kits

Mini kits are the easiest to carry, so there is really no excuse not to carry one. On the other hand, they provide the least amount of survival equipment, especially shelter items. Therefore, select your components wisely, always going for the smallest sized items and multi-purpose features.

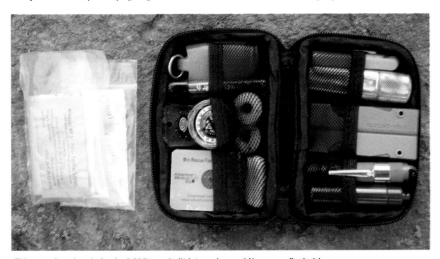

This complete, hand-sized mini kit was built into a zippered Neoprene flash drive case.

At least one item from each required component group can fit in an Altoids tin if the items are carefully selected and packaged.

This mini kit, built into a small plastic tackle box, contains items from all the required component groups.

This mini survival kit was built inside a Witz ID Locker that measures only 4.25" W x 3.25" H x .75" deep.

The mini kit in the plastic tackle box fits into the outside pocket of a small belt pouch. The back portion of the pouch allows for the addition of a survival blanket, emergency poncho and a full size base plate compass. The two side loops on the pouch allow the addition of a small flashlight on one side and a 1/2" Ferrocerium rod on the other. It now becomes a small kit!

Mini kits can be packaged in any small container, from an Altoids tin to a flash drive case. If the container is small and will hold the items you want and still fit in a pocket or small area, you can make it work. You can also carry a mini kit in a small belt case and supplement it with shelter items or other larger items like a full size compass. You can carry it as is, or always remove the mini kit and stick it in your pocket. The photographs illustrate some of the various configurations you can come up with.

## Small & medium survival kits

Once you move from a mini kit, you get more room to add more components, such as shelter, and larger items if you wish. There is nothing wrong with carrying a mini kit along with another kit, or in the case of a small kit, using the mini as part of it and adding items, as described in the mini kit section.

You will also find that, as you use your kits, you will make modifications to switch out components for new or better ones, or you might find other ways to make your kit more user friendly.

I showed a small survival kit in my first book that was built into a large tin, so I had a small pot for cooking or boiling water for purification. However, every time I wanted to use the tin as a

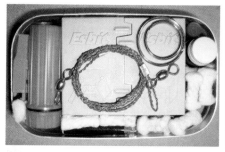

This small tin kit was shown in *Build the Perfect Survival Kit.* The bag was made to hold the contents so they could be lifted out to use the tin as a pot.

The small tin kit fits into a pouch which can be attached to a belt.

pot I had to empty all the contents and, when done, pack them all back in. After examining the problem, I designed and had my wife sew a small zippered bag that fit perfectly in the tin. I could then fill the bag with the survival kit components and just lift it out when I wanted to use the tin as a pot. When finished, I could just set the bag back in the tin. I also got a small belt pouch that the tin fit in, so the entire kit could be worn on a belt.

Various pouches are available that are made to carry water bottles, cross chest, over one shoulder. These bottle pouches have various pockets on the outside or the ability to add additional pouches. This makes them great containers for small survival kits, with room for the addition of a water bottle and even a cup or pot.

Maxpedition makes one called the 10x4 Bottle Holder, and Condor makes one called the H20 Pouch. It should be noted that Maxpedition, although very well made gear, has a proprietary system to attach various pouches to their products. The Condor products use the regular MOLLE (MOdular Lightweight Loadcarrying Equipment) fastening system, which is being used by the U.S. military, making the modular pouches of various manufacturers easily attached to Condor's products.

The Condor H20 Pouch comes with a shoulder strap for carry cross chest over one shoulder. A MOLLE pouch has been added to the back to hold an Esbit Folding Pocket Stove, and another pouch on the side for a signal mirror and mirrored compass. The large integrated front pouch holds a survival blanket, emergency poncho and a small survival kit in a waterproof pouch. The large central section holds a large titanium pot with a stainless steel Guyot water bottle inside the pot. By using a Nalgene cap on the Guyot bottle, instead of the large cap that comes with the bottle, a titanium mug fits upside down on top of the bottle. A bail for the Guyot bottle slides down the side of the pouch and the entire rig makes for a good day hike or short term survival kit.

I prefer the Condor H20 Pouch, as it is just slightly larger around and is less square than the Maxpedition 10x4 Bottle Holder. This allows me to more easily get a pot, which fits over my water bottle, out of the pouch when needed. Of course this is only personal preference and is in no way meant to recommend one over the other.

I have built several different day-hike kits in these type of pouches, as they allow me to carry a small survival kit with some minimal shelter items, as well as water, a pot, and, with a couple of additional small MOLLE pouches, a small stove, a compass and signal mirror.

I am not a big fan of hydration bladder packs for survival, as I find the bladders difficult to keep clean in the field. However, many people like them and they are especially handy for day hikes. Many of these small hydration bladder packs are ideal for supporting a small or medium survival kit with some additional shelter items.

The Maxpedition Jumbo Versipack

For medium size kits, there have been various side carry bags introduced which allow you to carry a kit, again, cross chest off one shoulder. Maxpedition offers various models such as the Fatboy Versipack and the Jumbo Versipack. 5.11 Tactical Gear offers a similar type product called the PUSH Pack. These bags are large enough for medium sized survival kits and are easily placed over one shoulder. The larger Maxpedition Jumbo Versipack even has an outside pouch fitted for a standard Nalgene or Guyot-type bottle. I have purchased various configurations of these side carry bags and, although they are becoming very popular with many people, I find the weight of the bag on just one shoulder uncomfortable over time, normally resulting in a stiff neck. This is especially true as they get larger.

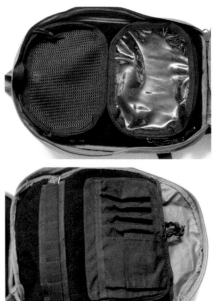

The Blue Force Gear Micro Pack is small but offers lots of internal options.

With the internal pallets of the Blue Force Gear Micro Pack, you can select for various configurations.

The Camelbak Mule with flap modification is my main day hiking kit and could sustain a person for a couple of days in a survival situation. You may not be real comfortable, but you would survive.

Depending on your needs, a kit can become large enough to fill a large backpack.

Another day pack I have been working with is the Blue Force Gear Micro Pack. It has the ability to add various pallets inside for organizing gear in different configurations. Each of these pallet pockets has Velcro inside and can be removed to grab a particular component group out for use. Still working on this one!

Another nice option for medium sized survival kits, especially if they will be for a waterborne situation or attached to an ATV or snowmobile, is a Pelican case. They are indestructible and waterproof. This is also a nice way to go for vehicle and aircraft kits.

In my first book, I showed a large survival kit built in a large back pack. The specific components were listed, showing how they were packed, etc. The specifics are available in *Build the Perfect Survival Kit*.

A medium sized kit built into a pelican case is great for waterborne operations or ATV and snowmobile configurations.

As you can see, there are many configurations for packaging a survival kit. As I indicated earlier, this book is not about building kits, and you know where to go for more information on that. The rest of the book is dedicated to the skills you need to effectively use your survival kit in a survival situation.

# ANATOMY OF A SURVIVAL KNIFE

**High Carbon Steel**
I prefer knives that are made from a high carbon steel, such as 1095 or 01. There are many, many quality steels when it comes to knives, but I feel that simple carbon steels work well for overall edge retention and toughness. A knife made with a high carbon steel that is fully hardened can also cast sparks with a piece of flint.

**Lanyard Hole**
A hole near the butt of the knife to allow a safety cord (usually 550 paracord) that can be wrapped and secured around your wrist.

**Full Tang Construction**
The Blade and handle are made from a single piece of steel without joints or welds.

**Square Spine**
When the spine of the knife is square it may be used as a striker / scrapper on a ferrocium rod (aka firesteel or Mischmetal).

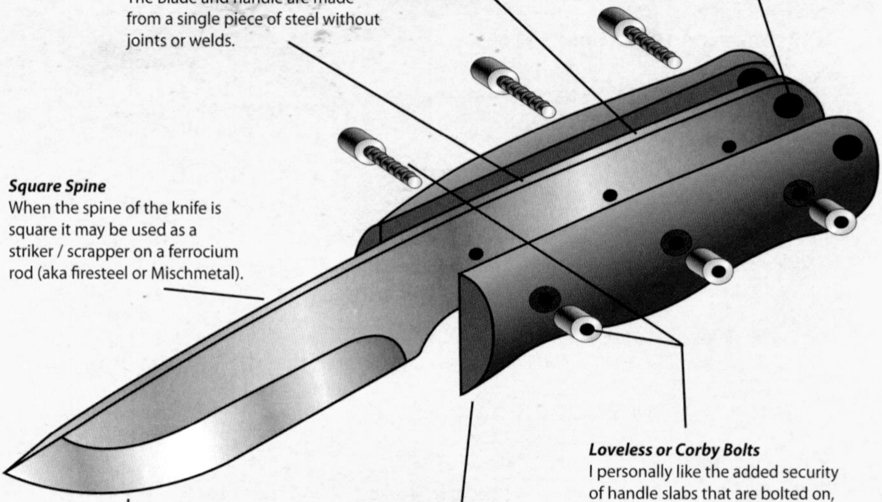

**Loveless or Corby Bolts**
I personally like the added security of handle slabs that are bolted on, rather than pinned or epoxied. Handles that are bolted on are much more secure.

**Micarta® or G-10 Handle Material**
Micarta in simplest terms is any fiberous material (paper, burlap, linen, etc.) cast in resin and compressed. G-10 is similar but cast in a fiberglass resin. Both offer stability, durability, water resistance and provide a secure grip even when wet.

**Scandi / Nordic Ground Edge**
A Scandi ground edge consists of and edge with a single bevel and no secondary bevel and is the grind shown in the illustration. Other types of grinds such as convex, full flat with a secondary bevel are suitible and common grinds for a survival knife.

Illustration by:
Rob L. Lyttle

Figure 4-1 Anatomy of a survival knife

*Chapter 4*

# Knives & Tools for Survival

**M**any survival experts agree that, outside of the brain, the most important survival tool is a knife. I have always agreed with an old Nordic Proverb, "A knifeless man is a lifeless man." Nothing is more true in a survival situation. If I could choose only one item for a survival kit or survival, it would be a knife. With a knife, I can make almost anything else I need in a survival situation. However, a discussion on knives is like a discussion on guns. It can be controversial and nobody will agree on all points. Because of its importance we will examine the issue.

I'm often asked what is the best survival knife. I always say that the best survival knife is the one that works for you and performs the tasks you need to accomplish. However, there is more to it than that. There are some specific characteristics that make certain knives better for the purpose of survival. Figure 4-1 describes characteristics desired in a survival knife.

Understanding the various knife grinds and points also helps you make a better decision in regard to an adequate survival knife. Figure 4-2 provides information that will help you better understand the types of grinds and points. Although I prefer a convex or Scandi grind with a drop point made from carbon steel for a survival knife, any of those described are suitable for survival.

Last, but not least, you should be somewhat knowledgeable about heat treating a knife. Knives come in a plethora of different steels, most of which are good as long as they are heat treated properly. A knife without a proper heat treat and proper tempering can end up being as useful as a butter knife. A bad heat treat can lead to a multitude of problems. If the knife is too soft it will not retain a cutting edge for very long and the edge can be prone to rolling. If a knife is too hard it can be brittle and end up chipping.

Heat treating and tempering procedures vary from steel to steel and are also dependent on the type and style of knife. Most knife manufacturing companies spend lots of time testing and perfecting the heat treating processes because it is one of the most important factors in the end product. The ideal Rockwell hardness for your average carbon steel or tool steel field knife is around 58 or 59, a couple of points up or down and you would be hard pressed as an average user to notice a difference.

# COMMON SURVIVAL KNIFE GRINDS AND POINTS

### Full Convex Grind

A full convex grind is fairly common blade grind that is suited for all purpose use. The grind starts at the spine and has a subtle arc all the way down to the edge. The egde is generally very, very sharp and can be easily maintained using a leather strop with some rubbing compound or a mouse pad with some very fine grit sandpaper. Even though the edge is thin and sharp it is also considered strong because there is more steel behind it than other common grinds.

### Saber Grind

The sabre grind has a flat primary bevel that usually starts in the middle or down a bit from the spine to the edge or secondary bevel. The edge bevel can be flat or convex. This type of primary grind is considered very robust and strong. Some of the most common military knives such as the Kabar® use the saber gring. The saber grind is built for heavy duty work such as prying, digging and chopping.

### Full Flat Grind with a Secondary Bevel

A full flat grind starts at the spine and goes until it reaches the point of the secondary bevel. It is a good all around grind because the edge or secondary bevel can be thin or thicker dependent on the purpose. A thin edge will excel at general cutting, slicing and skinning, where a thicker edge can be used on more robust materials such as hardwoods.

### Scandi / Nordi Grind

The scadi / nordic grind is a single bevel grind, basically one big edge. The scandi can be extremely sharp and is very common in the scandinavian countries and is consider thier everyday knife. I have found that this type of grind excels at carving wood. Due to the edge being thin and razor sharp the scandi grind takes a bit more to maintain and is more prone to the edge rolling when used against hard materials.

### Clip Point

The clip point tip is as it looks. The spine has a straight cut to the tip of the knife. The clip Can start as far back as the handle or at any interval from the handle to the tip. A clipped point drops the tip of the knife lower than the spine and makes for a strong and very pointy tip. Often clip point knives have a false edge that assists in penetration. They are commonly seen on military and fighting knives.

### Drop Point

The drop point blade has a curve drop from the spine to the tip. It is also used to lower the tip closer to the center to provide better handling and control. This type of tip is often seen on hunting and general camp knives.

Figure 4-2 Survival knife grinds and points

The hardness of a knife also varies based on the size and intended use of the knife. A big chopper-style knife can get away with being a bit on the soft side, as it is intended to be used more like an axe or hatchet than a small carving knife. And, a small carving knife can be a little on the hard side for better edge retention and less impact resistance. A machete, for example is really on the soft side of the Rockwell scale because its intended use is for brush clearing/chopping and it needs to be flexible. A machete is usually very long and thin, and if were heat treated to be hard like a field knife, it wouldn't last long and most likely the blade would snap.

My suggestion is always spend good money on a knife. As we have established, it is your primary survival tool, so don't cut corners here. Buy well-known brands and don't look for bells and whistles. The knife needs to cut, and cut adequately for your needs.

Two types of knives to avoid at all costs are hollow handle knives and double-edged blades. Hollow handle knives are intrinsically weak where the handle is attached to the blade. Not only are most of these very cheap knives, they will always break between the handle and blade leaving you with no knife. The exception to this rule are knives made by Chris Reeve, which are hollow-handle survival knives made from a single bar of A2 steel. If you must have a hollow handle knife, this is the one.

With regard to double edged blades, they are made for self defense, period. They are not, in my opinion, useful for survival purposes, at least in the wilderness.

## Non-primary survival kit knives

Now that we've established the ideal type of knife for survival, we must consider what type of knife will fit in our survival kit. There are always trade-offs, and my suggestion is to always carry a good fixed blade knife that meets or exceeds the characteristics described above. However, as my dad always said, you can't have too many knives. Therefore, let's examine some other types of knives that, if placed in a survival kit, could be a back-up to your main blade.

### Razor blades

Although not really considered a knife, razor blades are a cutting instrument that will normally fit in the smallest survival kit. Not intended as a major cutting tool, but something to use if all else fails, various types of blades fit this category.

Examples of razor-type blades include a surgical prep blade, utility knife blade, X-ACTO knife blade, a Warren Cutlery carving blade and a folding razor knife.

A custom kit knife made for the author, a CRKT Ritter RSK Mk5, a Gerber LST, a Gerber folding Utility knife, and a Victorinox Silver Alox Farmer. All of these knives fit easily in a small survival tin.

### Survival tin knives

Survival tin knives are any knife that fits into a small survival tin and are meant as a back-up to your primary knife.

### Multiple blade folders

There are many types of multiple blade folding knives on the market and they run from usable to ridiculous. If you choose a multiple blade knife, keep it simple. Some of these knives have so many blades that the handle makes them impossible to hold.

Various multiple blade folders that would work fine as a back-up knife for a survival kit: (in a clockwise direction, beginning at top left) an original Boy Scout knife, a military folding knife. a Victorinox Alox Farmer (without the saw blade showing), a Victorinox Hunter, and a Victorinox plain edge One Hand Trekker.

Some of my favorites are the original Boy Scout knife and military folding knife. Both have a good drop point blade, an awl, and a bottle and can opener. You will never regret having one of these in a survival kit. The next type are a little larger, but have the advantage of a saw and the best, in my opinion, are the Victorinox and Wenger. My favorite is the Victorinox Farmer, which I carry every day, and the plain edged One Hand Trekker, one of which rides in a shoulder strap pouch on each of my packs. Both of these knives have an excellent saw which is great for cutting the "V" notch in a fire board for a bow and drill or to start a notch on a trap.

The author has had this Ka-Bar folder (top) forever and it is still a good knife. In the second row is a SOG 4-1/2" drop point Flash II (left), and a Benchmade Griptilian drop point (right). The bottom row shows one of the larger folders made by Cold Steel called the Pocket Bushman.

### Single blade folders

There has been much discussion about a single blade folder being a primary survival knife, and the discussion will continue I'm sure. As I have established, my primary survival knife will always be a fixed-blade (full tang) knife. I once heard somebody say that a folding knife is one that is already broken in the middle. That is true of course, and that will always be the weak point of a folder. Don't get me wrong, I carry a Benchmade Griptilian, drop point, every day. I just don't consider it my primary knife, but a back-up blade.

If you do choose a folding knife as your main survival knife, make sure it is quality made and substantial. I always recommend a locking blade so the blade does not close up on your fingers, causing another emergency during a survival situation. A folder should feel comfortable in your hand and be easy to use. Don't get a big one just to have a big one. The size should be adequate to do the job, but not so big that it is uncomfortable to use. Again, as with all knives, buy quality.

### Primary fixed blade survival knives

As Figure 4-1 reveals, a primary fixed blade survival knife should have a full tang (no moving parts) and a grind that is conducive to the chores of survival.

A good way to determine a good size for a general purpose survival knife is to use your hand. Lay the knife blade across your hand, being very careful of course, and if the blade of the knife from the front of the handle to point is the width of your hand, then the knife will be a good choice as a general purpose survival knife. This is also a good measure for the handle, which should also be about the width of your hand.

My two favorite grinds for survival and bushcraft are the convex and Scandi grind. They are both excellent at wood work. I like the convex grind for its edge sharpness and strength, as I do a lot of batoning (more about batoning later) with a knife. The Scandi works well also, but we must all have a favorite. I have been known to carry both.

Some of the authors fixed blade knives (from left to right): an AF survival knife, a Marbles Ideal, a Pathfinder by Blind Horse Knives, two Mora's, a Skookum Bush Tool, a Bark River Bravo 1 & Fox River, and a Fallkniven F-1.

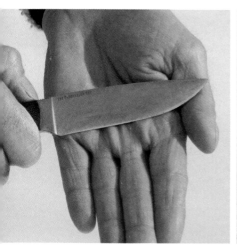

Using your hand to determine a good size for a general purpose survival knife, the length of the blade should be the approximate size of the width of your hand. The same goes for the handle.

The Skookum Bush Tool is high on my list of recommendations. The pommel ot the Skookum Bush Tool provides a large flat surface which can be used to hammer.

This unique Scandinavian type pocket sheath comes with the Skookum Bush Tool.

In regard to convex grind, you cannot get much better than a Bark River. They are one of the finest convex ground knives available for survival. They have an exceptional geometry of blade with an edge that doesn't quit when the going gets tough. I have put the Bark River Foxriver and Bravo 1 through extensive use and abuse, and they continue to provide excellent service. I am recently using the Bark River Gunny, which is a downsized version of the Bravo 1. Although slightly smaller than my usual main-carry knife, it is performing to the standards I require, and being I carry a fixed blade knife every day, it presents less of an impact hanging on my belt when at the mall.

A custom knife maker who also produces a fine convex grind is Dave Thomas of Chieftain Knives. He has made several custom knives to my specifications and they are excellent. The knife shown in the Neck Knife Survival Kit was made for me by Dave Thomas - very sharp!

When it comes to Scandi grind, my favorite is the Skookum Bush Tool which, although called a tool, is a knife designed by Rod Garcia with input from Mors Kochanski. It is definitely one of the finer knives designed specifically for bushcraft and survival. I had the distinct pleasure of spending a week in the field with Rod Garcia and he is not only a knife maker but well skilled in the techniques of wilderness survival. If you choose a Scandi knife, the Skookum Bush Tool is high on my list of recommendations.

Another fine knife maker that specializes in Scandi grinds is Blind Horse Knives. They have a good selection for survival and bushcraft purposes. They made the Pathfinder Knife shown earlier.

If you are on a short budget and desire a less than expensive knife with a Scandi grind, you can't go wrong with a Mora. The price in relationship to functionality is, let's say, "on the money."

## Large fixed blade knives (choppers)

There are two camps as far as opinions about large fixed blade knives, also called "choppers," and, as with anything dealing with knives, some are for them and the other half is against them. In my opinion, if it works for you then don't worry about what other people say.

I'm in the camp that believes that a large fixed blade knife is a good addition to survival edge-ware. It is always supplemental to my primary survival knife, but is functional for my purposes. Although you will rarely see me chop with a "chopper," you will often see me batoning with one. I find they work well at making larger pieces of wood into smaller pieces of wood. They are also multi-functional as they make a good draw knife, a good wedge and, of course, a good chopper, if chopping is something you need to do.

Some of the authors large fixed blade knives (from left to right): a TOPS Armageddon, Fehrman Extreme Judgement, Fehrman Final Judgement, Original Becker BK-9 with custom grips, Ontario RTAK-II and a Busse straight handle Battle Mistress.

Two of the authors machetes: an Ontario Sawback, a custom 16-inch Fiddleback Forge with micarta handles and an original Becker Patrol Machete (no longer available).

When it comes to a large fixed blade knife, I'm not interested in a "Rambo" style knife with bells and whistles, serrations, or any other thing that doesn't serve a purpose I have. I like them to have a thick blade for use as a wedge when batoning. I want them sharp and easy to sharpen in the field. My preferred large blade knives are now made my Fehrman and are extremely robust and will take a licking and keep on ticking. I have also spent countless hours with the TOPS Armageddon which has always performed as required. The original Becker BK-9 was a favorite for many years. The Ontario RTAK and RTAK-II were always just a little on the thin side for my personal liking. But you will decide what is right for you. If I am going to go thin, I might as well have a machete.

The bottom line is this: if you want to carry a large fixed blade knife, carry it as a supplemental blade to your primary blade. You make the choice that is right for you, and don't worry about what other people think. They can carry what they want.

## Machetes

Many people think of a machete when they think of a jungle, but don't let that fool you. They are an extremely versatile tool for any environment. They can clear brush, baton wood, be used as a draw knife and still have plenty of use left. They are a large, long, sharp instrument, so caution in use is recommended, especially when clearing brush. Anything sharp swung around in the air can cause a lot of injury if it meets the wrong target. Don't let it be you.

I prefer a machete, again, as a back-up to a main blade, and always carry one in my truck. Because of their length, machetes are more difficult to carry on your person, but can be strapped to a pack or slung over a shoulder. They are particularly handy in the jungle or a swampy area. They can also be included in a snowmobile kit, as they are handy for cutting snow to build a shelter.

There is a plethora of machetes to chose from. Ontario and Cold Steel both make a line of machetes. There are also some custom machetes available. I prefer those made by Andy Roy at Fiddlebackforge.com, as they are very well made, with an awesome edge and custom micarta handles.

## Fixed blade knife carry

There are many ways to carry a knife in the field. What you want to ensure is that your knife is safe from loss (remember it's your primary survival tool), easy to get in and out of its sheath and protected from the elements, and also that you are protected from getting cut. The primary means to secure a knife is a sheath. The two basic sheaths are leather sheaths and Kydex sheaths. I make all my own leather sheaths and prefer them for most outdoor activity. However, for long term survival in a wet environment I prefer Kydex, as they don't soak up the water and dry quickly. I also prefer Kydex for its ability to lock in a knife, especially if the sheath is worn upside down.

| A typical leather belt-worn sheath. | A secure knife-holding Kydex sheath worn in the upside down position. | A right-side-up leather neck sheath. |

Let's discuss just some of the basic ways to carry a knife in the field which provide for the above considerations.

### Belt carry

Belt carry is pretty straight forward. The sheath is attached to your belt with some form of belt loop or belt clip. For belt carry I usually prefer a leather sheath, but although the positioning at the right rear side does allow easy access to get the knife out, it is sometimes difficult to return.

### Neck carry

Neck carry is another way to keep your knife in a position for easy access. There are two main types of neck carry, right-side up and upside down. Determine what works best for you if you choose this type of carry.

I find that a pocket-type sheath needs to be carried right side up, especially if it does not have a pressure fit. A Kydex sheath which is pressure fit to the knife is the best, in my opinion, for upside down carry. Make sure the knife "clicks" into the sheath, and holds securely. I once had a knife with a plastic manufactured sheath (not Kydex) fall out of the sheath while under my shirt. It could have been a disastrous situation had I not felt it fall and land sideways at the belt line.

## Neck knife supplemental survival kit

The Kydex sheath can be modified to hold some survival essentials. The author's neck knife Kydex sheath has been wrapped with 100 feet of braided fishing line on the back and holds a ferrocerium fire-starting rod. The front has a small leather pouch which holds fishing tackle and a Clipper compass. It is not a complete kit, but is a good back-up for some of the required essentials.

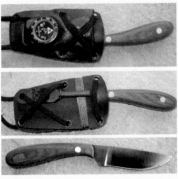

This neck knife was made by Chieftain Knives.

### Leg carry

Leg carry is another issue where people seem to love it or hate it. I have been wearing my large fixed blade knife on a leg rig for over 10 years and prefer it in the field. I normally piggy-back my primary fixed blade knife on the outside of the rig, resulting in quick access to either blade. They are easy to get out and easy to put back. I always use a Kydex sheath for both blades and hang it from the belt with heavy nylon webbing. This provides leeway for the sheath to move forward and back, allowing me to both sit and squat without any restriction. The

 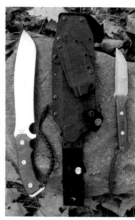

The author's leg rig holds a Fehrman Extreme Judgement, piggy-backed with a Barkriver Bravo-1.

lower end of the sheath always has a leg strap to keep the rig from swinging while walking or other movement. I prefer this type of carry in the field, but it is not for everyone. Just another option and, of course, the decision will be yours.

The author's custom Baldric rig adapter can be used on any of his belt loop sheaths.

The adapter can be attached to a knife sheath.

The Baldric rig adapter attaches to the custom leather shoulder strap the author made.

### Baldric rig

The Baldric rig has been around since ancient times. It is a shoulder belt or sling which has been used to carry a sword, knife (the Romans carried their knives on a Baldric rig), bugles, drums, etc. So why bring this up under survival gear? The Baldric rig is a convenient way to carry a knife or larger blade on the outside of a coat for easy access. Of course, such a rig could be used year round, but I usually use mine in the winter, when trying to get to a belt knife under a coat is rather difficult.

A Baldric rig can be as simple as using parachute cord to hang a belt sheath over your shoulder so that it is on the outside of your jacket or coat. Some people have begun to place rigs on their sheaths for the purpose of hanging them Baldric rig style.

I make all my own leather sheaths and they all have a belt loop. I don't want extraneous rings or loops on them when being used for belt carry.

Therefore, I decided that I would make a leather adapter that would slide into the belt loop of all my leather sheaths which would provide me with two "D" rings from which I could use any type of cordage to strap it over a shoulder. I can carry just the Baldric rig adapter in a small kit, and if I went to a jacket I could carry my knife on the outside. Of course, for everyday hiking I made a leather strap to match the adapter.

### Handling a knife

The first thing to learn about knives is safe handling. I know it sounds like it may not need to be said, but knives are sharp instruments and they can cut you quickly and deeply. I have seen it over and over again, and care must be taken at all times when handling a knife. I always recall the "Blood Circle" from the Boy Scouts and we make sure students at our school understand it, as they are often working in close proximity to one another. The "Blood Circle" is the area around you. Pretend you are holding your knife in your hand, and reach out and carefully turn all the way around. If there is anyone close enough to get cut by a knife if you had one in your hand, then you are too close to that person. If a knife slips when being used, it can be another person that gets stabbed or cut.

Most safety is common sense. Don't cut towards yourself with a knife. Don't hold a piece of wood below the area you are cutting with a knife, but hold it above the area being cut. Most cuts seem to occur on the thumb and forefinger of the hand not holding the knife.

If sitting, hold the item being cut out past your knees. Rest your elbows on your knees when possible which will ensure you are cutting out past your knees and legs. Many injuries occur when a knife slips and the user stabs or cuts their own legs or knees.

I have often seen cuts occur because somebody set their knife down while doing something else, then turned around or reached and were cut by their own knife. When you are not actually using your knife, place it back in its sheath.

# Lanyards for knife retention

Various types of lanyards can be attached to knives if a lanyard hole is available. A lanyard can be used to keep from losing the knife when working over water, etc. Some go over the wrist, and I don't prefer this type of lanyard. I want a lanyard to keep me from dropping the knife, as well as help me control the knife.

The lanyard I use on my knives which provides me with both security and controllability is shown in these pictures. As you can see, when the knife is dropped, all you have to do is turn your wrist, reach down, and re-grasp the knife handle.

The loop at the end of the lanyard goes over the thumb, and the lanyard lays over the back of the hand. If the knife is dropped, it is easily retrieved by reaching down and rolling the wrist to re-grasp the handle.

Because the lanyard limits your reach, you never have to worry about accidently grabbing the blade of the knife when reaching down. I also use this type of lanyard on my large fixed blade knives and it provides superior ability to control the blade.

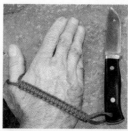

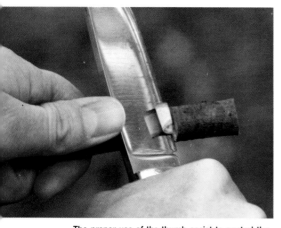

The proper use of the thumb assist to control the knife blade when cutting towards a notch.

When doing any type of fine work with a knife, watch your thumb. This is especially important if cutting around a stick, by rolling it. Don't have your thumb under the blade on the other side of the wood, but to one side or the other.

Don't cradle work in the palm of your hand if carving or cutting out a divot. If the knife slips or goes through the item your working on, you will stab yourself in the palm.

I could go on, but you can see that common sense and staying aware of what you are doing will help prevent unwanted injuries that can make any survival situation worse.

### Thumb assist

The thumb assist is a means to control a knife blade when trying to push a knife blade or when doing delicate work. It works especially well when cutting notches, such as for traps. With the thumb assist, you use your knife hand only to hold the blade of the knife in position in the area of the piece of wood where you want to make a controlled cut. You then use the thumb of the opposite hand, placing it on the spine of the knife blade, and wrap the fingers of that hand around the work. Holding the knife in place with the knife hand, the thumb of the opposite hand pushes the blade of the knife forward in a controlled manner. Again, don't push with the knife hand since, if you slip, you will take the desired notch right off the end of the stick.

### Cutting through a stick

If you need to cut through a stick, but you want a reasonable blunt cut, you will need to make a series of small cuts around the stick. Hold the stick in the non-knife hand, above where you want it cut. If the stick is long enough, support it under the arm pit of the non-knife hand. With the knife hand, start cutting in at a slight angle, using the thumb assist, and continue making cuts as you spin the stick. Once you are all the way around, you can continue in the same manner until the stick is cut through.

Use the thumb assist to cut around a stick.

## Cutting notches

The initial cut for a notch can be cut with a small saw, or by gently batoning. Once the initial cut is made, use the thumb assist to complete the notch. As previously stated, don't push with the knife hand, just hold the knife in position. The thumb of the non-knife hand will be providing the forward pressure.

## Cutting saplings

The technique for cutting down a sapling with a primary knife blade is quite simple. With your non-knife hand, bend the sapling so it bows toward your knife hand. Then take your knife and start a cut at an angle in towards the tree, at the point where the sapling is bending. Holding the knife securely, with downward pressure, rock the knife back and forth while keeping pressure on the sapling. When the cut is almost finished, start to release pressure on the sapling with the left hand, or it will break, causing additional cutting. It should only take several seconds for this process to be complete.

One method to make a notch is to use a small saw to start the notch, then use the thumb assist to carve out the other side.

Bend the sapling and initiate a cut. Then push the blade through the sapling using a rocking motion. Remember to release the pressure from the bent sapling before cutting all the way through.

## Batoning

As with most aspects of knives and their use, batoning is fraught with controversial opinions. I baton and I stand by that position. I have heard people say that they have never batoned and have never had the need to. Others do so all the time. Even though some say that anyone with common sense would never baton, I have usually learned my own lessons and based my decisions on those lessons. However, I do tend to listen to those more experienced than myself, and there are some experts who firmly recommend batoning. Some of those experts, whom I respect, are Ray Mears, Mors Kochanski, Chris Janowsky, Christopher Nyerges, Cody Lundin, Dave Canterbury, Jeff Randall, Les Stroud and Alan Halcon. After reading this section, you will ultimately make the decision for yourself whether to baton or not baton.

Okay, so what is batoning? It is simply splitting wood by pushing a blade through wood by hitting the back of the blade with a wooden baton. It's that simple. So, whay would you choose to baton?

### Better control

When you baton, you normally keep the blade of the knife perpendicular to your body. You then tap the back of the blade with a wooden baton, which can be any piece of wood. Control the blade and, if the blade does go through the wood quickly and unexpectedly, it will not hit your body. I always recommend batoning over a piece of wood, and usually use a short sump if available. The blade, after going through the piece of wood being batoned, will stick into the stump or wood, and not into you or the ground, which definitely is not good for the blade of your knife, or you!.

You can split wood with a hatchet or axe, but this requires swinging and energy. A hatchet and axe will never be as accurate as placing a blade on a piece of wood and tapping the back of the blade. I have known people with a pretty good aim with swinging an object, but even the best have had a hatchet or axe miss the target or, worse, bounce or glance off target. It is difficult to control where the edge goes once you follow through with the swing, and the blade takes off in an undesired direction. This is when accidents occur and the injury from the blade of a hatchet or axe can be severe to say the least – the last thing you need in a survival situation. If you are splitting wood in the back yard, that is one thing. But if you are trying to split some wet wood to extrapolate dry pieces from the center for kindling, batoning is a safer bet. Also, the energy expended by batoning is much less than with swinging a hatchet or axe.

### Precision cutting

Another reason batoning may be preferred is the accuracy of the cut. You may want to cut a spindle off the side of a board being shaped into a fireboard for a bow and drill. You can more precisely split a piece off the side while controlling the blade. That would be a difficult move with a swinging hatchet or axe.

### Energy conservation

Another reason for batoning is less stress on your body parts. I have often sat on a stump in front of another one and batoned for hours. In a survival situation, I would not want to be swinging a heavy sharp object that long. You can also baton while kneeling.

### Weight

One last factor to consider is the weight of a hatchet or axe versus a knife. In a survival situation, you will probably only be carrying a knife. A hatchet maybe. But an axe, probably not. So for the weight of a knife, you will still be able to split larger pieces of wood into smaller pieces.

The bottom line is you must make the decision yourself, not listen to the opinions of others.

## Can batoning break the knife?

Is batoning good for a knife? Well that depends. The proper way to baton is to place the blade straight across the wood being batoned. This allows the force of the baton, hitting the back of the knife, to direct that force straight into the piece of wood you are trying to split. You might have to hit the front or rear of the knife blade once it is past the top portion of the wood you are splitting, and the back of the blade is no longer available to hit. But don't start by hitting the back of the blade on the front end of the knife. This will stress the blade and it might break. It does happen and you must take this into consideration.

I have been batoning most of my adult life and after hundreds of times, I have never personally broken a knife blade. But, I am also careful. I try to get a feel for the wood, and if it feels to hard, I don't force it, but try another piece of wood.

I have seen many videos where people prove they can break a knife while batoning, and it normally occurs when trying to baton bricks or concrete blocks. My advice is don't baton bricks or concrete blocks. A knife is made to cut wood, so I would limit myself to those parameters.

Steady the blade (in this case, a Fehrman Final Judgement) so that the blade is flat across the piece of wood you will be batoning.

Baton by hitting the back of the blade with the baton.

A fixed blade knife works well for making kindling.

To make kindling, work from the outside taking off strips, as opposed to splitting down through the middle each time.

Hawks and hatchets are small enough to carry on a pack. The real small hatchet on the right of the front row is a Gransfors Bruks Mini Hatchet which is probably the lightest yet effective available. It can be carried in a medium size kit or custom carry rigs can be made.

Whenever possible, I try to avoid hardwoods, unless they are of small diameter.

My recommendation is to always use a fixed blade, full tang knife for batoning. As indicated, any type of batoning can stress a knife, especially between the blade and tang, so use the strongest knife you can. I'm often asked if you can baton with a folder. I don't recommend it, but for making kindling, if it is all you have, don't lock the blade. Leave the handle about, what I call, half cocked. Be careful, stick with small wood, and don't use major force with the baton.

## Hatchets and hawks

Hatchets and hawks are another option as cutting tools and are usually small and light enough to carry in a large survival kit or pack. I'm sure you are getting tired of hearing this, but these are another tool to carry at your discretion. They can be used to chop and baton. They can also be used with the hand chocked close to the blade for some fine work as well as planing a board flat, such as for a fire board for bow and drill.

The Mk-V custom hawk by Equinoxcoronado.com in a tiger stripe pattern.

One of the advantages of a hawk is that the head can be used in the hand, without the handle. A handle can be made in the field very quickly, and a very interesting YouTube video is available from IAWoodsman on that subject, called "Cold Steel Trail Hawk." You will be surprised at the versatility of a hawk in the field. After

The ECO Hawk comes with two angled blades on one end and a long angled blade on the other.

A quick hawk can be made using a limb and some parachute cord.

watching that video, you just might decide to carry only the head, and if a handle is needed, make one in the field.

If you are looking for some interesting hawks with some additional versatility, you might want to check out equinoxcoronado.com. They make the Mk-V Hawk with a custom composite handle which has a .50 caliber tube through the length of the handle. This tube has chloroprene plugs that are secured by turning stainless heads which expand the plugs to hold them in place. The tube can be used for various purposes, including as a blow gun or blow tube for fire, or to hold a survival kit. They also offer a product called the ECO-Hawk which is just a head with various blades. It can be handheld or easily attached to a stick to make a field hawk type tool.

A very small hatchet which can be carried in almost any small pack, or attached to a belt, is the Gransfors Bruks Mini Hatchet. Although very light, it is effective at small chores and with a very sharp convex grind works well at batoning. It also has a small hammer head allowing its use to pound stakes for a tarp, or other chores.

Another nice little hatchet is made by Gerber and is called the Sport Axe. It is 13-7/8 inches long and can be carried on or in a pack. Gerber makes various other lengths, but I find the Sport a good size for the money for larger kits or packs.

There are many other manufacturers of hatchets and another good one for a larger kit is the American Snow & Neally Penobscot Bay Axe (It is called an axe but, being 17 inches long overall, it's a hatchet in my mind). Although I have not personally used this model, a good friend of mine, Steve "Critr" Davis, the Lead Instructor for the Pathfinder School of Survival, has tested this model extensively and highly recommends it. I trust his judgment.

I have not addressed axes and do not want anyone to think they have been disregarded. They are large tools and are not normally carried with a survival kit. They are a handy item for a truck kit, if you are skilled in their use. If you want to carry one, that is your choice, but as an injury can be extremely severe, learn the proper use before planning to use one in a survival situation.

Dude McLean wears a custom shoulder rig made for a Gransfors Bruks Mini Hatchet which, like a Baldric rig, can be worn outside of a jacket for easy access.

Photo by Alan Halcon.

The cable saw can be used with a sapling as a bow saw or with hand holds made from branches. Rolled tightly, it can be carried in a mini or small survival kit.

Make hand holds from branches and place them through the split rings on each end of the saw.

Use the cable saw as a bow saw by bending a sapling and notching each end for the split rings to slide into.

The pocket chain saw is a clever device for some serious survival cutting.

## Saws

The are various type saws that can be carried in a survival kit. I have always found that their versatility makes them ideal for many survival situations. They come in many configurations and sizes, so let's look at a few that can easily be carried in different size kits.

### Wire saws

A wire saw is exactly that. It is constructed of eight strands of interwoven stainless steel wire. Split ring handles swivel providing twist-free performance. It can also be used to make a bow saw and will slide over itself, for use as an emergency snare, by placing the small ring through the larger ring. This saw fits in an "Altoids" tin survival kit.

When using with the split rings on the ends, I recommend cutting two short pieces of a branch and placing them through the rings instead of trying to saw with your fingers through the split rings. This provides a more substantial hand hold. When making a bow saw, get a sturdy bendable sapling and notch each end so that the split rings stay attached to each end without sliding up.

### Pocket chain saws

The pocket chain saw is a great addition to any survival kit. It features 124 bi-directional, heat treated steel cutting teeth that cut on both the upstroke and the down stroke. Also, since it is flexible, it wraps around the wood on three sides, increasing its efficiency. In a survival situation, this saw is safer than an axe or power chain saw since it won't bounce off a log into a leg or foot. By attaching a cord to each end, it can cut limbs in hard-to-reach places. It stores in a small metal can about the size of a small shoeshine tin and easily fits in a shirt pocket.

## Small folding saws

A small folding saw is something I am never without in the field. It starts with the small folding saw blade on my Victorinox Farmer and One Hand Trekker and goes up from there. Small pruning saws are invaluable for cutting wood to lengths with a flat end to facilitate batoning. They are also great for building shelters and many other purposes in a survival situation. Most can be carried in a small to medium sized survival kit, and when used wisely are safer than swinging a sharp tool.

One of my favorite pruning saws is the Bahco Laplander. This a robust folding saw and really cuts. Another option I have carried that is less expensive is the Gerber Sportsman's saw. This saw is very light and fits in any medium size kit.

## Large folding saws

Larger folding saws can make cutting wood a pleasure as opposed to a chore. Two of my favorites are the Trailblazer Sawvivor and Take-Down Bucksaw. The Sawvivor is one of the strongest saws for its weight and I carry the 15-inch version in my pack. It assembles in seconds, is easy to use and is an efficient tool. A unique tensioning system and a box frame provide for superior blade tension. This is a lightweight saw that really cuts. The rustproof aluminum handle is padded and stores two blades when they are not in use. This saw is available in both 15- and 18-inch lengths.

The Trailblazer Take-Down Buck Saw is one of my favorites, but is heavier than the Sawvivor. I carry one of these in my truck and when I am canoeing. The Take-Down Buck Saw is modeled after a classic wood saw design. The aluminum saw has a tension rod that tightens

Folding saws, both small and large, collapse for transport and assemble in seconds for use.

Another way to have a buck saw in the field is to carry just a blade and make one when you get there.

the blade until it twangs like a guitar string. The Swedish steel blade can be put to work cutting pieces of wood as thick as 15 inches. For transport, the saw collapses and its parts all fit inside the 19-inch round handle, along with up to two blades. Available in 18- or 24-inch length.

Another way to have a buck saw in the field is to carry just a blade and make one when you get there. A good friend of mine, Rod Garcia (remember the Skookum Bush Tool), carries a saw blade in a leather belt that holds the blade safely so he can wear the belt as a normal belt. He then makes a buck saw from available wood in the field. My wife fell in love with the saw when we were with him for a week in the field, and he was kind enough to gift it to her when we left. It was fun taking apart to fit in a bag for the flight back.

To avoid cutting your hand while using a buck saw, place the hand holding the work through the opening between the saw blade and frame.

The correct way to cut a supported piece of wood allows the cut piece to fall off when the cut is complete.

STOP! Holding the wood this way, if the saw bounces out of the cut being made, the blade will skid across the back of the hand holding the work.

STOP! Sawing the incorrect way, the downward pressure on the wood will cause the cut to close on each side of the saw blade, causing the blade to bind.

### Field tested tips for using a saw

Before moving on, I would like to mention saw safety. A saw can quickly bite you, especially if you use it incorrectly. I have had more than one saw blade jump out of a cut being made and skid across my hand. This always occurs when not paying attention.

When using a buck saw, place the off hand (the one holding the work being cut) through the opening between the saw blade and the frame. If the blade bounces out of the cut, the back top portion of the blade will bounce off the inside of the arm holding the work. The blade will not skid across the back of your hand.

A tip that will seem like common sense deals with cutting a piece of wood supported on something in order to cut it. The piece you are cutting off should hang over the support. If you try to cut the wood between the support, and where the other end sets on the ground, the downward pressure will bind the saw blade because the pressure applied to saw closes the cut against the blade. I have seen this many times with students and find it a tip worth mentioning.

### Snow saw

If you plan to be in snow country, a snow saw is a recommended item. A snow saw made by Life-Link is extremely light and carries well on a pack.

## Multi-tools

Another tool that can be handy in a survival situation is a multi-tool. I recall when they first came out and there was only one to choose from. That was the original Leatherman tool. I still have a few of the originals around. Now there are hundreds to choose from. I won't elaborate on them, but personally prefer a good pair of pliers with a cutter for wire, and various options like a file, scissors, etc. which aren't available in any of my Victorinox knives. My preference is still the Gerber, as it allows you to open the pliers with one hand using a fling forward motion with the hand holding the tool. The choice is yours in regard to how many tools they contain, but they can be a handy item in a survival situation.

## Trowels & shovels

### Small folding trowels

Small trowels are handy for everything from digging edible plants to making a trench fire pit to preparing a cat hole or digging a seepage basin to collect water. Although

Various multi-tools are available. The tool at the top is an original Leatherman.

not a necessary tool, it can be useful. They are made in plastic and stainless steel. Although the plastic models are lighter, I prefer the stainless steel trowel made by U-Dig-It, which comes with a nice cordura belt pouch.

The Life-Link snow saw is recommended gear for snow country.

The U-Dig-It stainless steel trowel comes with a cordura belt pouch.

### Large folding shovels

Although larger shovels are normally reserved for vehicle kits, they are useful for survival. The size and shape are limited by how much weight you are willing to carry. The old military folding shovel is still a viable option as well as a new smaller version made by Gerber called the Gorge. Although they are all heavy, the Gorge can be carried in a pack or large kit.

### Snow shovels

If you anticipate being in a snow covered area, then a snow shovel can be real handy for making snow shelters. There are many types, made specifically for carrying on a pack, where the handle separates from the shovel portion. I highly recommend one in snow country.

My preference is the Voile T6 Shovel w/Saw, in orange. The orange T6 scoop is one of the most durable shovel scoops I have found. It uses premium 6061-T6 heat treated aluminum. It also has deadman holes for use in a rescue sled or as an emergency anchor. The shovel houses a hi-tensile steel saw blade which is a do-all saw blade of amazing toughness. It can be used for avalanche pit work, shelter building or to cut just about anything. The blade stows inside the shovel shaft and is held in place with a double pop-button. The saw easily attaches to the telescoping shaft for extended reach. The effective cutting length for the saw blade is 10 inches. The shovel can be used with the handle short or extend. I keep one of these in my truck and it always goes on my sled when snowshoeing.

The Voile T6 Snow shovel can be used with the handle short or extended.

The Voile T6 shovel houses a hi-tensile steel saw blade that stows inside the shovel shaft. The saw easily attaches to the telescoping shaft.

The SnowClaw Backcountry Snow Shovel weighs in at only six ounces.

Another handy device which can be carried easily on or in a pack is the SnowClaw Backcountry Snow Shovel. It is very light, weighing in at only six ounces. One edge can be used for digging soft snow, and the other more rounded edge for hard snow. As a multi-use tool, it can be used as a shovel, snow anchor, emergency splint, plate, sled, waterproof seat, etc. It is made from high impact copolymer and is only 12 x 11.25 inches.

Chapter 5

# Fire & Light - Survival Assets

One of the most important skills in a survival situation is the ability to successfully start a fire. A remarkable array of benefits result from fire. It produces heat and provides light so you can continue activities when it becomes dark. You can dry your wet clothes. Both the light and smoke of a fire can be used to signal your location to searchers. Fire boils water to purify it for safe drinking. It also provides a means to cook in order to make food safe to eat, or more palatable. One overlooked benefit of fire is a sense of companionship, a friend in the dark that repels the noises of the night. Fire provides comfort and is a morale builder.

Although man has been making and using fire for thousands of years, what exactly is fire? Let's take a look at the technical aspects of fire, as it will help you better understand how to create it. After all, that is the skill you need to master.

The Fire Triangle

According to the American Heritage Dictionary, fire is "a rapid, persistent chemical change that releases heat and light and is accompanied by flame, especially the exothermic oxidation of a combustible substance." A real mouthful, but what does that really mean?

Fire is a chemical process. In order for this process to occur you must have oxygen, heat and fuel, often referred to as the "Fire Triangle." If you do not have all three elements, a fire cannot start or be sustained.

To make a fire, we need air, which is the source of oxygen for the fire. How many times have you seen someone fan a fire, or blow on it, to keep it going? That is oxygen being added to the heat and fuel to keep the oxidation process going. On the other hand, if you smother a fire, it will go out. No oxygen, no fire.

The heat can be generated by various means, including a spark, a hot ember or the concentrated beam of the sun's rays.

Fuel can be anything that is combustible. In a survival situation that will usually be some sort of tinder, like shredded bark, or other type of natural material (more on that later) that has a low flash point, followed by wood (if available) to maintain the fire.

If you have an adequate amount of oxygen, you must apply an adequate amount of heat in order to ignite the fuel. When the fuel is raised to its ignition temperature, combustion occurs and you have fire. Once a fire is started, it can be sustained as long as the three elements are maintained.

## Site selection & preparation

Before we get into actually making fire, let's begin by discussing site selection and preparation. When looking for a suitable site, try to locate an area that is flat and is protected from the wind and rain.

Whenever possible, fire making materials should be close at hand. Don't build your fire in an area where you must go and collect fuel and lug it back to the fire location. Build your fire as close to your shelter as safety allows. Too close will threaten you and your shelter; too far and no warmth is gained. When possible, build a reflector to direct heat from the fire towards your shelter.

Wherever you build your fire, clear flammable debris from a good three-foot circle or more around the fire location. Remove all leaves, brush, roots and other flammable litter. If there is snow on the ground, build a platform from green wood to start your fire on. If the snow is deep, remove as much as you can before building the platform.

To construct a reflector, pound two vertical uprights in the ground (about the width of the fire apart), leaning them slightly away from the fire, and stack small green logs horizontally on top of each other. You might need more vertical uprights in front of the horizontal logs to keep them from rolling off each other. Build this reflector on the back side of the fire, opposite of you. You can also build a reflector using rocks, if available. Make a three sided enclosure leaving the front, towards you, open. Either of these reflectors will help reflect heat back towards you.

## Tinder, kindling and fuel

Don't wait until you start the fire to think about gathering fuel. Collect it all before you begin. Fuel consists of tinder, kindling and fuel (bulk firewood).

### Tinder - manmade

Tinder is any type of small flammable material with a low flash point, easily ignited with a minimum of heat, even a spark. When it is raining or snowing and you need to start a fire, dry tinder is one of the more difficult items to locate in the outdoors. Therefore, let's first address man made tinder, as it should always be carried in a survival kit.

One of the easiest ways to make tinder from a survival kit is with petroleum jelly and cotton balls. Make sure the cotton balls are 100% cotton and not the synthetic type or they won't burn, they'll just melt. Apply petroleum jelly to the cotton balls, working the petroleum into the cotton balls with your fingers, so they are coated, but not saturated. For use as tinder, you only need a small piece of a cotton ball, which can be pulled off. You'll be amazed how flammable these cotton balls are and how easily they light by a spark. Keep them in a match case, an aluminum capsule or other such container.

Great choices for tinder include cotton balls with petroleum jelly, Tinder-Quick Fire Tabs and WetFire Tinder.

A good commercially-available tinder, one that I use in my survival kit tins, is called Tinder-Quick Fire Tabs, manufactured by Four-Seasons Survival. They resemble a cigarette filter. They are all-weather and even light when wet. Use them by pulling the tabs apart, avoiding touching or matting the inner fibers. Then ignite the fluffed fibers with a spark and they burn for two to three minutes. I find these tabs to be very handy, especially when making mini survival kits, like the one I make in an Altoids tin.

These Tinder-Quick Fire tabs are dry and can be pushed down into the various nooks, crannies, and open corners, which keeps the mini kit from rattling. For most of my mini kits these are my choice. I also carry two of these in my wallet, just in case!

Another commercial tinder product is WetFire Tinder, manufactured by Ultimate Survival Technologies. It is a small dry cube (approx. 1-3/4 x 1 x 1/2 inches), individually wrapped, which lights even setting in water. A small pile of shavings from one of these cubes is enough to start a fire. I have found that after several years they do dry out and will not light, which is a consideration for long term storage. I called the manufacture and they indicated that if the seal on the package breaks they will dry out, which affects their ability to light.

Some new tinder that has become available is MayaDust Tinder and TinderSticks which are both manufactured by Industrial Revolutions, Inc. MayaDust Tinder is shavings from MayaSticks which are made from Pino de Ocote, a fatwood pine cultivated in the highlands of Guatemala and Mexico. With 80% resin content, this tinder is easy to light even when wet, and produces an extremely hot flame. The MayaDust comes in a round plastic package measuring 2-3/4 inches diameter by 7/8-inch high. It only weighs seven ounces.

MayaDust Tinder and TinderSticks are two tinder choices from from Industrial Revolutions, Inc.

Jute twine makes great tinder when unraveled and worked into a nest.

## Tinder Tip #1

Almost everyone carries at least a small first aid kit, and alcohol pads are included in almost all of those kits. For use as a fire starter, or even a short term candle, just cut a small "X" in the top of the package and pull a small amount of the alcohol pad up through the "X." You can then light it even with the sparks from a Ferrocerium rod. This also works well with disinfectant hand wipes. Also, liquid hand sanitizer is very flammable. Just squirt it on your tinder, like Fire Ribbon, and it burns very hot.

The second product, TinderSticks, is also made from Pino de Ocote. I tested these sticks against some of the fatwood sold in stores, and these are the best I have found. The shavings I made from these sticks easily ignited with just a spark. They come in a package of eight to 10 sticks and they average about eight inches long. To carry them more easily in a pack or kit, saw them into shorter lengths and split them into smaller pieces by batoning.

A product that works great but is not actually sold as tinder is jute twine. It can be purchased in most hardware or gardening stores. Carry a small roll of this in your kit and you'll always have dry tinder. Simply cut off a piece and unravel the three strands it is made from. Then unravel these three individual strands, fluff it all up into a little nest and you are ready to ignite with even one spark. This tinder is inexpensive, effective and provides extra cordage to build a shelter!

Another manmade tinder usable in the field is a fine grade steel wool, preferably "0000" grade. Steel wool never actually ignites into a flame, but becomes a large ember which can be placed into tinder and blown into flame. To initiate an ember, pull a piece of steel wool into a long thin piece and bend it so each end of the steel wool touches the positive and negative side of a battery. An ember will appear almost immediately and travel through the steel wool.

Note that sufficient voltage must be provided, which I have found is a minimum of about three volts. One AA or AAA battery is only 1.5 volts, so will not ignite the steel wool. However, two placed in series will. Of course, most cell phone batteries are over three volts and work well for igniting the steel wool. The batteries of some new cell phones, such as the I-Phone, have a protection circuit built in which will not allow the battery to be shorted, which is basically what you are doing. If you ever plan on using this method as a back-up, try your battery before you need it. Of course, many flash lights, GPS units, etc. have two batteries of 1.5 volt.

## Tinder - natural

Natural tinder is any dry tinder you can find in the outdoors, again, that has a low flash point and is easily ignited with minimum heat, including a spark. Many books list various types of natural tinder available in the outdoors, but without knowing what they look like, many people have a difficult time identifying them when they see them. This chapter shows various types available, especially in the northeast U.S.

The first is bark and shredded bark of certain trees, beginning with Paper Birch. Very few people have not seen a picture of the beautiful bark of a Paper Birch, almost pure white, with pieces of bark peeling off like sheets of paper. This was the bark that was harvested over the centuries by the northern tribes of Native Americans. They used it to make canoes, houses, and fashion utensils such as cups and bowls. Small rolls of the bark can be used to start campfires, even in wet weather, as it burns even when wet. It has also been used to make torches.

However, other barks work well as tinder, but you must be able to identify them in the field.

One of my favorite finds in the woods is a Yellow Birch (often called "Curly Birch"). It is, in my opinion, one of the best tinders found in the woods. Yellow Birch has thin, paper-like, yellowish gray bark that peels from the side of the tree in curls. The trunk has randomly placed fine horizontal lines on it called lenticels. Leaves on the curly birch are alternate, simple, but you will identify it by the bark. The paper-like curls of bark can be collected quickly and, after buffing a small amount between the palms of your hands to break up the fibers and placing these on the remaining curls, easily ignites with just a spark. When you find this precious tinder, collect some in a zip-closure bag and carry it in your pack. I always have enough for several fires in my day pack.

**Several kinds of tree bark work well as tinder.**

Yellow "Curly" Birch    River Birch    Red Cedar

River Birch is my next favorite tinder, if the trees are not too old. When this tree gets older, the remarkable peeling bark becomes rough and ragged. However, where there is an old one you can often find a younger one. The younger bark is a salmon pink to bronze-brown and peels loose horizontally in sheets of various layers, and is easily harvested. Just shredding a few pieces without buffing is usually enough to ignite it with a simple spark. I have several of these trees in my yard, and even though they are about seven or eight years old, they are still considered young and the entire tree provides tinder year round.

Cedar, especially Red Cedar, is another one of my favorites. The outside bark can be pulled off in shreds and buffed into useable tinder. However, once the outside bark is removed, the tree can be scraped with the blade of a knife to get really fine shreds of bark that make excellent tinder.

Seed down from various plants makes a fine tinder, although some burns quickly (I call this a "flash-in-the-pan") and some burn reasonably long. The first is cattail, which has been called the grocery store of wild edibles. It is found in fresh and brackish marshes and shallow water. In the late fall, the female flower, which looks like a brown sausage-like head, starts to open and a

The seed down that is easily removed from cattails for use as tinder.

Milkweed pods offer tinder in the form of seed down in the fall.

Phragmites in the field have a silky, plume-like terminal flower cluster.

bunch of whitish-yellow fluff (seed down) exudes from inside, hanging on to the side. This is what you use as tinder. Collect a few of the sausage-like heads, and the contents of just one should be ample to start a fire. Pull the seed down out and, without pressing it together too tight, ignite with a spark. This is one tinder that is a flash-in-the-pan. Be ready with the rest of your fire starting materials because it doesn't last long.

The next seed down to consider is milkweed, which is found in dry soil, fields and roadsides. In the fall, the seed pods open and, like cattail, exude fluffy seed down. This is another flash-in-the-pan tinder, so ready to go with your kindling and wood. It is easily collected and can be kept in a pocket or zip-closure bag until needed.

The seed down from various thistle can also be used as tinder, but they provide a small quantity. If there's another option, use it.

Dried grasses make excellent tinder and are often available from fall through spring. I have collected dried grass that was sticking up out of the snow and was dry from the sun. Another often overlooked tinder is Phragmites, also known as Reed. These can usually be found in the same locations as cattail, but are often more abundant. In the fall they have a silky, plume-like, terminal flower cluster that not only ignites easily with a spark but stays burning for a reasonable amount of time - more than enough to get a fire going.

Another overlooked tinder item found in the field are bird nests. They are made up of fine dried grasses and shreds of bark, etc., and make an excellent tinder ball.

Another great tinder is the resinous wood from pine or other sappy conifers. Often called fatwood, it is made from the heartwood of pines that are naturally saturated with dried resin, also called pitch. This wood can come from stumps of trees that died standing. Under the right conditions after a pine tree dies, the heartwood will fill up with resin, which eventually crystallizes and hardens. This wood is resistant to rot and usually lasts until it is burned. It's the same material that amber is made from. It is common for the sapwood to rot away from the fatwood, and the fatwood is all that is left of the tree or stump. It only takes a small amount of fatwood kindling to start a fire. You can light a piece of fatwood fire starter directly with a match or lighter. With good fatwood, a pile of very small shavings can be lit with just a spark.

If you can't find fatwood, take any wood and split it several times by batoning so you have some pieces with the center revealed. Scrape the center with the blade of your knife at a 90 degree angle to the wood to get fuzzy scrapings. These will usually ignite with a spark.

You can also obtain tinder from the crushed fibers of dead plants. If you can find a rotting tree that is dry, break up the rooting part with your hand to make some fine tinder. Dried leaves can also be easily crushed for a fine tinder.

In order for natural tinder to work, it must be dry. It also must have fibers that can catch a spark. If the tinder has any hard bark or pith,

## Tinder Tip #2

I have been carrying a small pencil sharpener in my fire kit for years. It is my tinder maker. It is even effective when wood is wet, as I can scrape off the wet outside, then make plenty of shavings from the nice dry wood inside. Works real well on small sticks found laying around. My students always enjoy this tip, so try it, you'll like it!

remove it before use. Loosen the fibers by twisting the tinder, or rub it between the palms of your hands, which I call buffing. Buffing tinder can also help remove slight moisture that might remain in it. Or, pound the tinder with a rock or wooden baton to break up the fibers.

You want a fluffy bundle of tinder when you are done, loosely packed so when it takes a spark oxygen can circulate (remember the fire triangle).

One last hint about tinder: when you find it, collect it! Don't wait until you need it, as it might not be available. I don't think I have ever passed a Yellow "Curly" Birch tree without taking some of the curly bark and adding it to the zip-closure bag in my pack. I always know that I have dry tinder when I need it. As always, be prepared to survive.

### Kindling

Kindling is the next larger stage of fuel material. It should also have a high combustible point. For initial kindling, use very tiny twigs, wood shavings or sticks ranging in size from pencil lead up to the size of a pencil itself. They must be dry and easily lit from burning tinder. The next level of kindling can be from pencil size to larger than your thumb. This size is found lying around or dead but still attached under various coniferous tress. Larger wood can also be split into kindling size by batoning.

For fine tinder that will light with a spark, scrape the center of a piece of split wood with the knife at 90 degrees to the wood.

Make wood shavings using the blade of a knife.

Place the wood scrapings in a pile with the wood shavings sprinkled around them. The tinder is then easily lit with a single spark.

### Fuel

Fuel is any wood that is thumb size or larger. Be careful when adding fuel. Don't go from thumb size to wrist size. Add wood in appropriate sizes, working your way up to larger wood. I have seen a lot of students get a good fire started only to smother it using fuel that was too large.

Good fuel can often be found in trees that are "standing dead." In other words, the tree is dead and has been so for awhile, yet it is still standing. They are usually dry, as the water runs off them when it rains. Dead trees laying on the ground are often wet, having soaked up and retained moisture. If standing dead can't be found, look for trees that have died and fallen but are leaning up against another tree. These are also usually dry.

If fuel is wet, baton it, as it is usually dry on the inside. Instead of cutting fuel to length, burn them in half or pieces, saving a lot of energy on your part.

From left to right, strike anywhere matches, "Storm" matches and "Lifeboat" matches with their own waterproof vial. The bottom are extra long "UCO" Stormproof Matches.

## Instant fire

To start a fire you need a heat source. Various heat sources can be carried with you that will give you instant fire.

### Matches

Matches are an important component for any survival kit. They provide instant flame. However, regular stick or book matches are not advisable. Matches should be waterproof and windproof if possible.

The easiest way to obtain waterproof matches is to make them yourself. Book matches can be immersed in "Thompson's Water Seal" (found in most hardware stores) and allowed to dry. Although I don't recommend book matches, they make a small package when size is essential.

If you are making your own waterproof matches, my recommendation is strike-anywhere stick matches. Melt paraffin (the kind used for canning) by placing it in a small can and then set that can in a pot of boiling water (so the water heats the can but does not allow water to enter the can, like a double boiler). When the paraffin melts and becomes liquid, use tweezers to dip each strike anywhere stick match into the melted paraffin, immersing them completely. Lay them on a piece of aluminum foil until dry. They are then ready to use. However, there are many good commercially available waterproof/windproof matches available, and they will save you the time of making them yourself. These also have the added advantage of being windproof.

There are three that I recommend. The first are "Storm" matches which are wind and waterproof. They are made in the UK and imported by Pro Force Equipment. These matches actually burn in the strongest winds and rain, but they come in a match box and so should be repacked in a waterproof match case.

Another good product is "Windproof & Waterproof Safety Matches"; also known as lifeboat matches. They are NATO approved, made in England and imported by Pro Force Equipment. These matches are essentially the same as the Storm matches but come packed in a re-sealable plastic vial with a striker on the lid. My only complaint is that the striker is on the outside, which allows it to get wet.

# Striking Matches

When striking a match outdoors, especially if it's windy, hold the match between your thumb and forefinger. Then support the match with your middle finger when striking the match across the striker material. As soon as the match lights, cup the match inside your cupped hands. This protects the flame while moving the lit match to your tinder.

My new favorite wind and waterproof matches are the "Stormproof" matches by UCO. They not only burn in the harshest conditions, but are longer than all the matches discussed above. These matches are 2.75 inches long (the others being only 1-7/8 inches).

## Waterproof match cases

Waterproof matches, although initially waterproof, will not remain so if they are subjected to an over abundance of water. They may be fine if it is raining, but they cannot set in water for any length of time before the water eventually soaks in, usually through the ends. Therefore a water proof match case is always recommended to store matches for a survival kit. They can be made from various containers.

One of the more popular used to be a 35mm film canister. With the advent of digital photography, they are becoming more scarce. Various plastic medicine vials from your local pharmacist are waterproof and long enough for matches. When you store matches in a case, remember to include a striker, which can be removed from a package of book matches. The strike-anywhere matches will usually light without a striker if you have a dry surface, but sometimes a dry surface is hard to find when you're soaked. A striker maintained in a waterproof case ensures you always have a dry surface. Survival Resources sells a waterproof plastic vial that even fits the new longer matches.

From left to right, top: the Survival Resources Waterproof Vial and a commercial waterproof case. Bottom: both the long and standard size match case made by K&M Industries, Inc.

Many commercially-available match holders are durable and waterproof. Make sure you get one with a screw cap and rubber gasket. Some of these cases also have a small ferrocerium rod on the bottom of the container.

One of the best match cases I have found on the market is made by K&M Industries. These cases have a press-fit stopper with a double O-ring seal, which is held in place by the lanyard which provides a positive lock but allows quick and easy access to the match case contents. Each case is fitted with a quality Suunto, liquid-dampened jeweled compass, made in Finland. Each case has an interior striking surface for strike-anywhere matches. Each case is hand turned from solid bar stock, hand fitted and assembled to ensure a quality product. They are available in a standard length, approximately 3-7/8 inches long, which holds both Storm and Lifeboat matches, as well as strike-anywhere matches. They also make a long case, approximately 4-1/4 inches long, to accommodate longer matches such as the UCO Stormproof, or those made by REI. The K&M Match Cases are available in aluminum (really light) and brass. These are the Cadillac of match cases in my opinion.

Be careful with some of the cheaper match case models available on the market. Even though some include a compass for navigation, they are not liquid filled and are inadequate. Some have a built-in whistle for signaling, but most are "pea" whistles and are not very loud.

## Tip For Storing Lighters In Your Survival Kit

When storing a lighter in a survival kit, if it gets in a position where the gas lever is pressed, all the gas will escape from the lighter. When you want to use it for an emergency it will be empty. To prevent this, place a small cable tie around the lighter between the body of the lighter and the gas lever. Or, tie a piece of jute twine in the same position, which serves the dual purpose of also providing tinder.

### Disposable butane lighters

Another inexpensive item that provides instant flame is a disposable butane lighter. They are available in many shapes and sizes and can be purchased at any convenience store. There seem to be multiple schools of thought in regard to disposable butane lighters. The first is to carry standard, non-adjustable lighters, as they are simple and work. The other is to carry an adjustable flame lighter, so you can crank it up and get a larger flame. I recommend that you use the lighter that is right for you and works for you.

My favorite disposables are BIC lighters. They have small and medium-size lighters in various colors (blaze orange is my favorite as you can see them easily) for both mini survival kits and medium size kits.

A tip on disposable lighters is that they can still be used as a flint sparker even when they run out of fuel.

### Spark based firestarting

Many of the fire starters available for survival are spark based. They are an extremely reliable source of fire if used correctly. The real secret is to have good, prepared tinder to catch the spark.

## Ferrocerium and mischmetal

There isn't much dofference betwen these two materials, but in order to clear up some confusion in regard to many of the new mischmetal firestarters available today, I have separated the two terms for the purpose of this book. In the older days, all ferrocerium rods were called mischmetal. But there is a new generation of mischmetal rods.

I am not a scientist, nor do I play one on television, so I will try to simply explain the difference, at least in my mind, between the two terms. As a short background, my wife is from Switzerland and speaks fluent Swiss German and German. She was the first to voice confusion to me about the term mischmetal as it relates to ferrocerium. She explained that the term mischmetal is from the German word Mishmetall, meaning mixed metal. She said that a ferrocerium rod is made of a mixture of metal, and so according to the definition a ferrocerium rod is a mischmetal rod. It's hard to argue with the Swiss.

But the terms have taken on their own vernacular by the survival/fire starting community. The terms are used to distinguish between two types of fire starting rods or tools. Therefore, I will define how the terms are used in this book to discuss fire starting devices.

A mischmetal, also known as cerium mischmetal, is an alloy of rare earth elements, namely those from the lanthanum series. I already feel eyes rolling, so I won't go into detail about the elements. However, the resultant mischmetal by itself is too soft to use as a flint, such as used in a lighter. Therefore, it is blended with iron oxide and magnesium oxide. The resulting man-made material is called ferrocerium (probably because of the addition of the iron - ferro and the mischmetal -cerium, hence ferrocerium) and will produce sparks to ignite tinder when scraped by a sharp edge, usually a piece of steel. The scraper is usually called a "striker." For years, this was the only type of spark-producing fire starting device that came in a rod form, and was termed a ferrocerium rod or a mischmetal firestarter.

Enter the 21st century and a desire for a hotter firestarter rod. A new firestarter rod is introduced and called a "Mischmetal" rod. I know, I know, but what can I say. This rod allows the user to obtain both a sufficient ignition spark and an ample shower of hot burning flakes of magnesium used to ignite tinder. Without getting too technical, this is done by lowering the iron content and increasing the magnesium content. The increased amount of magnesium, relative to the decreased iron content, results in a softer rod. The pieces that scrape off are larger and, after being ignited by sparks, continue to burn after leaving the rod.

There you have it. For the purpose of this book, a ferrocerium rod (also known as a ferro rod) is harder, gives lots of sparks, but the sparks don't continue to burn. A mischmetal rod gives large burning chunks of magnesium that continue to burn after leaving the rod. So which is better for survival? It is really a user preference thing. There are advocates on both sides of the fence.

I, being old school, still prefer the ferrocerium rod. It is hard and, in my opinion, lasts much longer than a mischmetal rod. A ferro rod only gives you sparks, but hot sparks, and they have always been adequate for me to ignite tinder. The sparks are fairly easy to aim into a tinder pile.

The way a mischmetal rod is designed, large pieces are scraped off each time you scrape it. I have found that, because the mischmetal rod has large burning pieces of magnesium being carved off the rod, they seem to be more difficult to aim, at least for me. I have also found that the rods wear down in a much shorter time than a ferro rod. However, I have found that when the hot burning pieces of magnesium do find their way into the tinder, they burn longer. I have heard some old-timers comment that a mischmetal rod is for those that don't know how to adequately prepare their tinder. I've also heard others state that in a survival situation, the easier the better.

To make an intelligent decision, experiment with both and determine which is best for you. As I have always told students, you have to use what works for you!

## Spark-Lite Firestarter

The Spark-Lite Firestarter is a unique fire starting device, the first one-handed firestarter, invented by Oak Duke Norton, Jr. Oak was in the US Army, serving first in Korea and then in Vietnam in 1963, 1967 and 1968. While there, he discovered that the issue lighter in survival kits often leaked and, as with matches, unless they were sealed in a waterproof container, proved useless.

Sometime in 1979, Oak created a small two-handed device and called it the Spark-Lite. Oak also envisioned a one-handed model and, in 1984, he finally had a concept for a one-handed model. The original prototype was round and was difficult to hold when trying to spin the striker wheel, so Oak went back to the drawing board. He felt that if the device was square, it would be easier to hold between two fingers while spinning the striker wheel with a third finger. This new square prototype was tested and Oak found that it worked very well.

This original Spark-Lite was made from brass and had a small screw at the bottom so the flint could be replaced. Somehow, the Army Research Institute at Natick, Massachusetts, got hold of one of these early models and contacted Oak for further information. Oak visited the institute and discussed the product with them. They liked it, but it was heavy. They wanted it to be made out of plastic. If he could have them made from plastic they would buy it. As they say, the rest is history.

The Spark-Lite Firestarter Kit is still the smallest, most effective one handed fire starter on the market today, and is the official U.S. military firestarter. About the size of four matches, it measures only 2-1/4 inches long by 5/16-inch square, and comes in a case with eight Tinder-Quick Fire Tabs. It is certainly small enough to carry in a waterproof match case as a back-up to matches.

To use the Spark-Lite, hold it between your thumb, middle finger and the finger below that. This leaves your index finger sticking up, which is then used to spin the flint wheel. Direct the sparks into your tinder. They are still available in plastic in both OD green and orange. However, they have also introduced the Spark-Lite in aluminum, and have re-introduced the screw at the bottom so the flints can be replaced (an option that was not available with the original plastic units). They are manufactured by Four Seasons Survival, and I highly recommend that it be one of your fire starting devices.

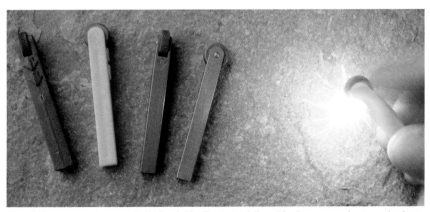

From left: a green and orange plastic Spark-Lite Firestarter, followed by the green and orange aluminum Spark-Lite. These devices produce effective sparks.

Top, left to right: the Mini, Scout and Army Swedish FireSteel by Light My Fire, followed by the Survival Resources Big-Stick Flint. Bottom: the BlastMatch and StrikeForce firestarters by Ultimate Survival Technologies.

## A Ferrocerium Storage Tip

If you are going to store a Ferro rod for any length of time in a survival kit, it will begin to oxidize and corrode. In order to protect the rod in storage, coat it with clear nail polish or lacquer. When you need to use the rod, just scrape the coating off and use it normally.

### Ferrocerium rod

The pioneers and mountain men carried flint and steel to start fires. Today we do the same thing, but the flint and steel has changed.

Today, they are called ferrocerium rods, and as previously described, they are manmade. They are used by scraping a steel striker along the length of the ferro rod causing sparks which you direct into prepared tinder to start a fire. Any steel can be used as a striker, including a carbon steel knife. A hardened stainless steel knife also works but does not provide as many sparks as a carbon steel knife.

Some of the best ferro rods out there are the FireSteel models offered by Light My Fire. Made in Sweden, they offer various sizes to fit anything from a mini kit to a large kit. The Mini, which measures three inches long with a 1/8-inch diameter ferro rod is my preferred model for mini kits and use on key rings. The Scout (three inches

# Using A Ferrocerium Rod

A ferrocerium rod is not difficult to use. However, I have seen complications with people who do not know the proper use. Some try to strike the ferro rod with the striker using short, choppy hits. Although a few sparks appear, you don't get a large spray of sparks, which is what you need to ignite the tinder. Others hold the ferro rod in place then scrape the striker forward towards the tinder, hitting the tinder with the striker and knocking it all over.

The first thing to do is prepare your tinder, so when the sparks start flying you are ready to make fire. Hold the striker in place next to the tinder pile. I like to firmly secure the striker by placing the palm of the hand holding the striker on the ground. Place the ferro rod under the striker so the striker is at the back of the rod, just ahead of the hand holding it. The striker should be at an angle to the rod, about 45 degrees. You want the sharp edge of the striker sliding along the rod, not a flat edge.

When you are ready to begin, hold the striker in place and pull the ferrocerium rod back towards you. While pulling the rod back, slide the striker along the entire length of the rod keeping steady, firm contact with the surface of the rod. This produces a plethora of sparks. Direct the sparks into the front bottom of the pile. If you hold the striker too high, the sparks will fly up and over the tinder. You want the sparks to enter the front and top of the tinder. Pivot the palm of the hand holding the striker to better direct the sparks.

Position the striker at about a 45 degree angle to the ferrocerium rod.

long with a 1/4-inch diameter ferro rod) and the Army model (3-3/4 inches long with a 3/8-inch diameter ferro rod) are good for medium and large sized kits. The Survival Resources Big-Stick Flint is my preferred ferro rod, and is especially handy for survival instructors who demonstrate fire starting. It measures four inches long, making it easy to hold, and is 3/8 inch in diameter. It provides a tremendous amount of usage, and yet, without a wide handle, it easily fits in all but the smallest survival kit.

Some larger ferrocerium rods are packaged with a striker built into the case that holds the flint rod, which saves you from losing it or having it separated from the rod. One of these is called the Strike Force Fire Starter, which was originally manufactured by Gerber, then Survival Incorporated, and is now manufactured and distributed by Ultimate Survival Technologies.

Another unit, also by Ultimate Survival Technologies, is called the Blast Match Fire Starter. This is another self contained unit and is advertised as being capable of being used one handed. The flint rod is on a spring inside the unit, and as you push on the rod it slides past the striker causing sparks. Several of my survival buddies and I have tested this unit. Although it can be used one handed, it often knocks over the tinder on the downstroke, resulting in having to collect and prepare your tinder again. I've also had the small striker break away from the holder, requiring the use of another striker in order to obtain sparks.

### Mischmetal rod

Mischmetal type rods are available from many suppliers. Not all, but most of the mischmetal rods are coming out of China. They come in many sizes, and most are just rods without handles. I have already explained what they are made of and, if you have decided they are for you, you can find many suppliers on the web.

Suppliers seem to be using the terms ferrocerium rod and mischmetal rod interchangeably. So, how do you know if you have a ferro rod or a mischmetal rod? You could ask before buying, but I have learned that some suppliers really don't know which they are selling. If you can't determine before buying, you will just have to buy one and strike it a couple of times. If you get nothing but a lot of sparks, you have a ferro rod. If large pieces of burning magnesium scrape off, you have a mishmetal rod.

While many of these rods come without handles, a new innovative approach is a device called the Aurora Fire Starter (patent pending). It is rugged and designed for the outdoors enthusiast. The Aurora Fire Starter uses a 1/4-inch diameter mischmetal rod. The rod is mounted inside a

Most mischmetal rods do not have handles (left). The silver Aurora Fire Starter has a built-in striking blade.

threaded cap which screws into an aluminum housing. The unit has an O-ring seal to make it waterproof. The body of the aluminum tube has a guide built in with a striking blade for striking the rod. Designed to function wet or dry, it is made from corrosion resistant aluminum and is available in silver or black anodized. It measures 3.5 inches overall and weighs 1.6 ounces.

### Magnesium fire starter

A magnesium fire starter is essentially a ferrocerium rod glued to a block of magnesium. Shavings from magnesium burn at approximately 5400 degrees (very hot) and yet the block of magnesium will not ignite (unless subjected to extreme heat). The advantage of a magnesium fire starter is that you scrape off a small pile of magnesium shavings (about the size of a quarter) using a sharp edged item such as a striker. You then use the sparks from the ferrocerium rod to ignite the shavings. The shavings ignite easily and burn extremely hot. Magnesium burns even when wet and will help ignite even damp tinder. I recommend carrying a magnesium fire starter as one of your ways to start a fire.

I carry a small magnesium fire starter on my key ring. I originally had it made for students, and it is now available from Survival Resources as the Mini-Match Firestarter. The Mini-Match measures 2-3/8 inches long. The magnesium bar is 1/4 inch in diameter and the attached ferro rod is 1/8 inch in diameter. I also have a larger tubular magnesium fire starter, the Maxi-Match, that I carry in my pack. It is 2-3/8 inches long. The magnesium bar is 1/2 inch in diameter and the attached ferro rod is 1/4 inch in diameter. The Maxi-Match is also available from Survival Resources.

## Using a Magnesium Firestarter

As always, get your tinder, kindling and other fire starting fuel ready first. Scrape the magnesium side of your magnesium firestarter with the edge of your striker or the back of your knife (don't use the edge of your knife as it will dull it). If it is windy, scrape the shavings into a curved piece of bark or something that will keep the shavings from blowing away. Once you have a pile of magnesium shavings about the size of a quarter, turn the magnesium firestarter over and use your scraper to direct sparks into the magnesium shavings. These shavings burn very hot, but very quickly.

Good choices for your survival kit include (from left to right) the Mini-Match & Maxi-Match Magnesium Firestarter from Survival Resources, and the Doan Magnesium Firestarter.

Another good commercially available unit is the Magnesium Fire Starting Tool manufactured by Doan Machinery & Equipment Co. It is provided in military survival kits and, being flat, is a good unit for all but the smallest survival kits. It measures three inches long by one inch wide and 3/8 inch thick, and has a ferro rod attached that is 3/16 inch in diameter.

## Strikers

A striker is the device that you scrape along the side of a ferrocerium or mischmetal rod to produce sparks. They come in many shapes and sizes. Basically, they are pieces of steel which have a flat side, providing a sharp 90-degree edge for scraping the rod. Many people just use the back of their knife blade, especially if it is a carbon steel blade. I have found that although stainless steel blades work, they do not produce as many sparks.

Many strikers are made from old or broken hacksaw blades. Some people grind off the saw portion of the blade. Others leave it on, providing both a striker and a minimal saw blade. Don't use the sawtooth part of the striker on your rods. It will only chew it up and waste valuable striking material.

Various types of strikers are commercially available, or make your own from a hacksaw blade.

The Corona Sharpening Tool lends itself to useful modifications.

An interesting item I found in a hardware store is a Corona sharpening tool. It was actually designed to sharpen various blades, such as garden sheers. I noticed it had a nice carbide blade and thought it would make a great striker. I bought one and it is probably the best striker I have ever used. We even started offering them at Survival Resources as "The Ultimate Striker." I have cut some down in length to carry it on my key ring. With the Corona, you not only have a striker on you, but a sharpener as well... truly a multi-use device!

## One-handed firestarting

There may be a situation where one of your hands is injured during a survival situation. In this case, you must be able to start a fire with one hand. There are probably as many one handed fire starting techniques as there are firestarters. Some are more difficult than others. The one I have found to work the best is as follows.

Find a stick, about thumb size or slightly larger, and lay it on the ground at the edge of a pile of tinder, between you and the pile. Have your other fire starting material ready.

Prop your knife against the stick with the back side of the blade toward the hand you will use to start the fire.

If you'll use your left hand to light the fire, the right foot holds the knife in place. With your left hand, pull the ferrocerium rod straight up, scraping it against the back of the knife. The shower of sparks are directed into the tinder pile causing ignition.

Next, lay your knife so that it is propped up by the stick, so the blade is protruding in an upward angle over your tinder, pointing away from you.

Now place the foot, opposite from the hand you will be using, on the knife handle, holding it securely in place on top of the stick. With your good hand, place the ferrocerium rod under the back of your knife blade. Holding the knife in place with your foot, pull up with the ferrocerium rod, scraping it against the back of the knife and shooting sparks into the tinder pile. Remove the knife as soon as the tinder ignites.

The blowing tube collapses for storage, extends for use, making it handy for encouraging a flame.

## Blowing tube

It is often necessary to get extra oxygen into a fire to keep it going. I recall, as a kid, my father taking off his brimmed hat and fanning the fire, which would always get it going. Years ago I wanted something small I could carry in my kit to blow air directly into the fire. However, a plastic tube didn't allow me to get close enough to the fire to be effective. Looking at a telescoping antenna on an old radio gave me an idea. I removed the antenna from the radio and cut off a short portion of the largest-diameter section. This allowed me to push the top, smallest diameter section out through the back. Now, in order to keep all the rest of the sections from falling out, I flared the last section (now the new smallest section at top). This allowed me to collapse the entire antenna or telescope it out.

On the back, largest end, I press fit a two-foot piece of plastic tubing that I got from a store that sold aquariums. I now had a blowing tube that collapsed to a small size with the tubing rolled into a small circle to easily carry in a kit or jacket pocket. To blow oxygen into a fire, I placed the end of the hose in my mouth, extended the antenna and blew new life into a fire. Many a morning I have found a small ember in the fire pit from the night before, put some tinder on the ember and used my blowing tube to revive an old flame.

## Magnifying lenses

A small magnifying lens is useful as an emergency fire starter and can be an additional item for a survival kit. Keep in mind it should only be a back-up device, as it only works if the sun is out and bright, and then only sometimes. Although small glass lenses are available, the small Fresnel plastic magnifying lenses also work. They are extremely thin and the one I use is two inches by 3-1/4 inches. I also keep one in my wallet. Keep in mind this is not a primary fire starting method. Here in the north east, where humidity is high, success often does not occur.

Focus the smallest circle of light on your tinder. Eventually, you'll see a wisp of smoke.

A useful, multi-purpose device, these lenses can be a back-up for broken corrective lens glasses, or used to help see when removing a splinter.

## Fire building

Once your fire is started, you have to keep it going. Remember, start your fire only after you have prepared your kindling and various stages of fuel to maintain it. I have seen so many students get a fire going only to have it go out while scrounging around for more kindling and fuel. Be prepared to maintain it right from the beginning.

Various firelays can be constructed after you get your initial fire going. These can actually be built right from the beginning, but it can be difficult to get the tinder ignited inside the structure. The exception to the rule is the tepee, which can be built before initiating your fire to protect your tinder from rain.

Gather and arrange your fire starting material prior to initiating the fire.

To construct the tepee firelay, place kindling sticks in a tepee style configuration over your initial fire. Begin by leaning two or three sticks together at the top, and then start laying other sticks against that structure. You might need to sharpen a piece of kindling and pound it into the ground at an angle so it leans over the fire and then lean other sticks against that first stick. The tepee style firelay is ideal for boiling water as it concentrates the flames up onto the pot or cooking vessel.

For a tepee firelay, stack kindling like a tepee around the initial fire.

A log cabin firelay gets lots of oxygen, so it burns hot and quickly creates coals.

Another handy firelay is the log cabin style, constructed by stacking fuel like a log cabin, with the tinder and kindling on the inside. It creates light and heat because the fire gets lots of oxygen. This firelay burns hot and therefore creates a lot of coals rather quickly. This is a plus for cooking, as you cook on coals. The log cabin firelay is also a good style for a signal fire, as green boughs, etc. can be placed across the top for heavy smoke.

There are many more firelays for various uses, but I have found these two to be most handy. Firelays can be built from long fuel to keep the entire length of your body warm when laying down. A reflector can be built on the opposite side of your location to reflect heat towards you or a shelter. If you locate yourself between a large rock surface and the fire, the rock surface will help reflect heat back towards you. With another reflector on the opposite side of the fire, you will have heat reflected on both sides of you.

## Fire pits

There are dozens of configurations for fire pits. Two work very well for both cooking and boiling water.

The first is a keyhole fire pit. It got its name because it looks like an old keyhole. Rocks are placed in almost a complete circle, but at the end of one side a rectangular section is built, so it is less wide than the circle. With keyhole fire pit, start a fire in the round portion of the pit, usually using a tepee firelay. This provides good flame for boiling water. As noted earlier, although you boil water with flame, you cook on coals. With the keyhole arrangement, you maintain the flames in the round end and rake coals over to the small rectangular end. You can make a small grill using green sticks and cook over the coals. This way, you can both boil and cook at the same time.

With a keyhole fire pit, you can use the flame in one end to boil water and rake coals into the opposite end for cooking. A grill can be made from green sticks.

The trench fire pit is another handy pit, especially if the ground is littered with flammable debris, it is windy or you have limited fuel. This pit works best in clay soil, as sandy soil will not maintain walls for a pot support. Also, be careful in areas where there are tree roots. Roots can smolder for days and travel back to the tree, causing the tree, especially if dead, to combust.

For this pit, dig a small trench in line with the wind, as you need a decent draft. The end facing the wind should be wider than the rest of the

Cook over a trench fire pit using a green stick grill, or a small grill cut down from a larger one. This can be carried in a small pack and used with a trench or keyhole fire pit.

trench and slanted down into the trench. Make a grill from green sticks to hold a pot over the fire or carry a very small grill made by cutting down a larger grill. When you are finished with a trench fire, make sure the fire is out and fill in the trench with dirt.

## Suspending pots over a fire

To effectively hang a pot over a fire, we need a way to suspend it and something to suspend it from. The first is called a bail. When I was a youngster (a long time ago) most pots for camping had bails on them. This made it easy to hang them over a fire or lift out of a fire. However, in today's world of ultra-light gear, bails seem to have gone by the wayside. If anything, you get some folding handles, as most of the pots are made to use over a small stove. But in survival, we normally need to cook over a fire.

Bails are an easy addition to any of your cups or pots. Some people drill holes and add some wire. I prefer free standing bails, so I drill holes in the side, and also make a half round groove in the lip. A pre-formed bail can be attached, and it stands up. When finished, it can be removed and stored with the pot.

Once you have bails on all your cups and pots, you need a way to hang them over a fire. More than a dozen ways have been devised for doing this, but it all boils down to four basic pot suspension systems.

Bails are an easy addition to any of your cups or pots.

A bail makes it possible to hang cups or pots over a fire.

A cup with a bail can be lifted using a lifter stick made in the field.

A prop stick suspends a pot over the fire. A forked stick driven into the ground holds down the back of the prop stick.

### Prop stick

A prop stick is a long stick propped against something, allowing you to hang a pot over the fire. The stick can be propped against a forked upright, a small tripod, etc. Hold it in place at the ground with a weight, such as a large rock or log, or when the ground is not frozen, a forked stick driven in the ground.

### Dingle stick

Another way to use a single prop stick, but adding the ability to swivel the stick, is a dingle stick. With a dingle stick, you use a support stick as in the prop stick method, but instead of holding the back on the ground with a weight or forked stick you attach a piece of cordage to the back of the prop stick, and then down to the bottom of the upright forked stick. This supports the pot over the fire, yet allows you to swivel the stick off and away from the fire.

With a dingle stick pot suspension system, the pot can swivel away from the fire.

### Spit

The spit uses to forked uprights with a green stick suspended across the two forks, allowing you to hang pots over the fire. This can be done using pot hangers made from green wood. For a pot hanger, use a sapling cut from just below the junction where a small limb comes off the main trunk. The trunk above this point can be as long as the pot hanger requires. At the length desired, trim off the remaining trunk, and on this end, cut a groove for the bail to hang from. Make sure the groove is made at an angle so the bail does not fall off. Trim the small limb so it will set over the horizontal suspension stick of the spit.

The spit uses to forked uprights with a green stick suspended across the two forks.

## Tripod

A tripod suspension system can be used any time, but is particularly useful in the winter if the ground is frozen. Made from three tall sticks of substantial diameter, they are lashed together using a tripod lashing. Pots can be suspended by various means, including a chain (something most people don't have in a survival situation), cordage or wire attached to a long pot hanger (especially when using cordage to keep the cordage away from the flames). I usually use a long green stick with a fork at top (like the small pot hanger described earlier). This stick allows you to hang a pot directly over the fire, and can have notches at various heights.

A tripod is particularly useful when the ground is very hard or frozen.

## Fire by friction: Bow and drill

Fire by friction is a primitive skill and beyond the scope of this book, as it is not something you would normally be carrying as part of a survival kit, and that is what this book is about. If you want to have at least something available for a bow and drill, then carry something for a socket/bearing. I carry a small antler bearing on my key ring, and have put sockets in some of my knife handles. It is a good skill to learn, and we teach it at our school in the intermediate course. There are various methods of fire by friction with the two most taught being the bow and drill and the hand drill. This skill is best learned in the presence of a competent instructor, as opposed to a book.

Various sockets for a bow and drill can be carried as part of a kit.

As a tip, if you go to a survival school to learn this skill, ask to use actual materials from the field. I once had a student attend our school who indicated he had learned the bow and drill method at another school and felt he owned the skill, as he had started a fire on his first attempt. He hadn't practiced since then as he felt it had been pretty easy. While

Collect materials from the field so you learn what to use to make your bow and drill. Even better, always carry three ways to start a fire!

attending our school he was having a difficulty getting a coal. I asked what he thought the problem was. He indicated that at the other school they were provided with kiln dried wood! Collect materials from the field so you learn what to use to make your bow and drill. I remember getting an email from this student later that year, thanking us for teaching him how to select wood from the field and he had been experimenting and felt much more comfortable with the skill.

Try not to be caught in a situation where you have to rely on a primitive method of fire making. Always have at least three ways to start a fire on you. It is difficult enough to start a fire with a device if you have already fallen through the ice and are going hypothermic. Although romantic, the chances of locating the materials and making a fire by friction are remote when you lose the dexterity of your hands and are shivering. You will probably die of exposure.

As always, be prepared to survive by having a means for starting a fire on you!

## Candles & lanterns

A candle is a handy item to have in a survival kit. You can light a candle with a match and then use the candle (protecting it from wind) to start a fire, allowing you to conserve matches. A candle can also be used for light and provides the all-important morale factor by adding comfort to a survival situation.

Candles come in all shapes and sizes, which is handy when you are trying to fit a candle in a specific kit. Candles that are especially practical for various survival kits include emergency candles, camping candles, tea light candles and those birthday candles that can't be blown out.

Emergency candles come in various lengths and diameters and are usually long burning. Most range in size from 3/4-inch to 1-1/4 inches thick, and five to 6-1/2 inches long. You can buy them in most grocery stores. They are usually white, but some camping stores sell them in a reddish pink color and call them Pink Lady candles. This type of candle is best for a medium to large kit. As always, choose components based on size as well as use.

Tea light candles (also called tub candles) are 1-1/2 inches thick but only 3/4 inch high. They are packaged individually in a little metal cup. Several of these can be stored in a medium size kit. They are handy because they don't fall over and have the added advantage of the metal cup, which can be used after the candle is gone. They don't last as long as emergency candles, but you can carry an equal amount in about the same space.

Candles come in all shapes and sizes, so there are options for every size kit.

Another handy candle that fits in most mini kits is the small birthday candle that you can't blow out. This works really well when the wind is blowing. Of course they are usually small, about 2-1/4 inches by 3/16 inch, but fit in very little space. They are only really good for fire starting, as they don't last very long. Regular birthday candles around the same size do not have the advantage of not blowing out.

Finally, the Nuwick44 candle is ideal for me-

Various Candle Lanterns are available from Industrial Revolutions, Inc., including (from left to right) the UCO Mini Candle Lantern, the UCO Original Candle Lantern, the Oil Insert for the Original Candle Lantern, and the Candlelier, a three candle lantern that is large but good for truck kits, etc.

dium to large kits. This candle comes in a can which is 1-1/2 inches high by 3-5/8 inches in diameter. The lid is replaceable so it can be re-used until the candle is used up (about 44 hours). It is unique in that it provides three movable and re-usable wicks which actually float on the wax.

Keep in mind that larger candles can be cut down to accommodate a desired container. I have one in an Altoids tin that is 3/4 inch thick but only 5/8 inch high.

Candle lanterns are another means of light for an emergency. The best out there, called UCO lanterns, are made by Industrial Revolutions, Inc.. The first is very small and can be carried in a medium to large kit or pack. It utilizes small tea light candles. I have carried this lantern with four tea light candles in it, one for use and three extra. When I want to use the lantern, I just remove the three extra and light the one in the bottom. It safely burns the tea light candles for three to four hours and has a bail handle for hanging or carrying. It measures four inches tall by 2.5 inches in diameter, and weighs 3.2 ounces.

The next size is the Original UCO lantern. This is a unique aluminum candle lantern which provides light and warmth, and helps reduce condensation in a tent. The candle is spring loaded to keep the flame height constant, while a small viewing window shows how much candle is left. The lantern itself collapses to a compact size for transport. The easy-slide glass chimney slides down into the lantern, making the candle easy to light.

UCO also makes an oil insert for the Original lantern. The UCO Oil Insert is a great option for the Original UCO lantern; it can be used instead of candles. Using lamp oil (liquid paraffin) instead of candles, it burns up to six hours. Simply unscrew the bottom of the Original lantern (like you are going to change a candle), and instead of putting in another candle, insert the UCO Oil Insert. It has a screw cap on top so the oil does not leak out when not in use. This a really handy item and adds versatility to the Original lantern.

The largest of the UCO lanterns is the Candlelier. This a larger version of the famous UCO Candle lantern. It is a three-candle lantern and is ideal for larger kits, such as truck, snowmobile, ATV, etc.

## Flashlights and headlamps

When it gets dark, we need light to see. Of course we have a fire (if we prepared) and candles to give us light. But a source of light that we can carry around with us and is water repellant or waterproof is obviously an advantage. This is where a flashlight comes in. They come in a thousand shapes and sizes, but we should think about some prerequisites before choosing one.

First, as usual, is size. Next, we will probably want it water repellant or, if possible, waterproof. We want it durable, and if possible, unbreakable. This eliminates many from our choices. We then must determine if we want an LED light (LED lights last longer than any other type light on the market), an incandescent type light bulb, or a bright Xenon type bulb. Battery life lasts the longest in LED lights, and discharge more quickly as we switch to incandescent and Xenon type bulbs, respectively. This eliminates more choices.

Next, we must decide where we are going to package the flashlight, so we know the size appropriate for the space. Obviously for a small place, like a mini kit, our options are further limited.

Headlamps are not a necessary item, however, they are handy and allow you to conduct activities using both your hands. For smaller kits I usually carry one of those elastic straps with a small loop sewed onto it. I can place a small light into the loop and wear the elastic loop around my head. This frees up my hands.

Mini flashlights fit in a mini kit or on your person. From left to right, the Photon Micro-Light II, a quarter for size comparison, the 10 Lumen Nano Light by Streamlight, the Pilot by Princeton-Tec, and a 5.5 Lumen, U.S. Made, ARC Flashlight.

Medium sized flashlights fit in small to large size kits.

For larger kits, you may want to include a headlamp designed for this purpose. Again, there are many choices. I normally use LED headlamps as they burn longer than the Xenon type bulb.

The smallest headlamp I have is the Petzl e+LITE headlamp, and it is one of the smallest I have seen. It has three white LEDs and one red LED. A rotating power switch controls light modes: maximum, economy and flashing strobe. For added versatility, the lamp can be removed from its headstrap and, using its integrated clip, mounted to a belt, cap brim or pack strap. The lamp source rotates 360 degrees on a ball joint, increasing versatility in tight places. It uses two CR2032 lithium batteries (included) that have a 10-year shelf life. This headlamp weighs one ounce and measures 1.5 by 1.25 by 1/2 inches. The included protective carry case measures 3.25 inches by 1.75 inches.

My primary headlamp for kits, is the Petzl Tac-Tikka Plus, which is a tactical version of the popular Tikka Plus headlamp by Petzl. It uses four LEDs and a push button to switch through four modes (low, medium, bright and blinking). This switching mode allows you to select the amount of light you need, and the lower the brightness, the longer the batteries last (up to 150 hours on the lowest setting). It also features a red flip down lens for night vision. It is powered by three AAA batteries, which is another reason for my selecting it.

Another headlamp whicht I keep in my urban bag is called the Petzl Tac-Tikka Plus. It offers three ultrabright LEDs and a single Maxbright LED. This unique combination provides for compact versatility. You have two settings, high or low, with the three LEDs for a wide angle, close in use. The single Maxbright LED also has a high or low setting but reaches out there and provides for distant spotting. It runs on three AAA batteries, and depending on the setting can run up to 200 hours. A pretty neat headlamp for various tasks and small enough for all but mini kits.

Surefire makes some very heavy duty, dependable flashlights, including the G2 LED in yellow, the EIE Executive Elite, and the E2E Executive Elite.

Headlamps free up your hands to perform other tasks. From left to right, top row: the Petzl e+LITE and Tac-Tikka (3 AAA batteries). Bottom row: the Princeton-Tec Remix (3 AAA batteries), and the Surefire Saint Minimus.

Even though the above headlamps are all quality built and robust in construction, if you are looking for a headlamp that is pretty much bomb proof, again we must go back to Surefire! They offer a new headlamp that is built for any situation called Saint Minimus. It features a hard-anodized aluminum housing that is lightweight yet extremely durable. It uses a solid-state LED that produces up to 100 lumens of light output with up to 50 hours of runtime at the lowest setting. It uses one CR123 lithium battery which is contained in its single-battery cap. A variable light output dial allows one handed selection of any light level from one to 100 lumens and features an emergency SOS mode. The variable light output dial also allows for continuous one-handed adjustment of light even with cold or gloved fingers (a nice feature for sure). Its micro-fiber headband system includes a washable moisture-wicking Breathe-O-Prene pad, low profile buckles and smooth stitching to eliminate pressure points. This is a great headlamp for heavy-duty situations, and I keep one with my G2 LED in my small urban go-anywhere bag.

There are many more units that are adequate from other manufacturers. Determine how bright you want them, how long you want them to last on batteries, and as with all items for a survival kit, what size you want. But carry some type of light in your kit. They are much easier to travel with than fire!

*Chapter 6*

# Shelter & Protection from the Elements

There has been rigorous debate about whether fire or shelter is the first priority for survival. I see them as equal in importance, and as two options where, ultimately, one is chosen depending on circumstances. If you are in a warm climate and it looks like rain, a shelter would be an appropriate course of action. However, if you are in the northeast in the winter and it is below zero, you need a fire, especially if you fall through the ice and get wet. You have a very short time to get warm and dry, or you're going to die. Once you are warm, you'll be able to build a shelter for protection from the elements. Again, the situation will dictate which of the two is the priority.

Since we covered fire in the previous chapter, let's now examine the ways your body heat can be transferred to the environment, and how a shelter protects you from the elements and helps prevent that loss.

## Heat loss mechanisms

The ways that heat from your body can be transferred to the environment are called heat loss mechanisms. In a cold environment they can all be detrimental, but in a hot climate some of these mechanisms can be used to your advantage.

### Radiation

Radiation is the primary cause of heat loss. Our body radiates heat to the environment much like the sun radiates heat to the earth or a campfire radiates heat to keep us warm. At 50 degrees F, 50 percent of the body's heat can be transferred to the environment through an exposed head and neck. We can also lose heat from our wrists, hands and feet. Have you ever had your mother or father tell you if you want warm feet to cover your head? Wearing a hat, scarf, wrist-overs or gloves can help eliminate loss of heat through radiation from your head, neck and wrists. A shelter can help reduce loss of body heat to the environment by holding it inside the shelter.

### Conduction

Conduction is the process by which we lose heat through direct contact between objects. This can occur when sitting on a cold or snow-covered stump or rock, when wet clothes come in contact with your body, by touching cold objects with bare hands, or by kneeling on the snow to build a shelter. Avoid these situations to prevent conduction of heat from the body to other objects. This is another reason to insulate between yourself and the ground in a shelter. In the winter, I carry a small closed cell foam pad, cut from an old military sleeping pad, in the back of my pack. I use it to insulate myself from a cold object when sitting down.

### Convection

Convection is loss of body heat due to movement of air or liquid across your skin. An example of convection is wind chill. Through radiation, the human body is always warming a thin layer of air next to the skin. The temperature of that layer of air is usually equal to that of the skin. When this layer of warm air is undisturbed, the body stays warm. However, if this warm layer is removed by convection, the body quickly cools down. In cooler environments, clothing is your first line of defense, as it helps hold that thin layer of warm air near your skin.

## Evaporation

Evaporation is a process whereby liquid changes to vapor, during which heat from the liquid escapes to the environment. In a cold environment, it is essential to wear fabrics that breathe. If water vapor from perspiration cannot evaporate through clothing, it will condense, freeze and reduce the insulation value of the clothing. This will cause your body temperature to go down. However, in a warm environment evaporation can be used to your advantage. Have you ever, on a hot day, worn a wet T-shirt or a wet bandana around your neck? This is also evaporation at work, because as the water is evaporated it pulls heat from the body, cooling you. It is called evaporative cooling. At our camp, we use this method in the summer by placing wet towels on water containers to keep the water cool.

## Respiration

We lose heat through our normal breathing process. You can observe this when you see a person's breath on a cold day. This is heat from the body lost to the environment. It is also difficult to prevent this loss, as we have to breathe.

## Heat regulation in the human body

### Hypothermia

Often called "the killer of the unprepared," hypothermia is a real threat to survival. The three main elements leading to hypothermia are cold, wind and wetness. Keep in mind it isn't necessary for temperatures to be at or below freezing for hypothermia to occur. Many instances of hypothermic death have taken place in temperatures over 50 degrees F. Hypothermia is heat loss at the body core, and it results from exposure to cold with the addition of other heat-loss mechanisms or nature's elements.

Normal body temperature is 98.6 degrees F. If core body temperature drops below 95 degrees F, your body will not generate enough heat to maintain normal body functions and hypothermia sets in. If your body temperature drops below 92 degrees F, you won't be able to help yourself survive!

In the case of mild hypothermia (between 91 and 95 degrees F), normal shivering begins and ranges from mild to severe. You might have a cold sensation and have goose bumps, your hands can be numb and you might not be able to perform complex tasks with your hands.

In moderate hypothermia (between 82 and 90 degrees F), shivering becomes intense. There is an obvious lack of muscle coordination and movements become slow and labored. Violent shivering continues, and speech, thinking and gross muscle movements become difficult. The use of hands often ceases and stumbling becomes frequent. This is a serious situation.

In severe hypothermia, below 82 degrees F, you are in major trouble. All shivering stops and exposed skin becomes blue or puffy. You are confused, unable to walk and muscles become stiff. You lose awareness of others, if present, and the pulse and respiration are erratic. At this point, unconsciousness occurs and death usually follows.

A good survival kit should contain the items you need to avoid falling prey to hypothermia. You need to be prepared in order to protect yourself from the cold and effects of hypothermia.

### Hyperthermia

Hyperthermia is elevated body temperature which occurs when the body fails at thermoregulation; and the temperature control system becomes overloaded. The body is normally able to cool itself through sweating, but under some conditions sweating is not enough and body temperature can rise rapidly. If the temperature continues to rise, it can damage the brain and other vital organs and result in death.

There are three levels of heat related injuries: heat cramps, heat exhaustion and heat stroke. Heat injuries are a serious matter.

As indicated earlier, normal body temperature is 98.6 degrees F. When your temperature is between 99 and 100 degrees F, you are at risk of heat cramps, the least serious heat injury. Heat cramps normally result from over-activity in a hot environment and are connected to dehydration and poor conditioning. Initially, you'll begin to feel cramps in the abdomen and legs. You'll have hot sweaty skin, may feel nauseous or dizzy, and may have a headache. When this happens, rest, drink water and, if possible, move to a shady, cool environment. Evaporative cooling, discussed above, and staying hydrated can help prevent this stage.

In the next stage, heat exhaustion, the body temperature rises to 101 to 102 degrees F. Symptoms can include extreme thirst, headache, nausea, rapid pulse and breathing, and exhaustion. These symptoms also describe the early stages of shock. Persons at this stage may often feel cool because of profuse sweating.

The last stage, and most severe, is heat stroke. This occurs when the core temperature is between 103 and 106 degrees F. Victims of heat stroke may have a sudden change of behavior, become disoriented, hallucinate, become irritable or speak incoherently. A heat stroke victim will have elevated and rapid breathing. Seizures are common in heat stroke victims and, if left untreated, death follows.

As you can see, heat injuries can be dangerous and even fatal. We will discuss treatment for both hypothermia and hyperthermia in Chapter 11, Wilderness Hazards & Safety.

## Clothing as a defense against hypothermia and hyperthermia

The clothing you have on your back or with you when a survival situation occurs is always your first line of defense as shelter from the elements. Understanding the advantages of various types of clothing, and the proper layering of that clothing, helps you to protect yourself from the heat loss mechanisms.

First, let's address a cold environment. One of the keys to preventing hypothermia in cold weather is to dress properly. The best way to dress for the cold is by layering. There are three basic stages to proper layering, the base layer, the insulation layer and the protective shell layer.

### Base layer

The base layer is the clothing next to your skin. This layer should be material that will wick moisture away from your skin, and could be synthetic, such as polypropylene, or made from natural fibers, such as merino wool or silk. Merino wool is an exceptionally good choice since it absorbs moisture while still feeling warm and dry to the touch. It also does not absorb skin oils, which helps to avoid that "been-living-in-these-awhile" smell.

Avoid cotton in the winter for any layer, and definitely never use it as a base layer. Cotton absorbs water like a sponge, takes a long time to dry and, when wet, feels damp and clammy. No matter what you layer over it, you will quickly feel chilled.

The base layer should fit snugly without binding or chafing and allow for freedom of movement.

### Insulation layer

The second layer is the insulation layer. This layer should also be breathable and trap a layer of warm air next to the body, keeping body heat in and cold out. This layer would include your shirt, pants, sweaters (wool preferred), and a wool or fleece jacket. This layer must maintain its ability to insulate even when wet, and then dry quickly.

## Protective shell layer

The third layer is the outside protective shell layer. This layer protects you from the wind, rain or snow, and should be wind and waterproof while also ventilated to allow moisture to evaporate or escape. Some fabrics to consider are Gore-Tex or laminated or treated nylon.

## Other considerations

Remember your legs! Long underwear covered by pants and an outer layer of nylon wind pants are a good example. Fleece lounge pants make a good insulation layer as well. Keeping your legs warm can go a long way to keeping your whole body warm.

In today's high tech world, it is possible to get all three layers in one garment, but that is not desirable. You have to wear it all or nothing, and this eliminates the option to shed layers to regulate your body heat.

When dressing for the cold, the hands, feet and head are often overlooked. Wear polypropylene-lined Gore-Tex gloves or fleece or knit wool gloves and under nylon mitts or gloves. Carry a spare pair of thin fleece gloves in a pocket; these feel warm even when they're damp.

Wool socks are recommended for warmth and dryness. Today's wool blends are soft and comfortable, and come in every size, shape and color. I prefer SmartWool socks, which come in light hikers to heavy crews and are made from a high percentage of Merino wool and nylon. Smart-Wool makes some other good products such as Merino wool base layers. When buying socks, make sure you get the correct size for your foot so they are smooth and comfortable against your skin, or blisters could result.

Boots should have the same qualities as the layers you wear on your body. They should wick away moisture, have a layer of insulation and be both water resistant and breathable so moisture can escape. Be leery of boots that have plastic-based uppers. Opt for leather or coated nylon, or even rubber if it's real rubber, and not a plastic imitation.

The top of your head can be your biggest source of heat loss, even if you have a full head of hair. A leather, wool or fleece hat makes a world of difference in keeping you warm. While it may not be the fashion statement you want to make, a leather hat with sheepskin lining and ear flaps is a great way to keep your head warm.

Wearing a scarf around your neck can do more than keep your neck warm. It can seal off the top of your coat and prevent heat from escaping and, at the same time, allow moisture to escape. Don't tie the scarf in a knot; if it gets snagged on something it should pull off. I normally put a scarf inside my coat.

Don't forget your wrists, even if gloves are not required. I have often worn light polypropylene wrist-overs, which can be worn with or without gloves. They prevent heat loss through radiation. I also have a pair of fingerless wool gloves from Filson which not only prevent heat loss from the wrists but last a lot longer around a fire. Fleece and nylon gloves tend to melt when you get them close to a fire or have a spark land on them.

If the rest of your body is warm, you may not need to cover your face unless you are in windy conditions or doing an activity that creates wind, such as skiing or snowmobiling. A scarf pulled up over your mouth and nose may suffice, or you may prefer a neoprene, knit or fleece face mask.

Now that we have covered a cold climate, let's discuss a warm climate. The heat loss mechanisms are the same. In the same way you use those principles to prevent heat loss when cool or windy, utilize them to cool you when hot.

As stated previously, evaporative cooling can help. Although "cotton kills" in a cold environment, it can be used to your advantage in a hot climate. As we know, cotton soaks up water, which in this case would be your sweat. As the moisture evaporates from the shirt, it will cool your body. The same goes with a bandana tied around your neck.

In a hot environment, the goal is to protect your skin from the radiation of the sun. There is a lot of new clothing available that is designed to protect you from the sun's ultraviolet rays. In the heat, sweating helps cool the body. If you look around the world at those who live in a desert environment, you will see a lot of loose layered material, protecting the body from the sun yet allowing adequate air flow.

It is often the small things that are forgotten, so remember to carry sun block and sunglasses. They are paramount at protecting exposed skin and your eyes.

**Desert dress must protect the skin from the sun's radiation.** Photo by Alan Halcon.

## Clothing and personal protection

Since clothing and other personal protection devices that you have on you are your first line of protection, let's examine some important items.

### AeroVest

A very interesting item is the SolaTec AeroVest. It is an emergency cold weather survival vest offering protection against the cold for unexpected and changeable weather conditions. The AeroVest is small, light (just two ounces) and easy to use. It can fold as small as a cell phone or pack of cigarettes, so it can be carried in a pocket, pack or small survival kit. It consists of a two-layer metalized vest which is inflated with air, creating a third layer of insulation and a thermal barrier. The inside metal layer reflects back 90% of your core body heat. The outside metal layer blocks the wind and rain. Just two or three puffs of breath per side inflate the eighteen air pockets with 98.6 degrees F air to help prevent hypothermia.

I did some testing of this product during the winter to determine if it really worked, and it did. It worked particularly well over a sweater and under a coat. I did some further testing to determine if I could sit comfortably in the vest, as well as lay down. Both were accomplished in the field with no problems.

The AeroVest can fold as small as a cell phone.

The AeroVest is a two-layer metalized vest which is inflated with air, creating a third layer of insulation and a thermal barrier.

Just two or three puffs of breath per side inflate the eighteen air pockets of the AeroVest.

## Head gear

A hat is a good item to have in a kit for protection from radiation. Although I normally wear a brimmed hat in the field, I also carry a wool watch cap in my pack. A watch cap, whether wool or acrylic, can go a long way to keep your head, ears and neck warm. I have slept many a night wearing a watch cap to help keep me warm.

Also remember that, whether a watch cap is wool or acrylic, you can wet it in a hot climate and wear it for evaporative cooling of the head.

When it is hot out, you want to protect your neck and face from the sun. A "Boonie" type soft brimmed hat can easily be carried in a pack or kit. If you only have a ball-style cap, use a bandana, scarf or other material to hang over your head and hold it in place with the ball cap. This will protect your face and neck from the sun. When really hot, for evaporative cooling, wet a bandana or other material and wear it "dew rag" style. As it dries, you can re-wet it. Lastly, I find that a good quality waxed canvas brimmed hat works well unless it is very hot. It is rain resistant, shades your face from the sun and keeps from losing heat through radiation when cold.

Another item that can help protect the head in a buggy area is a head net. There are various types and some need a hat to hold them away from the face. I prefer the Repel Deluxe head net, as it has under arm loops to keep the netting tight to your clothing.

A wet dew rag can be used for evaporative cooling.
Photo by Dave Tameling.

A waxed canvas brimmed hat is rain resistant and shades your face from the sun. Photo by Janice McCann.

## Bandanas

A bandana is an extremely useful device that can be used in various ways, and I recommend carrying at least one. I always carry one in my right rear pocket and more in various kits. Buy a large one, as they fold down small. Cotton is preferred. In my packs I carry an old military handkerchief as a bandana, which are 28" long x 24" wide, and fold down fairly small.

First of all, a bandana can be used as a bandana. If it is hot, wet the bandana with water and wear it tied around your neck to keep you cool. If you are sweating, use it as a head band. Wrap one around your head, dew rag style, for protection from the sun when hot or for protection against heat loss when cold. If your nose is running, use it as a handkerchief. If it is windy or dusty, use it as a nose and mouth cover. For medical emergencies it can be used as a bandage or a sling, to tie a splint, etc.

The bandana is more than just a personal protection device. If you need to filter the sediment from water before purifying it, pour it through a bandana. It also works well as a napkin, wash cloth, small towel or a pot holder when folded several times. This is another component that packs small and can perform many tasks. Carry a couple.

## Gloves (for warmth and working)

Your hands can take a lot of abuse during a survival situation, so you want to protect them. Against the cold, all survival kits, except a mini, should have at least a small pair of polypropylene gloves. In my fall and winter kits, I also carry a pair of Filson wool gloves, both half finger and full finger. When working around fire all the time, you will come to appreciate wool, as it doesn't melt every time an ember lands on it.

If your kit is large enough, I suggest a good pair of leather work gloves. They really help protect your hands when dragging logs, building shelters, etc. If the space is available, throw a pair in.

## Sunglasses

It is important to protect your eyes from the sun, so try to carry a pair of sunglasses in a survival kit. They are also handy when working around water and to prevent snow blindness. With the small fold-flat Emergency Sunglasses, available from Survival Resources, you should never be without a pair in your kit. They take up little space, have an adjustable cardboard temple and one size fits all.

Sunglasses protect your eyes from the sun, and can help prevent snow blindness.

### Skin protection

To protect your skin from the elements and bugs, carry sun screen, lip balm and bug repellent in your kit. Lip balm can also be used on tinder for fire starting. There are various manufacturers that offer sun screen and bug repellent in small tear-open envelopes, which are easily stored in a small survival kit. Carry what you can to protect your skin.

## Shelter construction materials

Items that will help you build a shelter or protect you from the elements are extremely important components of a survival kit. The larger the kit, the more, or better quality items you can carry. Don't cut yourself short; carry the most that the size of your kit allows.

### Survival blankets

A good survival blanket is one of the most versatile and useful items to put in your survival kit. They come in various sizes, but the bigger the better. Three that I recommend are the Space Emergency Blanket, the AMK (Adventure Medical Kits) Heat-Sheet Two-Person Survival Blanket, and the Space All Weather Blanket.

The smallest of these, the Space Emergency Blanket, is available with silver on one side and either silver, orange (more a gold color), or olive drab on the other side. These blankets fit in all but the smallest kit and can be carried in a jacket pocket as well.

The AMK Heat-Sheet Two-Person Blanket is 20% larger than the Space Emergency Blanket. It features a bright orange side, an easy to spot universal distress color, and has survival and first-aid instructions printed directly on the orange side.

My favorite, which goes in anything I can fit it in, is the Space All Weather Blanket. This is a substantial blanket, reflective silver on one side and either orange or olive drab on the other. It has grommets on the corners which, as you will see later in the chapter, makes for a quick shelter. It measures a substantial 60x84 inches. I even carry one of these in the game pocket on the back of my Filson Double Mackinaw Cruiser coat. They also make great ground cloths for under a shelter, or even as a reflector by the fire.

Space also makes a Sportsman Hooded Blanket. This is similar to the All Weather Blanket, but has a hood and handholds in two corners. We did determine that although the packaging

From left to right: the Space All Weather Blanket, Space Emergency Blanket and AMK Heat-Sheets.

gives the same dimensions as for the All Weather Blanket, it is actually 59" x 69". Being shorter, it does not work as well for a shelter, but is great for setting in front of a fire and reflecting heat to your back. They are reflective silver on one side and either red or olive drab on the other.

## Poncho and rain gear

Rain gear is an important shelter item. As we know, once we get wet it is more difficult to stay warm. Ponchos are a multi-purpose item, as they can be used directly over the body for protection from the rain, and can be unsnapped at the sides to be used as a

The Space Sportsman Hooded Blanket.

shelter. Some have grommets which make them even more versatile. Many people like the old style military poncho, and they are quite functional. However, I like the Equinox ultra light silicone-impregnated ripstop nylon poncho, as it folds down to nearly nothing for packing, yet provides an adequate shelter. I carry the extended model, which is longer in the back – helpful in the event you wear it over a pack. This makes for an even larger shelter.

The emergency poncho, although light and thin, can be carried in almost any kit but a mini. It is more than adequate to keep you dry, except they are a little short for tall people, so your legs will get wet. They can also be used to cover an emergency shelter or as a light ground cloth. For their size, I throw one in every pack and kit.

Remember to choose rain gear that serves more than one purpose (as with all survival kit components). Generally, do not choose a rain suit over a poncho, as a poncho can be used for other purposes, as described above. However, in my larger kits I carry a small Marmot rain suit, which folds down to be relatively compact compared to most rain gear, but always accompany it with the ultra light poncho. In smaller kits, I carry just the ultra light poncho.

The Emergency Poncho folds up to be quite compact. One of these can be placed in almost any kit.

With the Emergency Poncho, your legs might still get wet.

### Tube tents

A tube tent is a lightweight emergency shelter sold by many camping stores and is basically a polyethylene tube. It can be set up as a shelter by stringing cordage through the tube and tying the ends between two objects, such as trees. I have seen these as part of many commercially available survival kits. They are reasonable light but don't pack very small and are not very durable. However, in a survival situation, they will provide you with protection.

### Tarps

Most tarps, although rugged and waterproof, are just too big, heavy and awkward to be included in most survival kits. There are various companies that make ultra light tarps out of silicone-impregnated ripstop nylon, and I prefer those made by Equinox. They offer three sizes, 6x8, 8x10 and 10x12 feet. They have grommets along the outside perimeter approx. every 2.5 feet and lightweight ties on the center seam for multiple pitching options. I find the smallest size fits in almost any kit made in a fanny pack, small pack, etc. I carry one in my day pack along with the ultra-light poncho. Between the two, you end up with a lot of options for shelter. In my larger pack, I carry the 10x12-foot tarp, as the pack size is not that much larger than the 8x10, but provides a larger shelter.

### Bivy sacks

A small bivy sack basically provides you with a small sleeping bag. Although not as adequate as an actual sleeping bag, it does provide you with an emergency option if stuck out overnight. AMK makes two different sized bivy sacks that will fit most but the smallest survival kit.

The AMK Heatsheets Emergency Bivy weighs only 3.5 ounces. This is ideal for those occasions when you take a wrong turn and are forced to spend the night out. It's now available with an ultra light stuff sack, allowing for repeat uses. Made from a newly developed polyethylene material that is vacuum-metallicized to reflect back 90% of your body heat. Unfolded, it measures 36x84 inches, and in the sack it is 3.5x2.5 inches. The stuff sack is made larger than the original rolled bivy so you can get it back in after use.

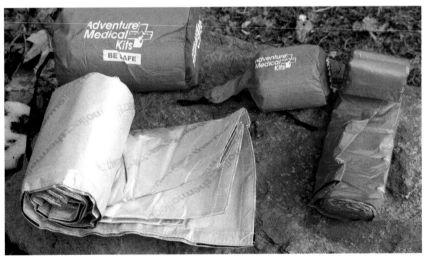

The AMK Thermo-Lite Bivy in and out of the stuff sack on the left and the AMK Heatsheets Emergency Bivy on the right.

The AMK Thermo-Lite 2.0 Bivy is an ideal survival/emergency bag for day-hikes, backpacking or larger survival kits. It is a year round sack ideal as a light weight replacement for your sleeping bag when temperatures are above 50° F. It reflects and retains up to 80% of radiated body heat. The Thermo-Lite non-woven fabric is waterproof and windproof while still producing an ultra light, warm weather sleeping system. It comes in an ultra light stuff sack that allows you to conveniently store it before and after use. It measures 36x84 inches unfolded and weighs only 6.5 oz.

## Miscellaneous shelter items

Some of the best, most versatile items you can put in your kit are contractor garbage bags. They measure approximately two feet-nine inches x three feet-nine inches. I recommend, if you have room in your kit, to carry three. That way you have one for use as a poncho and two for use as a tube tent. Their use in a survival situation can only be limited by your imagination. Fill one with leaves and use it as a mattress to insulate you from the ground. Fill another one and use it on top of you as a comforter. Cut one open and use it to waterproof a makeshift shelter. Use it to collect rain, funneling the rain into a water container. The uses go on and on.

To use one as a poncho, just cut a hole in the top if you have a good brimmed hat. If not, then cut a hole in the side, which provides you with a hood but does not leave as much length. However, it does provide room in the back for a small pack because of the opposite corner sticking up. I don't recommend cutting arm holes unless absolutely necessary. I have found that if you just squat down, you can extend your arms out from under the opening for many chores, such as batoning wood, etc. Of course, if you need real movement, such as to build a shelter, arm holes might be necessary. Only cut them if you really need them.

A contractor garbage bag can be used as a poncho with a hole cut at the top.

A poncho made by cutting a hole in the top, side, allows space in the back for a pack.

The Orange Survival Bag from Survival Resources is 84 inches long by 36 inches wide

Another great item that is also quite versatile is the Orange Survival Bag available from Survival Resources. This is a BIG survival bag! It is 84 inches long by 36 inches wide and is made from three-mil, really rugged polyethylene. Great for making an emergency shelter – poke a hole through one of the bottom corners and run a ridgeline through it to use as a tube tent, or use the technique shown at the end of the tube tent heading. Use it to cover a shelter to waterproof it, use as a ground sheet or just climb inside and huddle. Many other uses include using it as a signaling panel, a waterproof sleeping bag, or a mattress or comforter filled with leaves.

I have also been known to carry a large piece of painter's drop cloth. This is rather thin plastic and folds down small. You can carry a piece approximately 10x12 feet in very little space. It can be used to waterproof a shelter, as a ground cloth or to throw over yourself in the rain. It's a really inexpensive alternative for a multi-purpose device.

### Parachute cord

Parachute cord is something you cannot have enough of in a survival kit. It is probably the best utility cord available for survival purposes. But what is it? Parachute cord, also called 550 cord, is actually 550-pound test parachute shroud line that was used by the military. It is 1/8 inch in diameter and has a continuous filament nylon shroud with seven inner nylon lines. These inner nylon lines are also strong and can be separated from the shroud for various uses such as sewing, fishing line, making nets, making snares, etc. If you had 25 feet of parachute cord with you and you separated the inner lines, you would have 175 feet of inner lines plus 25 feet of shroud for survival use.

In order to separate the seven lines from the shroud, cut a short piece of shroud off each end (just enough to get by the melted part). Push back the shroud until you see the seven inner nylon lines. Hold onto the seven lines with one hand, without touching the shroud. Now hold the shroud on the other end, without grabbing the seven inner lines. With the hand holding the inner lines, pull them through the shroud, working slowly so you don't pucker the shroud, until the seven lines are completely out of the shroud. You now have seven individual nylon lines.

But wait, there's more! If you need thin nylon lines for sewing or making a fine fishing line, each of the seven inner nylon lines can be un-twisted providing another three lines. These thin lines are really twisted but can be used individually.

But wait, there's still more! Don't throw away the empty shroud. It is strong and can be used for lashing. Keep in mind that separating the inner lines from the shroud is difficult with long pieces, so use only short pieces of cord, about four to five feet long.

 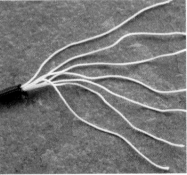

Made up of seven inner strands within an outer shroud, parachute cord offers more than meets the eye.

Although I advocate cutting parachute cord for the purpose of removing the inner nylon lines, do not cut it for other uses. The nylon shroud will continue to fray, revealing the inner lines. You don't want this for normal use. Always use a lighter to cut the cord, burning entirely through it, which melts the ends closed (sort of cauterizing the ends). Be careful after doing this, as the ends will be hot and the melted nylon likes to stick to your fingers and continue to burn (don't ask me how I know this, I just do). When I am not in the field, I use a small butane soldering iron with a hot-blade attachment. This cuts the cord nicely for those hanks I'm going to carry in my kits.

Be aware that not all parachute cord is created equal. There are various camp stores, etc. that sell "Para Cord," which sort of sounds like parachute cord but is not the real thing. You can tell right away when you pull back the sheath and exclaim, "where are the seven inner lines?" Instead, you find a single bundle of some sort of fuzzy nylon which cannot be separated into individual lines. As they say, buyer beware!

## Choosing a location for your shelter

Okay, you are in a survival situation and need shelter. Before initiating construction, several factors must be considered. First, think ahead. It is much easier to build a shelter in the light than in the dark. Don't wait too late in the day to get started. If you know you'll be spending the night out there, start early, get your shelter built and get comfortable.

The weather is another factor. What do you have to protect yourself from? In the summer, it might be rain, wind or a drop in temperature. In winter, you have more to consider. Temperatures will be much lower and insulation will be more important.

As with real estate, think location, location, location! Try to locate your shelter near sufficient shelter-building materials if you need them. Try to be near water (but not too close), fuel for fire, a signal/recovery area and food, if available. Is the location safe for a fire?

When possible, choose a location that is dry and well drained. Don't set up your shelter in a water run-off area, as you might get swept away in a downpour. Avoid animal trails, since you wouldn't want a large animal trampling you at night as they travel down their trail.

Try to have an open southern exposure, with the entryway facing east or southeast. You want the wind to the back or side of the shelter, depending on the type of shelter. What you don't want is the wind blowing directly into your shelter.

You need a location that is large enough for you to comfortably lie down but small enough to conserve heat. Look for natural barriers that could help to block wind or reflect heat from a fire.

Avoid areas that could pose a threat from flooding, avalanches, mud slides, rock slides and falling trees. I always tell students, "look up." Nothing will ruin your sleep like a dead tree or limb falling on your shelter in the night. Large dead limbs are called "widow makers" for a reason.

## Immediate action shelters

I've examined a lot of material written about survival and survival shelters, and I find that many times shelters are described as down-and-dirty, made-from-natural-resources shelters. Sometimes this is necessary, and we

Wrap yourself in a Space All Weather Blanket for protection from the wind or rain.

In a sudden storm, you can quickly hunker down in an Orange Survival Bag.

will be discussing these types of shelters later in this chapter. But let's back up a bit and discuss shelters that can be quickly erected with minimum effort from items that should be in an adequately equipped survival kit. I call these immediate action shelters.

One of the quickest ways to get out of the rain or wind is to simply get out a Space All Weather Blanket, sit down, tuck the back under your butt and wrap up. This works particularly well for a sudden thunder storm, and you can easily wait out the storm while staying dry. This would also work using a poncho or small tarp. Or, just climb inside the Orange Survival Bag!

### Bent sapling shelter

Another quick immediate action shelter can be made with the Space All Weather Blanket and a springy sapling. Simply bend the sapling over and tie the top end down to another tree at the base or, if a tree is not available, a stake made from a short stick. Either way, this holds the sapling bent over so you can throw the All Weather Blanket (or any other material for that matter) over the sapling and tie out the four corners. This can all be accomplished in minutes, especially if you keep tie-offs attached to the grommeted corners.

### Tube tent shelter

An often-carried item in medium to large survival kits is a tube tent. A tube tent is essentially a large tube of light plastic material. As mentioned earlier, a tube tent can also be constructed by cutting the bottom seam of an Orange Survival Bag or the bottoms seams of a couple of contractor garbage bags.

Constructing a tube tent shelter is pretty straightforward. Simply tie one end of a ridge line to a small tree and feed it through the tube. Then tie the

Bend a sapling for a quick shelter. Tie the top end to a tree or stake to hold it down, then place an All Weather Blanket over it. Note guy lines from corners.

Feed the parachute cord, which is already tied to a tree, through the tube tent before tying off the other end. Use logs inside to hold out the bottom edges. A tube tent offers considerable room inside.

Push a small smooth stone into the side of the tube tent from the inside. Create a slip knot on one end of cordage, place it over the protrusion on the outside and pull tight. Pull the other end of the cordage and stake it or tie it to another tree or root.

other end to another tree, an appropriate distance from the first, to fully expand the tube to its length. Hold the bottom sides out by laying logs inside the tube, the length of the tube on each side, which is also reasonably quick. The sides can also be held out by placing large rocks on the inside at the bottom of both sides. I prefer the log method if available.

The sides of a tube tent can also be tied out. Do not to try to cut a hole in the material for the guy lines, as the material is thin and will rip. Instead, use a small smooth stone or rolled up bunch of leaves or dried grass. Place the stone or a ball of other material inside the tube tent and push out. You will see the protrusion on the outside. Put a slip knot in one end of a piece of cord, place the loop of the slip knot around the protrusion and pull the loop tight around the protrusion. Now pull the cord out and peg it to the ground or tied it off to a tree or root.

There is another way to make a tube tent if you only have an Orange Survival Bag or other large contractor bag. The advantage with this technique is you don't have to cut a hole for the ridgeline to pass through. This technique was invented by my stepson Jonas, who ironically is on a scholarship at Miami University for a five year architectural program.

On one end of a piece of parachute cord, tie a double overhand knot. Slide that knot inside to the top corner of the bag.

With another piece of parachute cord, tie a slip knot and place over the protrusion made from the first knot inside the bag.

Tie the two ends to suspend the bag between two trees. You now have a ridge line without cutting a hole in the corner of the bag, leaving the bag usable for something else without having a hole in the bottom.

### Tarps

Tarps, such as the previously-discussed silicone-impregnated ripstop nylon tarps, are light and easy to carry. They can be used to quickly make an immediate action shelter. Of course, there are many ways to put up a tarp. I have been told that a tarp is not pitched, but flown. My feelings are that, in a survival situation where you need a shelter now, the quickest way is the best.

One of the quickest ways to make a shelter from a tarp is to locate a ridge pole and wedge it into the fork of a

In under five minutes you can make an immediate action shelter from a ridge pole leaned against the lower limb of a tree and a tarp. Hold the sides down using two old logs or heavy objects found nearby.

tree or over a low limb. Throw the tarp over the ridge pole and pull out the sides, then hold the sides down using logs, rocks or any other heavy objects you can find. That quickly you have an immediate action shelter.

Another way to put up a quick shelter with a tarp is to string a ridge line with cordage and throw the tarp over it. Tie out the sides with cordage using stakes and you're set to go. Remember to place the side of the shelter to the wind, not one of the ends, or the wind will blow right through your shelter.

There are various ways to make a quick lean-to shelter using available material. However, the lean-to is my least favorite type of shelter, as it provides the least protection from the wind and rain. Without a reflector fire, it is difficult to heat.

## Improvised shelters

An improvised shelter is one that is reasonably easy to construct, but requires more time and effort than an immediate action shelter. It can be built using what you find in the wilderness, or with a combination of material you have with you and items found in the wilderness.

### A-frame shelter

An A-frame shelter is easy to make if material is available, but is time consuming. It can be built entirely out of material found in the wilderness, but the addition of a poncho or tarp over the top helps to make it waterproof.

The first thing you need is a sturdy ridge pole which can be leaned into the fork of a tree or over a lower limb. If neither is available, lash two sturdy sticks together using a shear lashing, then spread open the bottoms, making an "A" shape. Lean the ridge pole in the notch at the top of the "A." Make sure the ridge pole is longer than you are tall, as the bottom three feet or so will not be usable inside. If you are six feet tall, I would recommend a ridge pole about 10 feet long, not including the portion that extends over whatever you have it leaning on.

Lean sticks of various lengths against both sides, at an angle to the ridge pole. The angle should allow adequate room inside for you to get in and lay down. I would suggest about four feet, two feet on either side of the ridge pole. Of course this depends on the size of the person that will be us-

Building an A-frame shelter is one of many skills taught in survival courses.

# Modified A-frame shelter

While on a 10-day trip to the wilderness canoe area of the Adirondacks in New York, I wanted to experiment using birch bark to fill in the sides of an A-frame shelter after the initial frame work was up. I found a large white birch that was down and had been for quite some time. The bark was easy to peel in large strips. The ridge pole was leaned against two sturdy sticks that were shear lashed together.

Check the ridge pole for adequate size for a modified A-frame shelter.

Create the initial framework.

Harvest strips of birch bark from a downed tree. Never peel bark from a live tree.

Weave the strips of birch bark between the framework.

Weave birch bark over the ridge line after completing the side.

Add leaves to the sides of the shelter.

Layer leaves from the bottom up, building a wide base.

Layer the leaves on both sides to ensure adequate insulation.

An orange All Weather Blanket can be added to the top and held in place with several logs. This allows the shelter to be observed from the air, as well as adding some waterproofing over the ridge line.

ing the shelter. Continue leaning sticks against the sides until there is very little space between the sticks. If you are going to place a tarp, poncho, or plastic material over the frame, make sure you do not extend the leaning sticks very far above the ridge pole. Try to keep the ends blunt, and all about the same height from the pole.

Next, add large pieces of bark on the sides, if available, or even pine boughs. Finally, place leaves and other fine debris over the skeletal frame. If the shelter is being built for warmth, the covering of leaves for insulation should be about three feet thick.

Also insulate the floor inside the shelter, especially if you don't have a sleeping pad. Fill the inside with leaves if they are available. Once you get a bunch inside, lay down on them and compress them well. Then continue in this manner to ensure an adequate insulation layer. You could also use pine boughs, and if you carry contractor bags or the Orange Survival Bag, this is the time to fill one with leaves or other debris and use it as an insulation mattress.

### Tree root shelter

In the woods, you may find a large tree fallen with the root ball pulled up out of the ground. The root ball is usually standing vertical. If facing the correct direction against the wind, this makes a good starting wall for a shelter. Logs and large sticks can be leaned against the root ball to make a roof and sides. Boughs or other materials, including a tarp, poncho or plastic, can be added to the top to make it waterproof and hold debris.

Often a depression is left in the ground when the roots are pulled up, so be careful in the rainy season, as the depression can fill up with water. You might wake up in a small swimming pool. You can fill the depression using debris, or find a fallen tree that did not leave a large depression. Many times the roots pulled up because they grew over a rocky area. This may not leave a hole but does leave a rocky surface. It is easier to pad a rocky surface than it is to fill a depression. And remember, if it is winter, rain isn't as big of a problem as in the summer. As usual, it is all about trade-offs.

### Desert shade pits

If you are stranded in a vehicle in the desert, use the vehicle for shelter but don't stay inside it, it will become an oven. Dig a pit under the vehicle about 15 to 18 inches deep on the end opposite the engine compartment. Take your time and avoid getting too hot. Your vehicle will provide shade from the sun. Open all the doors and windows for ventilation, which will help reduce heat buildup inside the car. If your lights come on when you open the doors, disconnect the battery so it will not discharge while the doors are open. Crawl into the pit you dug and enjoy the shade.

A desert shade pit can be made to provide a place to rest during the day and lower the temperature approximately 30 degrees. Try to build it during the early morning or evening hours. Until then, use a tarp or other material to erect a sun shade.

The easiest way to build a shade pit is to locate an area that has rocks or dunes on both sides, a little wider than your body, with an 18- to 24-inch depression. If you cannot locate such an area, then you will have to dig a pit 18 to 24 inches deep. Make the pit as long as your body and wide enough to crawl into. On the entrance side, remove additional sand or dirt so you can slide your body down into the pit.

You will need two pieces of material or a large one to cut into two pieces. Build up walls around the outside on three sides using the sand or dirt you dig out of the pit. The fourth side will be the entrance. Stretch one piece of material over the hole, holding it taut with rocks, sand, or dirt around the edges.

To build a snow trench shelter, shovel a trench, add framework over the top of the trench, then cover with a tarp. Add snow first around the edge of the tarp, then over the top. A large bag filled with snow or a large pack can be used as a door.

Now build up the four corners with rocks. If you can't find rocks, then you will need to build up four pillar-type structures using sand or stones. Stretch the second piece of material about 18 inches above the first. Try to leave space on all sides for air to move through between the two pieces of material. The top piece of material can be held in place using guy lines, attached using a small rock or other material, as shown for the tube tent above. These guy lines can be tied to a rock if available. If not, make an anchor with a piece of wood or other debris, burying it perpendicular to the pull. You can also fill bags with sand if you have them, and bury them to tie off.

## Snow trench

Talk of shelters made in the snow invokes the imagination of many who recall images, probably seen in movies, of a dogsled pulling up to an igloo. Snow shelters take considerable time to construct and require a lot of energy. An igloo takes time, material, tools and knowhow. Snow caves, which many of us made as children, are also time consuming, and you can probably recall getting real wet crawling around in the snow. They also require some real deep snow. The snow mound shelter, also known as a "Quinzhee," is made by piling up a bunch of your equipment, or whatever stuff you can find, and covering it with snow. Then the inside is excavated by removing the equipment or material you used to mound the snow on. Again, a labor-intensive effort.

The above shelters are beyond the scope of this book, as they are usually made entirely out of snow, and not with material you have in your kit. However, a shelter that is practical is the snow trench. Because it is easy to make and requires the least amount of effort, it is ideally suited for emergency use. Another advantage of making a snow trench is the minimal contact you have with the snow, decreasing your chance of getting wet while building it. Each snow trench shelter should be for one person.

A snow trench is usually just a trench about three feet deep and slightly longer than your body. If the snow is not deep enough, build up the sides using the snow from the trench as well as snow from nearby. It is handy to have a shovel or something to use to move snow. Even the end of a snowshoe could help. Once the trench is excavated, place long sticks, limbs, etc., over the trench, placing them from side to side, not the long way. One end should have an open space to crawl into the shelter. Once the basic roof framework has been placed, cover that framework with boughs or, if available, a tarp. The tarp works well for this purpose. Secure the tarp by placing snow, first around the outside edge. Then place snow over the top, making sure the framework is strong enough to hold the weight.

On the inside, you will need insulation from the ground. If you were prepared, you'll have a closed cell foam sleeping pad or self inflating sleeping mat. If not, locate debris such as leaves (difficult to find in heavy snow), pine needles or boughs. This is another good time to have contractor garbage bags or the Orange Survival Bag. They can be filled with pine needles or other debris for use as insulation from the cold ground.

As you can see, the more material you have available to assist you with building a shelter, the quicker you will be protected from the elements. As always, be prepared to survive!

*Chapter 7*

# Water Collection & Purification

**Y**ou will learn in any good survival course that the human body needs water to function normally and to survive. Without water, dehydration sets in and your chances of survival diminish quickly.

Your body by weight is 75% water. This water helps to maintain your body temperature. Water lost through sweat, evaporation and other bodily functions must be replaced. An average individual needs two to three quarts of water each day when performing normal activity. If performing strenuous activity, such as during a survival situation, or in an excessively hot or cold climate, the amount of water required may increase to four to six quarts.

The "Rules of Three" indicate that you can go three minutes without air, three hours without shelter (from heat or cold), three days without water and three weeks without food. Although this is a generalized rule, it shows that you can go a lot longer without food than water. It also depends on the environment. In an extremely hot environment, your ability to function will diminish quickly if you don't remain hydrated.

Your urine is often a good indicator of dehydration. The darker the color of your urine, the more your body is dehydrated and the more water you need to drink. Dehydration can cause weakness, dizziness and decreased mental capacity and coordination, something a survivor doesn't need.

I am often asked if water cannot be purified for drinking, should they go without drinking. My feeling is that you should always try to purify water when possible. However, the bottom line is, if you don't drink you will certainly die. If you drink unpurified water, you have a chance of getting sick, being infested with parasites, etc., but you will live and be able to talk about how terrible it was while the doctors are pumping you full of medicine. Again, I don't recommend drinking unknown water as a general rule, but it beats the alternative.

## Water containers

The best way to ensure that you have water when you need it is to carry it with you. Therefore, before discussing how to locate or purify water, let's discuss containers for carrying water. These containers can be used to carry water with you, and provide you with something to collect water in when you find it.

I prefer to carry a primary water container that allows me to carry a cook pot over it. This eliminates the additional space required for a pot. If you need to boil water or melt snow, you are going to need a pot of some sort.

Various water containers are substantial and can survive heavy field use. From left to right: a 32-ounce and 48-ounce BPA free Nalgene Bottle, the Guyot 32-ounce stainless steel bottle, the Nalgene Oasis and an old stainless steel military canteen.

Different types of pots can be placed over the bottom of water containers, maximizing the use of space in your kit. From left to right: a stainless steel Alpine Mug, an old style military canteen cup, a Vargo Ti-Lite Mug and a Snow Peak Solo pot. All of these can be used for boiling water or cooking and take up no additional room.

Place split rings through the holes drilled in the lower rim of a Guyot Stainless Steel bottle with a bail. A lid from a standard Nalgene bottle fits on the Guyot bottle with the split rings in place.

The new Nalgene bottles, which are BPA free, are heavy duty bottles with wide mouths. I prefer wide mouths, especially when you are trying to fill them from a source of water in the field.

My preferred bottle is the 32-ounce Guyot stainless steel single wall bottle. You can boil water right in this bottle – very handy in a survival situation. It also lets you melt water that freezes in it in a cold climate. Or, place hot water in it, put it in a sock and use it as a foot warmer in a sleeping bag.

The military style canteen does not have a wide mouth but fits inside the old style military canteen cup, which is one of my favorites for boiling water or cooking, and being metal (stainless steel) provides the options listed for the Guyot bottle.

Before moving on to other containers, I would like to explain how to make a bail for the Guyot stainless steel bottle. As you saw in the chapter on fire and light, I like to hang my bottle from a bail, like all my cook pots. However, if you drill holes into the side of the mouth of the bottle, it ruins the watertight seal when the lid is screwed on. I drill holes into the lower rim of the bottle, one on each side. There are then two ways to attach a bail.

The first way is to attach a small split ring into each hole drilled on the lower rim. Then make a bail with bends that pass through the split rings and lift the bottle. With this method the bail will not stand in an upright position unless you hold it. I use a lid from a Nalgene bottle on my Guyot bottles as they are smaller around than the Guyot lids. Just my preference, but the lid still goes on the bottle, even with the split rings installed.

I still wanted a bail that would stand up on the Guyot bottle, and after bending some 3/32-inch piano wire in various configurations I finally got what I was looking for. The new bail uses only the two holes drilled in the lower lip, and the split rings are not required. The bail is slid under the lower lip (the one with the bail holes) and the two short upright ends are inserted up into the holes on the lip. As you start to lift the bail, it slides up through the holes until it is caught by the "U" shape of the bail. Once the bail is upright, the side pressure of the bail locks it in an upright position. The bail can be carried in the container with your bottle.

The bail slides through the holes drilled in the lower rim of the Guyot bottle. The bends in the piano wire hold the bail upright.

For secondary water containers, I prefer a flexible container that packs down small. They supplement your primary container and provide additional storage for water. These containers, manufactured by various companies such as Nalgene and Platypus, are made from a clear flexible plastic laminate and can be folded or rolled up when not in use. They come in various sizes, even one that is designed to fit in the leg pocket of BDU (Battle Dress Utilities) trousers. They can be carried rolled or folded in a kit for use when needed, or carried filled and then rolled or folded for storage after use. They have leak proof caps, and some have gusseted bottoms so they will stand up when filled. These flexible canteens are available with small mouth and large mouth openings. This is often a trade-off, as the small mouth packs better, but the wide mouth is easier to fill.

Soft canteens made from clear flexible plastic laminate can be folded or rolled up when not in use.

One of the best flexible water containers is the Aqua-Pouch, which I designed specifically for survival kits, is available only from Survival Resources. The one liter Aqua-Pouch is a free standing, zip-closure, water storage container designed for use with water purification tablets. The pouch has a line marked for one liter of water for easy measuring when using water purification tablets.

The Aqua-Pouch is a 5.2 mil, extremely sturdy, FDA-approved food grade pouch. It has a gusseted bottom and measures 6.5 inches wide by 10 inches high, can be rolled or folded for easy storage, and is free-standing for easy filling and pouring. This pouch will hold boiling water (for those who purify water by boiling), and it can be frozen and then thawed by placing it in boiling water. Because of the large top opening, you can put snow in it and carry it between your clothing layers for melting. The Aqua-Pouch also has grommets at the top which allow you to attach cordage, such as parachute cord, to transport the pouch or attach it to a pack.

Even though the Aqua-Pouch fits in most small survival kits, you might require a smaller container for use in mini-kits. A recommendation often made is to carry a non-lubricated condom. It is small (can even be carried in a mini kit) and can hold a considerable amount of water if it is supported in a sock, sleeve or trouser leg. I carried one or more in my kits for years.

The Aqua-Pouch, featuring a line marking the one-liter level, lays flat and rolls up to carry in a survival kit.

Attach cordage to the grommets of the Aqua-Pouch to carry it or attach it to a pack.

I always keep my eyes open for survival kit items that pack small, are durable and can be used for multiple purposes. After watching my wife use oven bags for turkeys, I started playing with them. They are constructed of a Mylar-type material and are durable, so I started using them for mini kits. I cut them down to half their height, filled with one quart of water and drew a horizontal line on the outside with a small permanent marker indicating the one-quart level. When I needed to use the bag to purify water, I filled it to that point and knew how many purification tablets to use. For bags that I didn't cut down, I also marked it at the two- and three-quart level.

Water leaks from most oven bags. However, when tied at the bottom they hold a considerable amount of water.

This worked great for many years, but as with all things today, the manufacturer changed the way they manufactured them and they started to leak. I now find that almost everyone I get leaks right out of the box. I have moved on to a new product, as I will describe next. However, if you still want to use oven bags, don't cut them off, instead tie a knot in the bottom of the bag. This keeps them from leaking, but makes it almost impossible to pre-mark the bag with a one quart line and they no longer fold flat.

Since the oven bag, I have found a small soft water container that folds up flat enough to fit in a mini kit. It is called the Emergency Water Bag and has a gusseted bottom. It is sold at Survival Resources with a one-quart water line marked for use with water purification tablets. It can be folded up very small, yet allows you to carry a quart of water. It is four mil. thick and is sterile (there is a tear off tab on the top to open the bag for the first time). It has a roll-down top which is secured shut with wire tabs specially designed so the ends are covered to prevent puncturing the bag. You simply roll the top down three times, curve the ends together and twist the tabs to secure. Although this bag is not as sturdy as

The Emergency Water Bag folds down small to fit in a mini kit.

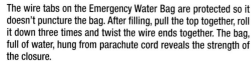

The wire tabs on the Emergency Water Bag are protected so it doesn't puncture the bag. After filling, pull the top together, roll it down three times and twist the wire ends together. The bag, full of water, hung from parachute cord reveals the strength of the closure.

the Aqua-Pouch and not as stable standing, it is a great alternative, specifically for mini kits because of its ability to fold down very small. They are packaged three per bag.

As another option, carry freezer zip closure bags in your kit to carry water in an emergency. They are also useful for other things such as collecting tinder, edibles, etc.

## Sources for water

In a survival situation, watch for any of various sources to obtain the water you need.

### Surface water

Surface water, including streams, ponds, lakes, rivers, and springs, is the easiest way to obtain water. It is usually easily located. If you don't know where it is, use various indicators to determine the best place to look:

**Terrain:** Study the terrain around you. Look for drainage areas. Flowing water such as rivers and streams flow downhill, so drainage areas might indicate running water will be located in those areas. Lakes and ponds are normally in low-lying areas, but not always. They can also be found on the top of mountains. Swamps and marshes are wet areas and water will usually be found there.

**Vegetation:** Look for vegetation. If everything around appears dry, but one area seems to have lush vegetation, it might indicate water is located there or just below the surface. If you see vegetation intrinsic to swamps and marshes, such as cattails, phragmites, etc., you will likely find water there. To suport this vegetation the ground is at least moist, so it is a good place to dig for water.

**Animals:** Like humans, animals need water. Many large game animals drink at dusk and dawn, and the trails they leave can lead you to water. Many times, various animal trails will converge to a main trail. Often this main trail will lead you to water. Another sign could be animal droppings. Animals have been known to defecate after drinking, so multiple droppings might indicate you are close to water.

**Birds:** Flocks of birds often circle a water source during the day. Birds also gather near water in the early morning and late afternoon. Watching the direction of birds in flight during those times might lead you to a water source.

**Insects:** Insects are known to swarm around a water source. Bees are usually within a few miles of a water source. Mosquitoes breed in water and large numbers of them indicate you are near a water source. It may be a swamp, but it is water.

Learn to be cognizant of what is going on around you, and observe. Many of these indicators can be subtle, but are there if you notice them.

## Subsurface water

Anywhere the ground appears damp or looks like a water drainage area is a good place to dig for water. Dry stream beds may also provide water by digging a hole, but not always. Try at the concave bend, as this is where water moves the slowest. Dig a hole about two or three feet deep, and if no water is found, start another hole.

If water does start to seep into the hole, dig down a little further. If the ground is soft and the sides start to fall in, you will have to line the hole with wood, rock, etc. When the hole is full, let the water set for a while to let sediment settle to the bottom. Carefully scoop the water out with a cup or pot if available, and filter further.

Consider any water obtained to be contaminated, and purify it before consumption.

## Water collection techniques

There are various ways to collect water if you haven't found a major water source. Learn to use all the means available so there are options in a survival situation.

### Rain water

Rainfall is free water for the taking. I have often laughed at students who run for shelter when it starts to rain, with little thought of collecting it.

Set out containers to catch the rain water or direct the water to containers by various means. Use whatever material you have, including plastic, ponchos, a survival blanket or tarp, to improvise a gutter to direct the water towards your container. This method increases the amount of water collected when rainfall is limited. You can use other items to direct water, such as long pieces of curved bark. The idea is to get as much as you can while the rain is falling.

Another method is to dig a hole and line it with plastic material to make a catch basin. Even faster is to take four short pieces of log and make a square. Hold them in place with rocks, so they don't roll back. Then put a piece of plastic down inside the square hole, draping it over the outside, and you have another catch basin. Improvise with what you have!

After it rains, look for areas where water has collected. Carry a piece of plastic tubing so you can collect water from rock depressions or other places the water is contained.

## Ice and snow

By volume, ice yields more water than snow and requires less heat to do so. Find ice in the form of icicles on plants and trees, as well as on the surface of streams, ponds, rivers, etc. When taking ice off plants and trees, try to take only ice above waist high – below this is the average height that animals can urinate. If ice is obtained from over water, such as streams, ponds, etc., it is no purer than the water from which it came. Be sure to purifiy it, as the water may be contaminated.

A water generator melts snow in an oven bag hung over a fire using a tripod. Use an All Weather Space Blanket as a reflector to increase efficiency.

If near salt water, only use ice that is crystalline with a bluish cast, as it has little salt in it. If the ice is gray in color or opaque, it is salty and should not be used.

In snow country water is everywhere, just in a different form. First, don't eat snow or ice. Your body gives up heat to melt snow. Eating snow or ice can reduce body temperature and will lead to more dehydration. Doing so for days can also cause swelling of the mucous membrane in your mouth which makes it so raw that it can prevent eating and drinking until the inflammation subsides. Yes, dogs can eat snow, but we can't.

When collecting snow, use snow closest to the ground and, of course, select snow that is not discolored (especially yellow). Snow closest to the ground is packed and yields more water than the upper layers.

To melt snow for water, place a small amount in the bottom of your container and place it near a fire. Allow the container to warm until the small amount of initial snow has melted and you have water in the bottom. Then add snow a little at a time, floating the snow in the water, so that the mixture remains slushy. This prevents burning the bottom out of the container. Don't pack the container with snow, as snow absorbs water if packed and will form an insulating airspace at the bottom of the container. When this happens, the bottom of your container may burn out.

I have found that using an oven bag over a fire makes a good water generator. Tie a knot in the bottom of the bag (the bags often leak), then tie the top with a knot on each side. Using parachute cord, make a slip knot around each knot on the top two corners and hang the bag on a tripod next to a fire. On real windy days, I often use an All Weather Space Blanket wrapped around two sides of the tripod. The reflected heat creates almost a little oven and the snow melts quicker.

Another way of melting a small amount of snow is to use your own body heat. Only use this method if you are traveling or active. Place the snow in a plastic bag and hang it between your insulation and outer layer. The Aqua-Pouch is ideal for this purpose, as it has grommets to hang around your neck. Again, if you are inactive, take it off or your body heat will be conducted into the cold bag.

Wear an Aqua-Pouch between layers of clothes to melt snow while you're traveling or active.

Lightload towels and small PackTowels are handy for collecting dew.

### Collecting dew

The time to collect dew is early in the morning, before it starts to evaporate. Dew can be collected from grass, leaves, etc. with any absorbent material. Tie a bandana around each ankle and walk through the grass and see how fast they get soaked. Ring them out into a container and go again. If you don't have any material such as a bandana with you (unlikely after reading this or my first book), tie tufts of grass around your ankles and walk through the dew. Not as effective as cloth material, but something is better than nothing. Small PackTowels are handy for this, as they are absorbent and I carry one anyway. Another possibility is Lightload Towels, which come compressed into a small round package measuring only 1-3/4 inches by 7/16-inch thick and expand to 12 by 24 inches. Either of these can be used to collect dew and be wrung out into a container.

### Solar stills

Most people who write about solar stills can be divided into one of two groups: proponents and opponents. The first group usually talks about the in-ground solar still, borrowing diagrams from old military manuals, and touting their effectiveness. Many of these people have never built one. Those in the second group usually have built one and have determined they don't work very well. They have learned that you lose more water from your body through sweating than you gain from the still.

### In-ground solar stills

I have built several in-ground solar stills in the northeast during the summer, and even though they require a lot of work, they have produced water. However, we have plenty of water here and if the hole doesn't fill in with water on its own, the heavy rain knocks it down.

Where you need it, in an arid area, you can only obtain the water if it is present to begin with. I've been told to put lots of green vegetation in the hole before covering with plastic, as it will help produce water. Now, if I have found an area with lots of green vegetation I would probably dig there first, as water will probably percolate into the hole.

A good friend of mine who has written ten books on survival is Christopher Nyerges. He teaches survival in California and spends a lot of time in the desert with his students. After explaining how to make an in-the-ground solar still in his book, *How To Survive Anywhere,* he asks, "Now is all this practical? As with most things, it works best when you really don't need it - that is, when there is plenty of moisture in the soil. In very arid environments, with wind, we have had some stills produce zero. Others produce just a few tablespoons. But in very moist conditions (when we probably could have obtained all our water simply by digging a well), we have obtained two quarts a day, which is quite good. But what was the cost in body water?" Christopher agrees: too much!

There is a simpler way to capture water with a still, and in my opinion, much more effective. Let's examine that technique.

### Transpiration bags

A transpiration bag is a solar still that requires very little effort to produce water compared to an in-the-ground solar still. All you have to do is carry some large, clear plastic bags and a small amount of cordage in your kit or pack.

The first thing to do is find some deciduous trees or bushes (be sure you do not use a poisonous plant – this is a time the ability to identify specific trees and bushes comes in handy). The larger the better, as the larger the plant the larger the root system. It is the roots that gather the water. Clear bags work better than colored bags as the sun can shine through the bag. This allows for photosynthesis, which provides for the transpiration.

I find that the clear trash bags, measuring 30 by 33 inches, work well, are inexpensive, and easily carried in a small space.

Set up the transpiration bags where they will get the most sun throughout the day. For instance,

Place a transpiration bag over some limbs of a deciduous tree after pulling them together in a bunch.

in a large field with a woodline on the north side, as the sun rises in the east and sets in the west, the transpiration bags get continuous sun for most of the day.

Pull a bunch of branches together to fit as many branches and leaves into the bag as possible (the larger the bag, the better). Pull the bag up over the branches and tie the bag off, around the limb, using a small amount of cordage. Make sure the seal is tight, you do not want any air leaks. Pull down one corner of the bag to create a place for the water to collect. Use a small stone to hold this corner down, or tie the corner of the bag to a stake in the ground.

Place a small rock in the corner of the bag to hold a corner away from the vegetation.

The sun causes the clear bag to heat up, which draws water from the leaves. This water evaporates and condenses on the inside walls of the bag. With the corner of the bag held down lower than the rest of the bag, the drops of water condensing on the inside walls travel down the inside wall of the bag and accumulate in the lowered corner. The transpired water is now purified and ready to drink.

If you take the bag off in order to retrieve the water, you must start all over again. Instead, use a

**Water collects in the bag.** Photos by Robert Mustin.

tube to get the water out of the corner. Place this in the corner of the bag when you first set it up, and have it exit where you tie the bag to the limb. Be sure to seal this tube with a small plug, such as whittled from a piece of wood.

With this tube technique, the water often has debris, bugs, etc. in it that accumulated in the corner. If you just snip off the very corner of the bag (the corner that is accumulating the water) and fill your container with the water, you can filter the water through a bandana, coffee filter, etc., to eliminate debris. Then tie a tight knot in the corner and let the process continue.

So how much water do you get? Well, we average between a cup or two a day, depending on the sun and cloud cover, and often more. That's quite a bit of purified water for little effort. And if you put out several of these transpiration bags, that's more water. The tree should continue to provide water for 2-3 days, at which point you should move the bags. This is an effective and nearly effortless way to collect water in a survival situation.

### Water purification

It is my opinion that any water found in the wilderness should be considered contaminated and purified before consumption. There are four water-borne enteric pathogens that can contaminate water: bacteria, viruses, protozoan cysts and parasites. Any of these can cause sickness or worse, and obviously this is undesirable in a survival situation. Contamination can also be caused by various other sources, such as chemicals, etc. Therefore, no matter how clear water may appear, always attempt to purify any water found in the wilderness.

Without carrying anything in your kit, water can be purified by bringing it to a boil. This assumes that you have the means to make fire, a container to boil water in, and the time to do so. It is better to carry a means to purify water, which requires less energy.

### Pre-filters

Before discussing water filters, let's first review pre-filters. When using chemicals to purify water, the length of time the chemicals take to properly purify the water is affected by the turbidity of water. Always start out with the clearest water possible. If using a mechanical filtering device, the filters can become easily clogged by sediment and other debris in muddy or cloudy water. My suggestion is to pre-filter water before attempting to purify or filter it.

When water is located in the field, it is not always clear and often contains a lot of debris or sediment. Pre-filtering reduces the turbidity. Keep in mind, this does not purify water, it only removes solid particles from the water. Pre-filtering can be as simple as straining the water through a bandana or t-shirt to eliminate as much debris or sediment as possible. Let's examine some other options for pre-filtering water.

### Pre-filter Support Sheath

Various companies include "cone" coffee filters in their survival kits for pre-filtering water. What they don't mention is that a cone coffee filter will not hold water unless it is supported. The seams are only pressed together in a corrugated fashion, and those grooves and ridges will only hold together if it is supported, like they are in a coffee maker.

My wife, Denise, and I experimented with various ways to support the filter during use and finally came up with a solution that is effective, yet folds up very flat. It is called the Pre-Filter Support Sheath, made from six mil. poly material, and it works very well. We manufacture this device and it is offered through Survival Resources as part of a water purification system that combines this with an Aqua-Pouch and water purification tablets. It is called the Aqua-Pouch Plus.

To use, insert the pre-filter into the sheath and place it on top of your water container. Pour water into the filter to filter out debris, sediment, bugs, etc. The water flows through holes on the side, which are placed above the seam of the filter, and down into your water container. This does not purify the water, it only pre-filters it.

Use the Pre-Filter Support Sheath to filter out bugs, sediment and debris prior to purifying the water.

## Seepage basin

Another way to pre-filter water is called a seepage basin, also known as a sediment hole. This works well if you are in an area where it is swampy or water has a lot of scum on it. With this method, you use the soil present to filter the water. Just dig a hole three to four feet from the tainted water. The hole should slowly begin to fill with water and it will be clearer than the water from the source. If the sides of the hole keep falling in, use wood or stone to shore up the sides. Make sure you cover the hole with something when not in use to protect it from additional debris or animals.

## Three-layered filter

A three-layered filter can be constructed from available material. Many of the military manuals show using a tripod, on which to attach the material, and this technique is shown in many other books on survival. I never really carry any material that has three equal sides, and if I fold a bandana to make a triangle, it is too small to use on a tripod.

# QUADRIPOD WATER FILTER

Place filter material in each layer of the filter.

A water filter can be made with only parachute cord, bandanas and short sticks with notches in the ends.

Therefore I suggest that you build a quadripod using four long sticks with a sheer lashing at the top. You can now use three square pieces of material, such as bandanas. Just tie a knot in each corner of the three bandanas which makes them in the shape of a container, or dipped pocket. Using cordage, such as parachute cord, place a slip knot around each corner knot on the bandana and tie each of these cords to a separate leg of the quadripod using a clove hitch or other knot.

Each bandana should now make a dipped pocket into which we can place our filtering material. Place grass in the upper section, sand in the middle section, and charcoal in the bottom section (charcoal can be obtained from the burned wood in a fire, which is actually activated charcoal). Place a container to catch the filtered water under the center of the bottom section. Now pour water into the top section and let it filter through each section, into the next, until it ends up in your catch container. You now have filtered water.

If you do not have four long sticks, but have short ones, you can make a filter by using just parachute cord and the bandanas. Simply tie the bandanas directly to the long lengths of parachute cord and hang from a tree branch. Use two short sticks with notches in each end. Place them crossed corner on each bandana, so the sticks cross each other. The sticks will hold the bandanas open so they still make a pocket for the filtering material. This technique was devised by my stepson, Jonas.

## Chemical purification

Iodine-based water purification products are for short term or limited emergency use only, and should not be used on a continuous basis. Also, although iodine based products have been found effective against viruses, bacteria and Giardia lamblia, they are not effective against Cryptosporidium. And, iodine-based systems leave an aftertaste in the water.

Iodine tablets make questionable water bacteriologically safe to drink. A major brand of iodine tablets is Potable Aqua, which is manufactured by WPC Brands, Inc. They come 50 tablets to a small glass bottle (two inches tall by one inch in diameter). If this is too big for you, Survival Resources sells a small amber glass vial with a Teflon screw Cap (necessary for re-packaging iodine tablets) which measures only 1-3/8 inches tall by 5/8 inch in diameter. It only holds half as much, but is great for mini kits. Two tablets treat one quart or one liter of water. Directions are printed on the label.

Another Iodine purification option is a product called "Polar Pure" by Polar Equipment. Although the bottle is larger than Potable Aqua (three inches tall by 1-5/8 inches in diameter), it is handy if the space is available. To use, you simply fill the bottle with questionable water and shake. There are iodine crystals in the bottle and in one hour you have an iodine solution for

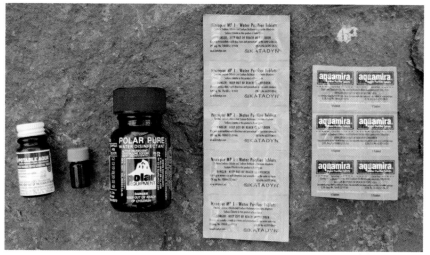

From left to right: Potable Aqua, a small re-packaging vial, Polar Pure, Katadyn Micropur, and Aquamira, chlorine dioxide-based tablets.

purifying water (and the solution can be carried in the bottle so it is ready when you need it). There is a thermometer built into the side of the bottle with directions to indicate how many capfuls of the iodine solution to use per quart or liter of water, depending on the temperature. Also, the bottle is manufactured with an insert that prevents the iodine crystals, which must remain in the bottle, from falling oft when pouring out the iodine solution. It will purify up to 2000 quarts of water.

My preferred method of chemical treatment in the field is chlorine dioxide, which is effective against, viruses, bacteria and cysts, to include both Giardia lamblia and Cryptosporidium. There are various chlorine dioxide-based products available, and I prefer the tablet form. The other thing I like about chlorine dioxide is that the water has no aftertaste after using the chemical.

The first to offer chlorine dioxide tablets as a means for purification was Katadyn with a product called Micropur. This system uses one tablet per liter of water. Each tablet is in a foil capsule with 10 capsules per sheet. They are available in 20 packs (two sheets per package) or 30 packs (three sheets per package). Many other companies are now also offering Chlorine Dioxide based tablets including Aquamira and Potable Aqua.

Aquamira also offers a two-part liquid purification system that when mixed produces chlorine dioxide. One of the two bottles also has a mixing cap on top. You place seven drops from each bottle in the mixing cap and let stand for five minutes. Fill a container with one quart or one liter of water and add the mixture from the cap. Shake or stir and let stand for 15 minutes (30 minutes if the water is very cold or turbid). Although effective, I don't prefer this system, as you have to carry two bottles of chemicals and accurately mix the two components. I find the tablets easier in a survival situation.

## Water filters

Most water filters only filter water, not purify it. And, although there are some units that both filter and purify water, most do not. Depending on the size of the filter (and you must check before buying), a filter will eliminate protozoa (such as Giardia & Cryptosporidium), and most

The Katadyn Hiker filter is easy to use and pumps alot of water rapidly.

bacteria. They will not eliminate viruses, such a Hepatitis A, or bacteria smaller than the size listed on the filter (normally 0.2 – 0.3 microns).

One thing I have learned about filters. If they are ceramic filter based systems, they remove waterborne enteric pathogens down to 0.2 microns. But if they are a pleated glassfiber media they only remove down to 0.3 microns. However, I have also found that the ceramic get clogged easier and normally pump slower. The smaller the holes in the filter media the more effort to force water through it. Just my observation and, as with everything in survival, involves trade-offs.

From left to right: the Katadyn Mini, Hiker, Vario and Pocket filters.

Most water filters are too large for most mini or small survival kits and will only fit in most medium and large kits. I find purification the best option, but water filters can filter considerable water in a short time, and if in doubt, you can always purify the water after filtering it.

A handy unit that is fairly small (good for a survival pack or large kit) is the Katadyn Hiker Pro. It uses a 0.3 micron pleated glassfiber media type filter, which has an activated carbon core to reduce unpleasant tastes and odor from water. It uses two hoses, one for the input and one for the output, and it weighs 11 ounces. I have used this on various survival trips and it is easy to use and pumps a lot of water rapidly. I like this filter.

Katadyn makes a very nice little filter called the Mini. It is small enough to fit in a coat pocket or fanny pack. It utilizes a 0.2 micron silver impregnated ceramic filter. It is very light at only eight ounces.

A new filter by Katadyn is the Vario, which weighs 15 ounces and combines both ceramic and pleated microfiltration. A cleanable ceramic disc lengthens the life of the primary 0.3 pleated glassfiber microfilter with a carbon core. It can be attached directly to a water bottle or used with an output hose.

The last Katadyn filter I will discuss is the Pocket filter. This is a heavy duty device, and used by the military and other professionals around the world. It is the heaviest, at 20 ounces, because it's very well made from metal and is incredibly strong. It uses a field-cleanable 0.2 micron ceramic depth filter and can output up to one quart/liter per minute.

Another filter I have used is the MSR Miniworks, which is a ceramic filter based system. It is designed so that a wide mouth Nalgene water bottle screws to the bottom (like the Katadyn Vario) so a second hose is not required. I thought this was a nice feature, so I tried it. However, like other ceramic based filter systems, it seemed to clog easily and pump slowly.

A small handheld filter is the Frontier Filter by Aquamira Technologies, Inc. Basically it is a small filter (3-7/8 inches long by one inch in diameter). A small plastic straw (included) attaches to the filter, and the filter body is inserted directly into water, with care taken not to submerge or otherwise contaminate the straw. You then drink directly from the straw. It is small enough to be carried in a small kit. The Frontier Filter is certified to remove 99.9% of Giardia and Cryptosporidium, but is not certified to remove bacteria or viruses. Therefore, for maximum protection, use the Frontier Filter in conjunction with some form of water purification tablets.

The Aquamarine Frontier Pro with a quick disconnect.

The Aquamira Frontier Pro can be used on a bladder system, connected to a commercial water bottle, or with a bladder as a gravity flow system.

A new filter being offered by Aquamira Technologies, Inc. is the Frontier Pro. Though larger than the original Frontier Filter (It measures 6-7/8 inches long by 1-1/4 inches in diameter) it provides a lot more versatility. It has an adapter for water bladder systems, can be attached to most commercial water bottles, and something I really like, can be converted to a gravity flow system. Again, even though this device is certified to remove 99.9% of Giardia and Cryptosporidium, it is not certified to remove bacteria or viruses. Therefore, for maximum protection, use the Frontier Pro in conjunction with some form of water purification tablets.

Again, keep in mind that most filters only filter water. If the product you buy does not specifically state that it both filters and purifies, then it only filters. Filters are a handy item, but when in doubt, use them in conjunction with a chemical treatment.

## Water purifiers

A water purifier actually purifies water by inactivating all water-borne enteric pathogens, to include viruses, bacteria, and protozoa cysts (or at least 99.9%). Unlike filters, purifiers actually make water safe to drink, no matter what the pathogens are.

Katadyn makes the MyBottle Purifier which is the only EPA-registered purifier. It is a convenient alternative to pump-style water purifiers and filters, and is handy for those kits where you already carry water bottles. This system is built inside a bottle, which you fill with contaminated water and then drink directly from the integral drink spout. The cushioned mouthpiece folds flat to prevent leaking. This bottle allows you to prepare clean drinking water anytime and everywhere. Just fill the bottle and drink without pumping. The three-phase

The SteriPEN Adventurer Opti comes with a belt sheath and solar charging case.

water filter has the highest safety level and eliminates bacteria, protozoa (Giardia, Cryptosporidium), plus kills 99.9% of waterborne viruses, as determined under the U.S. EPA, and the ViruStat purification cartridge purifies water on demand (no waiting). This purifier treats up to 26 gallons (100 liters) per replacement cartridge, depending on water quality. The water bottle holds 24 ounces after cartridge displacement. It measures 10x3 inches and weighs eight ounces.

Various water purifiers are available from SteriPEN. The one I thought might be best for a survival kit is the Adventure Opti. This is a small unit that can be carried in a small provided belt sheath or carried in a case that doubles as a solar charging unit.

The SteriPEN creates ultraviolet (UV) light that disrupts the DNA of microbes in seconds. Without functional DNA, microbes can't reproduce or make you sick. The SteriPEN exceeds the U.S. EPA Guide Standard and Protocol for Testing Microbiological Water Purifiers, destroying over 99.9999% of bacteria, 99.99% of viruses, 99.9% of all protozoan cysts, to include Giardia and Cryptosporidium. It has a patent-pending Optical Water Sensing System that turns the unit on only when it is correctly submerged in water. It purifies 0.5 liters of water in 48 seconds, and one liter of water in 90 seconds.

I liked the idea of the unit having the option of being carried in a belt sheath, or inside the solar charging case. Even when carried in the sheath, the extra batteries can be charging in the solar charging case, which has a clip on it to attach to the back of your pack while on the move.

However, even though it has a great reputation, I'm still on the fence with this one. It works well if you have a means to get the water in your container without getting it all over the threads and mouth. You press the on button once or twice, depending on if you have one half or one full liter of water, and place the UV tube portion in the water in your container. When

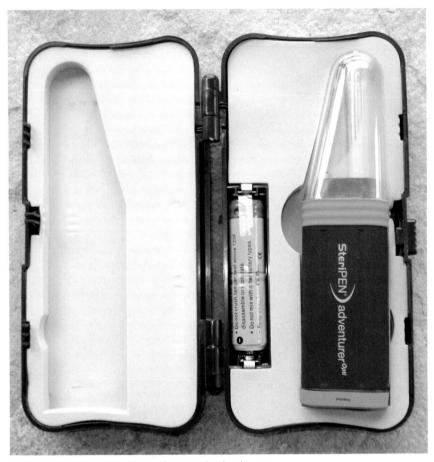

The storage case for the SteriPEN doubles as a solar charging case.

you place the UV tube portion of the SteriPEN in the container holding the water, it will turn on automatically when the optical sensing system senses the UV tube is submerged. You must continually agitate the water while the purification process occurs. Although the water should be purified at the end of the process, it does not purify the threads or outer rim of the bottle. With water purification tablets, once you mix the chemical with water, you can loosen the cap and turn the bottle upside down to allow the water to flow over the threads to ensure they are purified. The SteriPEN doesn't provide for this option and I'm not certain how you purify anything other than the water inside the container. Just a thought.

The SteriPEN directions also indicate that the water you are going to purify must be above 32 degrees F (0 degrees C), and if it is not, you should bring it up to that temperature before purifying. The directions also indicate that the unit is intended for use, and is most effective, in clear water. If clear water is not available, you should first try to filter the water. If it is necessary to treat turbid, murky or cloudy water in an emergency situation, then they provide further instruction, including using two treatments.

The other thing that I am always concerned with in a survival situation is depending on anything that runs on batteries or can be broken. Even though this device is getting a lot of positive reviews, I would recommend carrying an alternative, like chemicals, in the event the unit is lost, broken or the batteries go dead and there is no sun to help you recharge them. I am also surprised that the solar charger indicates that the batteries may require between two and five days to fully charge. As with all survival kit components, it will be your call whether this water purifier adequately meets your needs. I would probably include this in a travel safety kit, where I want to purify water while on a trip and suspicious water in a hotel or restaurant needs to be purified.

The last water purifier I will discuss is the MSR MIOX Purifier. It is a handheld device that works by creating a powerful does of mixed oxidants (MIOX), which is added to untreated water, inactivating viruses, bacteria, Giardia and Cryptosporidium (protozoan cysts). It requires two CR123 batteries and salt to operate. Simply, you must make a solution of water and salt, using the MIOX Purifier, and then add that to the water you want to treat. It takes various amounts of time for the various bacteria, viruses, cysts, etc, with four hours required for Cryptosporidium.

I must admit I have never used this device, as it uses batteries, can be broken, you need to carry the salt, and it is a two step process requiring the making of the solution and then treating the water. It has received a lot of positive reviews in various hiking circles, but for the technology and time involved, I will probably continue to carry Micropur tablets for ease of use in a survival situation.

As you can see, there are choices to make. I like things in a survival situation simple and I have found the least technology, and battery requirement, the better for my needs. You will decide what is best for you.

## Hydration systems

A type of water container that I didn't discuss under water containers is the hydration system. It is basically a flexible water reservoir (or bladder) that is contained in some type of carrier for protection. It has a long tube that hangs out, with a drinking valve (most have to be bitten when drinking, so the water does not run out when not in use). Many are now being offered in various packs.

These hydration systems are being manufactured by various companies, with one of the originals being Camelbak. They make many different designs from small hydration fanny packs to small, medium and large hydration back packs. Another company that makes various size designs is Blackhawk. They call their product HydraStorm, and their units are military-type gear. There are other manufactures, such as Gregory, who offer these units.

I find these systems hard to fill and keep clean in the field. They are handy for day hikes, etc., where they do not have to be maintained for any length of time in the field. You will have to experiment and decide for yourself if they are adequate for your survival kit needs.

*Chapter 8*

# Signaling For Help

**A** nother important activity in a survival situation is to signal people who might be trying to locate you. Most successful rescues occur because the person is able to assist in their own recovery. Rescue efforts that fail are often because the survivor lacks the knowledge and/or ability to signal for help.

The first step toward a successful rescue occurs before you leave home: let someone know where you are going and when you will be back. Obviously, in some situations this isn't possible, but most of the time you can. If you do so, you know that if you don't return at an expected time, someone will be looking for you and have a general idea of where you might be.

Signaling is a survival skill that you should take seriously. You should be equipped and skilled in the event your trip takes a turn for the worse and you need rescuers to find you. Always have the ability to signal by various means depending on the environment, weather, and situation.

## Signal mirror

Every survival kit should have a survival mirror. It is the most underrated and valuable daytime means of signaling. There are various shapes and sizes, and as usual, your choice will depend on the size of your kit.

Glass signal mirrors are the heaviest, but provide the best reflection available. The finest I have found are manufactured by Vector 1, Inc. Mirrors like these were originally developed for the U.S. Air Force for use by downed pilots and their crew. The Vector 1, Inc. Air Force-type signal mirror is one of the leading survival signal mirrors on the market today, and is made of 1/4-inch laminated, shatter-resistant glass.

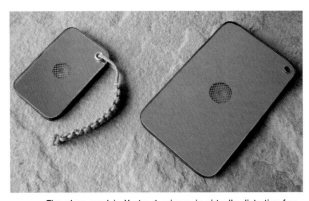

The unique feature of the Vector 1 Air Force signal mirror is the center viewing hole and sight targeting retro-reflective grid. This special feature allows the lost party to direct up to six million candlepower of reflected sunlight onto the rescue target with pinpoint accuracy.

The Japanese glass used in Vector 1 mirrors is virtually distortion-free, allowing the reflected sunlight to travel 25 or more miles. This is two to four times further than the light travel from

**The glass used in Vector 1 mirrors is virtually distortion-free, allowing the reflected sunlight to travel 25 or more miles.**

metal or acrylic mirrors. Each mirror has a reinforced lanyard hole and comes in a protective foam pouch. Use directions are printed on the back of the mirror. They come in two sizes, 2x3 inches and 3x5 inches. I carry one of the 2x3s in a specific pouch mounted to the shoulder strap of my smaller packs, and a 3x5 in my larger packs. Survival Resources makes custom padded cases for each of these mirrors, which help to protect the glass mirrors.

Another good signal mirror made by Vector 1, Inc., called the "Vector 1," measures 2x3 inches and fits in all but the smallest kit. The Vector 1 signal mirror was developed to offer the best of both worlds in signal mirror technology. The reflective mirror is glass, providing superior flash distance (up to 25 miles), encased in durable and break resistant acrylic. The sight grid offers a retro-reflective mesh aimer providing truly accurate aiming ability. The acrylic case is waterproof, floats and provides a lanyard hole. Use directions are printed on the backside of the mirror. It weighs one ounce.

Another good signal mirror is the Rescue-Flash Signal Mirror manufactured by Adventure Medical Kits. It is made of durable LEXAN polycarbonate with a mil-spec retro-reflective aiming aid (which is the grid produced by Vector 1, Inc.) for one handed use. Visible to over 20 miles,

The Vector 1 and Rescue-Flash signal mirrors feature retro-reflective grids.

A signal mirror is the most underrated and valuable means of signaling during daytime.

it has instructions printed on the back. The mirror is covered by a protective cover to prevent scratches while stored in a survival kit. It has a lanyard hole and measures 2x3x1/8 inches and weighs 0.7 ounce.

Another mirror, super light but not in the same class as the mirrors above, is the Featherweight Mirror manufactured by Sun Company. Larger than the Vector 1 and Rescue-Flash, it measures 4-1/4x3-1/8 inches and is only 1/32-inch thick. It is of shatterproof metal construction, is bendable and can be slid into tight places in a kit. It also has a sighting and lanyard hole.

The retro-reflective aiming grid is a screen mesh material installed at the center viewing hole of a signal mirror.

### Retro-reflective grid

Without getting too technical, the retro-reflective aiming grid is a screen mesh material installed at the center viewing hole of a signal mirror. This screen mesh grid is coated with spherical beads of high angularity, which causes the light striking them to reflect directly back in the same direction, as opposed to another angle. This is known as retro-reflectivity. This is the same principle as the light from your headlights that hits street signs at night. The light, instead of reflecting off at another angle, reflects straight back at you. Anyway, because of the mesh screen, light from the sun's rays are free to pass through. As you look through the grid and the sun strikes it, you see a burst of light in the viewer. As you move this burst of light to your target, the light reflected off the mirror is directed straight to the target. This allows a signal mirror with a retro-reflective grid to be aimed very accurately.

The light burst observed through the aiming indicator is not the sun, but a reflection on the grid from the sun. As you manipulate the mirror and turn it towards your target, in this case a tree, the reflected light from the sun on the surface of the mirror is being directed exactly where the light burst is aimed.

When using a mirror with a retro-reflective aiming grid, first reflect light from the mirror onto a nearby surface. Slowly bring the mirror to eye level and look through the sighting hole. You will see a bright light spot on the aiming grid. This is your aiming indicator. Hold the mirror close to the eye and slowly turn or tilt the mirror until the bright light spot is on the object you want to signal. Slightly tilt the mirror back and forth and the flash from the mirror will be aimed directly at the target. Make sure you keep the bright light spot on the target as you tilt the mirror, in order to keep the flash on the target.

### Alternate signal mirror aiming technique

If you have a signal mirror with a hole which does not have a retro-reflective grid, or any mirror for that matter, you need a different technique to aim the mirror. This is also true when you have a retro-reflective grid but don't have the angle between the sun and the target to see the light burst in the viewer. In this case you should hold the mirror in one hand and outstretch the other hand. With the raised outstretched arm, spread your index and middle finger (like a "V"). Now use the mirror to reflect the light from the sun onto your two fingers. If you can see the outline of the mirror on both fingers, then you know the reflected light from the sun is going through the V. Now carefully move your fingers toward the target, keeping the reflected light from the sun on and through the V. Get the target between the V and the reflected light should be directed towards the target. Slightly tilt the mirror back and forth, while maintaining aim through the fingers, to flash the target.

### Improvised signal mirrors

It is not difficult to make a signal mirror yourself. You can buy a kit in many auto parts supply stores called "Easy-Stick Replacement Mirror." It is bendable plastic material that comes in a sheet 7x10x1/16 inches thick and only costs a couple of dollars. You can cut a mirror to the size you want with scissors and have plenty of material

Use two fingers to aim a signal mirror. Reflect the light off the mirror onto your fingers. Direct the reflected light between the "V" made by the fingers. If the target is between your fingers, it will see the flash.

A compact disc can be used as a signal mirror in an emergency, and auto repair mirror material can be cut to make an improvised signal mirror.

left over for other kits. I have made mirrors in various sizes for specific applications and punched a small sighting hole in the center using a leather punch. It has the added advantage of the self sticking side in the event you want to stick one in the lid of a survival tin (although in so doing you lose the advantage of the sighting hole).

If you carry a survival kit tin mini-kit, you can polish the inside lid of a survival tin and use that as a survival mirror. As long as you have your kit, you have your mirror.

One last tip on signal mirrors. If you are stranded in a vehicle in a survival situation and you have a CD, it makes an adequate signal mirror. It is highly reflective on one side and already has a sighting hole. Of course, you could also remove the rear view mirror from the car as a means to signal.

Keep in mind that an improvised mirror is never going to be as effective as a mirror designed for the purpose of signaling. I am an advocate of carrying the real thing. But, in an emergency situation, anything is better than nothing!

### Signal whistle

A whistle is a useful device for signaling and is easy to carry. It is much easier to blow on a whistle than to yell, and the sound from a whistle travels further. Also, a whistle can be incorporated in a survival kit, or it can be carried around your neck on a lanyard or on a key ring.

The first thing to remember about a whistle for survival is this: don't get a metal one. In freezing weather it can freeze to your lips. The second thing is get a pea-less whistle. As with everything in survival, the more parts something has, the greater chance that it won't work when you need it. Also, if the pea is lost, the whistle won't work. I will discuss a few that I think are effective for survival needs. Three blasts on a whistle is an internationally-recognised distress signal.

Manufactured whistles have much more range than a human whistle. In some documented cases, signal whistles have been heard up to a mile away. Whistles are easy to carry on your person or in a survival kit. Children especially should always carry a signal whistle on them in the event they become lost.

The first two whistles I'll describe break the "no pea" rule, but they are the loudest on the market. The whistles are manufactured in the U.S. by the All-Weather Safety Whistle Co. and designed with the pea inside an internal chamber so it cannot be lost.

The Storm Whistle is the loudest whistle on the market. On land, it can be heard up to 1/2 mile, and its unique patented design allows it to be heard under water up to 50 feet because the sounding chamber purges all water when the whistle is blown. A high-impact, non-corroding thermoplastic protective housing is easy to grasp, and the patented double chamber allows it to be blown when held right side up or upside down. It's perfect for emergency signaling and creates a clear, high frequency sound, with a power rating over 75% greater than other safety whistles.

The Windstorm is considered to be the second loudest whistle on the market. Tests show that the Windstorm whistle produces a sound that is heard more easily than other popular whistles. This whistle performs in all conditions, in any weather or safety situation. Both of these whistles are very loud and have been adopted by the U.S. military.

All of the following whistles are pea-less. The Fox 40 Classic whistle has a harmonically tuned, three-chamber pea-less design. It can't be overblown; the harder you blow, the louder it gets. It works when soaking wet and produces an omni-directional sound, heard in all directions. This whistle is extremely loud and is being issued to the military and Coast Guard. This is the whistle I carry on my key ring and pack.

Another pea-less whistle good for survival purposes is the Fox 40 Micro, which is flatter than the Fox 40 Classic, thereby fitting better in smaller survival kits. It is extremely loud and exceeds SOLAS and USCG specification. It also is a triple-frequency whistle and has a lanyard hole. I use this whistle in my tin kits.

The ACR Signal Whistle was designed for aid in both land and sea rescues. It has a unique flat design and is only 0.25 inch thick, great for packaging in a survival kit. It also meets USCG/SO-

Top row, from left to right: the Storm Whistle, Windstorm and the Fox 40 Classic whistle. Bottom: the Fox 40 Micro, the ACR Signal Whistle and the Marine Safety Whistle.

LAS requirements and has a loud, shrill, dual tone. It measures only 1x2x0.25 inches and weighs only 1.4 ounces.

Last, but not least, is the Marine Safety Whistle. It is a high pitched, NATO-approved whistle which can be used with a lanyard or clipped directly onto a belt or pack using a built-in retainer clip. A streamlined design incorporating an enhanced ergonomic feel makes the whistle easy to hold.

Several whistles have been designed as survival whistles with various added features. One is called the Four Function Whistle. It is a whistle, a thermometer and a compass, and has a small magnifier. It is not very loud and appears easily breakable. There are many of these type whistles sold in camping stores and they are not, in my opinion, adequate for survival. Buyer beware! I recommend getting a good quality whistle that will provide the volume required for a survival situation.

## Improvised whistles

In a survival situation, items can often be found in the field to use as survival tools. This is true for making whistles. Two items you can find in the wilderness to use as a signal whistle don't even need modification. One is the cap of an acorn from an oak tree and the other is cap from a water bottle - yes water bottles are often found in the wilderness.

Place both thumbs over the acorn cap or bottle cap, leaving a small V-shaped opening at the front. Blow across the top of your thumbs, so that the air goes across the opening. You may have to adjust your thumbs a couple of times to get it right, but when you do you will know it. You now have a whistle made from debris found in the wilderness. It won't be as loud as the whistles discussed above, but as with everything in survival, something is better than nothing.

Improvised whistles can be made from an acorn cap or the cap from a water bottle.

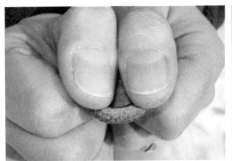

To blow a whistle made from an acorn cap, place your thumbs over an acorn top, leaving a V-shaped opening. Blow across the tops of your thumbs in order to get a whistling sound.

# Making A Can Whistle

A whistle can also be made from any old can found in the field. The technique was originally in *Boys Life*, a Boy Scout magazine, back in the 1950s. My father, who was an Eagle Scout as well as my Scoutmaster, used to have our troop make these. Of course, back then cans were tin and thicker than they are now, but it still works.

Again, this whistle will not equal a real whistle in loudness. Caution should be used as the edges of this whistle can be sharp and you can cut your lips if you are careless.

Start by cutting the top and bottom off the can, then cut the center piece from top to bottom. You can discard the top and bottom at this point. Carefully unroll the center section so you have a flat piece to work with.

Cut a strip that is approximately five inches long and 3/4-inch wide. This can be done by scoring a line and bending the material back and forth, which will give it a clean edge.

Take the piece you just cut and cut 1.5 inches off the end, again, by scoring and bending. Now you should have one piece approximately 3.5 inches long by 3/4-inch wide, and one that is 1.5 inches long by 3/4-inch wide.

Lay the short piece over one end of the long piece, crosswise and centered. Bend the ends that hang over on each side down and around the long piece.

## Making A Can Whistle *continued*

Press hard so it remains attached to the end of the long piece.

Right behind the piece you added, bend the remainder of the long piece down at a 90-degree angle.

Bend the piece back up and around, making a round whistle shape. This piece should bend up and around and, leaving the last part straight, should just about meet up with the crossed piece that you attached. You'll start seeing a whistle shape, minus the sides.

Take an item like the small blade of a knife and slide it in between the crossed piece and the long piece you wrapped the short piece around. Don't make too big of a gap, just something you can blow air through.

Close the sides of the whistle with the thumb on one side and your index and middle finger on the other side. You will probably need to adjust the top so that the air coming through the front blows across the flat section of the top. It takes some work, but you should get it to blow. If your fingers are too small to completely close in the sides, try holding the whistle between your palms. It is more difficult to adjust the top this way, but it can work.

## Emergency strobe

A signaling device that should be in all survival kits for waterborne operations or activities (especially for large bodies of water) is an emergency locator strobe. It can also be used for marking a campsite or a disabled vehicle. They come in various shapes and sizes and should be USCG approved.

A good unit for any medium to large survival kit is the Emergency Strobe by Grabber Outdoors. This small, lightweight battery powered strobe light creates a beacon that is visible up to three miles. It is waterproof and flashes 50-60 times per minute for up to 16 hours. It uses a Xenon strobe module that produces a 300,000 candle power light and operates on one D-cell battery. It is red in color. It also has a safety pin-type holder (actually a stainless steel locking pin) so you can wear it on a PFD (personal flotation device), in the event of a "man overboard" situation at night. The unit is 4-1/2 inches high and weighs eight ounces, and it is U.S. Coast Guard approved.

A combination emergency locator strobe and flashlight called the Firefly Plus is available from ACR Electronics. It is U.S. Coast Guard approved. This international orange unit is waterproof and operates on two AA alkaline batteries. The high intensity strobe can be seen for over one mile and the unit floats. The strobe will operate for up to 10 hours and the flashlight for up to two hours. It measures 5.3x1.5 inches and will fit in most medium to large kits. It is also supplied with a wrist strap.

Leland Limited, Inc., manufactures an emergency strobe light, similar in appearance to the Emergency Strobe, called the ESL-I - Emergency Strobe Light. It is offered in red, orange and yellow, with a Xenon bulb USCG approved strobe light. It operates 8-12 hours at 50-60 flashes per minute, and then automatically switches down to 20-30 flashes per minute for another eight-hour shift. It has a stainless steel clip for webbing, straps or a belt, and the bottom has bayonet fitting to accept accessories such as magnets, threaded adaptor or a wind proof base. The strobe is waterproof and can be seen for three to five miles, depending on atmospheric conditions. It comes with a clear lens, approved by USCG, and offers other lens colors in red, blue, green, amber and slime yellow-green. It uses one D-cell alkaline battery that must be replaced every year.

The Emergency Strobe and the ACR Firefly Plus are both good strobes.

Leland also makes a strobe similar to the ACR Firefly Plus called the ESL-II - Strobe Light with Flashlight. This unit is available in black, yellow and

The Guardian by eGear is more a safety strobe than an emergency strobe, but is visible over one mile from a front view, and 1/4 mile from the side view.

orange. It also uses a Xenon bulb, and like the ACR unit, has a flashlight built in to make it even more useful. The switch is magnetic and can easily be activated with gloved hands. The unit is double o-ring sealed and withstands up to 100m (300ft) under water. It does float if dropped on the surface. Due to the unique nature of this module, only a clear strobe is offered.

An extremely small unit called The Guardian is manufactured by eGear. It is more a safety strobe than an emergency strobe, but is visible over one mile from a front view, and 1/4 mile from the side view. It is a dual function safety light with both steady on and flashing modes. They are available in clear or red lenses, are waterproof, and operate on one coin cell lithium battery. They only measure 1-5/8 inches long by 1-1/4 inches wide by one inch high. They are small enough to carry in a small survival kit and provide you with at least a small strobe. A small clip is included which allows you to attach the unit to almost anything.

## Rescue laser lights

The Rescue Laser is a new innovative approach to survival signaling made by Greatland Laser, LLC. Unlike "point" lasers, these lasers give off a long beam of light which increases in width as the distance increases. At a distance of eight miles the beam is 3,000 feet wide, and at 16 miles it is 6,000 feet wide!

The Rescue Laser Light is a hand-held, day and nighttime laser signaling device that provides a convenient, effective way to signal a rescue party. It's waterproof and the rugged design combines the safety of a laser signaling device with the convenience of a flashlight.

Unlike pyrotechnic flares, the Rescue Laser Light is non-flammable (so it can't catch the forest on fire), is environmentally safe, and can operate continuously for five to72 hours (depending on the model) on a single, long-life, replaceable lithium battery (included). Pyrotechnic flares, which are visible at long distances, only last for a very short duration. A Rescue Laser light can be seen up to 20 miles away at night for the red light unit, and up to 30 miles at night for the green light unit. These units can also be seen during the day at two to three miles.

I really like these devices and have been carrying the small red laser, pocket-sized unit, for several years and it is awesome to see at night. You signal by fanning the laser line back and forth. I have shown the light to students on a close tree, with the laser line in an up and down position. I then shine it on a tree across the field and they are amazed at how, in just the short distance, the laser line has increased significantly. The small pocket-sized unit, Rescue Laser Light, which has a red laser light, is great for all small survival kits.

The Rescue Laser Flare Magnum also has a red laser. It is approximately twice as long as the pocket-sized unit and is still small enough for all but mini survival kits. It runs on two AA batter-

A Rescue Laser light can be seen up to 20 miles away at night for the red light unit, and up to 30 miles for the green light unit. They can also be seen during the day at two to three miles.

ies and can be seen up to 20 miles at night and one to three miles during the day.

The Green Rescue Laser Flare is a green laser unit, just a bit shorter than the Magnum. The green laser is the most expensive, but the distance is increased by 50% over the Magnum; it can be seen up to 30 miles at night and three to five miles during the day. It runs on a single CR123 lithium battery.

These rescue lasers are really a great signaling tool for an emergency situation, both at night and during the day. I would recommend the inclusion of one of these units in a survival kit.

The Rescue Laser gives off a long beam of light which increases in width as the distance increases.

## Additional ready-made signals

### Flares

Survival flares are another useful item for a survival kit, especially if you are on water. They are used for aerial signaling so searching aircraft can locate your position. One that I have found to be reliable is the Skyblazer Flare by Orion. It is compact, USCG approved, self contained, waterproof and floatable. This disposable flare can attain an altitude of 450 feet, has an average of 16,000 candlepower, and burns for 6.5 seconds. They are available from Orion Safety Products, along with various other flares, including the pocket rocket. These are small flares fired from a small pocket sized launcher, like a large pen.

### Dye markers

Another small device that can be carried in a survival kit, especially if you are on water or in snow country, is a dye marker. They are small (two ounces) and packed in a waterproof container. They can be deposited on water or snow and are visible from aircraft during the day. Orion Safety Products offers a package of two that contain a green dye that covers up to a 50 square foot area and is environmentally safe.

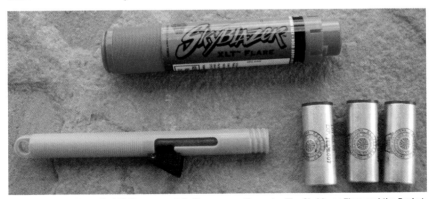

Flares are a useful survival kit item, especially if you are on the water. The Skyblazer Flare and the Pocket Rocket are available from Orion Safety Products.

Dye markers from Orion come two to a package.

### Smoke signals

Various companies manufacture smoke signals designed for survival use. These small devices give off smoke (usually orange) and are usually waterproof. They burn from 45 seconds to a minute and are an option for a survival kit if you don't have time to build a fire, or are on the water. Shipping them requires a hazmat charge.

## Making your own signals

### Ground signals

There are various ways to make ground to air signals, with numerous factors to consider in order for them to be effective. The type of signal you construct will depend on the material you have available. Ingenuity in the use of that material will also play a role in the effectiveness of your signals. Let's examine some of the parameters.

**Size and ratio:** Any signal you make on the ground should be as large as you can make it. In order to be seen from the air, the general rule is the signal should have no line less than three feet wide and 18 feet long. If you are making an X on the ground, each leg of the X should be three feet wide by 18 feet long. However, if you are making letters, such as SOS, then the shortest dimension (this would be across the S) must be 18 feet wide. In order to maintain the proper ratio, the S would be 18 feet wide, so the height would have to be higher than the width. Of course each letter must be three feet thick.

**Angularity:** You never see straight lines in nature, so patterns made with straight lines and square corners are preferred. This makes it obvious that the signal was manmade, and not an anomaly of nature.

**Contrast:** A signal has to stand out sharply against its background. You want the signal to look larger than it really is. In a field, knock the grass down or turn it over. Even a burned grass pattern can be effective. In the snow, fill the inside of stomped down snow for the signal with something of a different color. Use pine boughs, sticks or burned wood from a fire. Make the outline of the signal stand out against the snow. I have even used dye markers, meant for the water, to color the inside of a stomped out signal in the snow.

Shadows can also work here. Utilize shadows to make something appear larger. If you can't make a trench in the snow for a signal, build up mounds of snow in the shape of the desired signal, or use mounds of boughs or rocks. The shadow cast by the mounds will make the signal look bigger. If you are using signal panels, use upright sticks to raise the panels up off the ground, again utilizing shadows to increase the size.

Avoid disrupting the area surrounding the signal and use only one path to and from the signal.

**Location:** As in real estate, location is very important. Make sure the signal is located in an area where it can be seen from all directions. Avoid areas where shadows from other things such as trees or overhangs might disrupt or conceal the signal. A large clear area, as high as possible, is preferred.

A dye marker helps enhance the contrast of the signal against the white snow.

### Type of signal

Types of signals include various letters and arrows. I find that most people don't remember what they mean when they need them, unless they carry a guide of ground signals with them. For this reason I prefer a large X, as it is easy to make and means "unable to travel." It lets rescuers know you need help. Another one that is often used is SOS, and although certainly effective, it takes much more effort to construct than an X.

### Signal by fire

You can also attract the attention of rescuers using fire and smoke, and it is one of the best known signals. If people know you are missing and they are looking for you, then one fire should usually be sufficient. However, if nobody knows you're missing and you need help, three fires evenly spaced apart and arranged in a triangle or a straight line serves as an internationally known distress signal.

If using at night, have a very bright fire. If used during the day, you will need smoke, as much as you can produce. Smoke signals are only effective on clear, calm days, where they have been known to be seen up to 50 miles away. However, high winds, rain or snow can disperse the smoke and make them much less effective. Smoke tends to be less effective in heavily wooded areas, so try to get the smoke generated from a clearing if possible.

The smoke you produce should contrast with the background. White smoke created by using green vegetation, or even water, is best used against a dark background. Against snow, a dark smoke works best and can be created using oil, rubber or plastic, if available.

To create smoke when you need to signal, the material must be gathered before you need it. Have a fire going at all times, such as for heat or cooking. Have the material to create the color smoke desired at the ready to place on the fire when it comes time to signal. You can also build a smoke generator and have it ready to go. When the time comes, transfer fire from your maintained fire to the smoke generator.

A smoke generator can be constructed by various means. One version is made from a tripod structure. Make a tripod frame, leaving the tops of the three poles sticking up above the lashing. Then build a small platform almost half way up. This can be done by lashing two sticks horizontally across the three uprights. This doesn't have to be fancy, as you will basically be burning this structure up. Lay green sticks across the sticks you lashed to the uprights to make a small platform.

A tripod smoke generator starts with the tripod and platform for the fire. Boughs are then added to produce the white smoke. Photos by Alan Halcon.

Before you start to cover it, collect tinder, kindling and small fuel and set it on the platform you built. Collect a bunch of big green boughs and hang them over the side of the structure, suspending them from the three protruding ends of the uprights at the top of the tripod. Continue to cover the structure with as many green boughs as you can, leaving a small opening on one side so you can reach in and start the fire.

When you are ready to signal, reach inside the opening and get the fire going. It won't take long before you have white smoke pouring off the smoke generator.

Another way to build a smoke generator is to use the log cabin firelay discussed in Chapter 5. Again, cover the log cabin structure with a pile of green boughs, leaving a small opening in order to start the tinder and kindling inside.

## Hand signals

At least eleven different hand signals can be used to signal a pilot in the air. However, most people can't remember them when they need them, or use the wrong ones. I prefer to remember just two, the right one and the wrong one.

Many people want to wave to a pilot when they see them coming, hoping the pilot or other searchers on the craft will see their hand waving. The waving of one hand means "All OK, Do Not Wait." Always wave both hands together over your head. This means "Pick Me/Us Up." If you want to be left there, then wave just one hand. If you want help, wave both.

Waving one hand at a pilot means "All OK, Do Not Wait."

Waving both hands together over your head means "Pick me up!!"

## Electronic signaling

### Personal locator beacons (PLBs)

Personal locator beacons, also called PLBs, are small, portable, lightweight transmitters which can transmit a personal emergency distress signal (beacon) to your nearest rescue services. When activated, such beacons send out a distress signal, which can be detected and facilitates locating the person in distress. A GPS position can be encoded into the signal, allowing instant identification of the user and their location. When activated, a PLB transmits a signal on a dedicated world-wide frequency for distress beacons. The signal is initially received by a satellite

**An ACR SARLink PLB.** Photo courtesy of Dave Laplander.

of the Cospas-Sarsat international satellite system for search and rescue. The signal is then relayed to a receiving station on earth which forwards it to the appropriate rescue response unit.

I am not an authority on these devices, but Doug Ritter is very knowledgeable in regard to PLBs and their use. Doug has done some impressive and extensive testing of most of the PLBs on the market. He also does continuous updates in regard to new technology, recalls, etc., in regard to PLBs. You can find this testing on his website, Equipped To Survive, at www.equipped.org. He is, in my opinion, an authority on personal locator beacons.

There are various makes and models by different manufacturers, to include ACR Electronics with the SARLink PLB and McMurdo with the Fast-Find 210 GPS-PLB. All of these devices are evaluated on Doug Ritter's website.

### Spot satellite messenger

A SPOT Satellite Messenger is not considered a PLB, but a satellite messenger. A PLB uses a digital signal in the 406.0 & 406.1 MHz frequency band and is transmitted to government operated search and rescue satellites. The SPOT uses a private company to receive its signals. Although the SPOT is cheaper than a PLB initially, yearly subscription fees can run the price up after a couple of years.

The positives are you can set up contacts before you leave and write a specific message. When you hit the "OK" button, it sends a message to those on the contacts list, along with your location on a Google map. When you hit the "HELP" button, your location along with a help message (which you set up ahead of time) is sent to your contacts so they are aware of your problem, but the signal does not trigger a search and rescue operation from the authorities. The "911" button will continually send your location to a private rescue coordinator, the GEOS alliance, who then has the responsibility to convey that information to the local search and rescue authorities.

The SPOT Satellite Messenger uses a private company to receive its signals. Although the SPOT is cheaper than a PLB initially, yearly subscription fees can run the price up after a couple of years.

I'm not recommending a SPOT vs. a PLB, just providing information that might help you choose the device best for you. Again, if you want more information, or review testing, go to Equipped To Survive, at www.equipped.org and review Doug Ritter's extensive data.

© 1998 Tim Bottomley.

*Chapter 9*

# Navigate Your Way Back

**N**avigation skills are essential for survival and you should be well versed in using both a map and compass. Either one will assist you in the ability to navigate, but together they are a team that can't be beat. This chapter provides the basics of how to select the proper equipment, and what a map and compass can do for you. Although the basics of use are provided, I highly suggest that you take a good course where you can get hands-on instruction. The use of a map and compass takes practice, and there are no shortcuts.

## Maps and their use

A map is nothing more than a pictorial representation of the surface of the earth, drawn to scale and reproduced in two dimensions. If you are a driver, you know there are all kinds of maps, such as road maps, etc. Although these maps can get you from one place to another using the highway system, when you go into the wilderness, they are of little use. What you need is a topographical map.

Although there are many makers of topographical maps, we will limit our discussion to USGS maps with a scale of 1:24,000. The smaller the number to the right of the "1" in the scale of a map, the more detail you will find. Although larger scale maps show a larger area, for the purpose of navigation, I suggest a map with a 1:24,000 scale which provides enough detail to be usable.

A topographical map provides a three-dimensional representation, viewed from overhead. It portrays terrain and landforms in a measurable form using contour lines. However, before we get in to the specifics of contours, a discussion of the information provided on a maps borders, and colors used to identify specific features, is important.

# Information provided around a map

Adjoining maps: At the top and bottom in the center, and on each side in the middle, the name of the adjoining map is printed. In each corner of the map, printed at an angle, is the name of the adjoining map for that corner. This allows you to effectively join maps together from the same series.

UNITED STATES
DEPARTMENT OF THE INTERIOR
GEOLOGICAL SURVEY

73°52'30"       ⁵94000ᵐE                                    ⁵95
41°45'                                            350  QUAKER

The top left of the map provides information in regard to who made it, in this case, The United States Department of the Interior, Geological Survey. This is known as a USGS map.

PLEASANT VALLEY QUADRANGLE
NEW YORK—DUTCHESS CO.
7.5 MINUTE SERIES (TOPOGRAPHIC)

27 MI. TO N.Y. 82
2.1 MI. TO U.S. 44
⁶02            ⁶03                              73°45'
                                                41°45'
                                       Tyrrel

The top right provides the name of the map, the state, and the series.

41°37'30"      ⁵94                    ⁵95 .630 000 FEET        ⁵96
73°52'30"

Mapped, edited, and published by the Geological Survey
Control by USGS and NOS/NOAA
Topography by photogrammetric methods from aerial photographs
taken 1955. Field checked 1957
Polyconic projection. 10,000-foot grid ticks based on New York coordinate
system, east zone. 1000-meter Universal Transverse Mercator grid
ticks, zone 18, shown in blue. 1927 North American Datum
To place on the predicted North American Datum 1983 move the
projection lines 6 meters south and 35 meters west as shown
by dashed corner ticks
Fine red dashed lines indicate selected fence and field lines visible
on aerial photographs. This information is unchecked
There may be private inholdings within the boundaries of
the National or State reservations shown on this map
Revisions shown in purple and woodland compiled from
aerial photographs taken 1980 and other sources. This
information not field checked. Map edited 1981

The bottom left provides further information about the map, such as which agency did the mapping, and how the revisions were compiled.

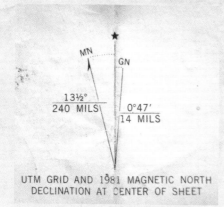

UTM GRID AND 1981 MAGNETIC NORTH
DECLINATION AT CENTER OF SHEET

QUADRANGLE LOCATION

Between bottom left and center is where you will find the True North and magnetic north symbol, called the Declination Diagram.

Between bottom center and right is where you will find a small diagram of the state with a small black rectangle, representing the map you are using, showing where that map is located in relationship to the rest of the state.

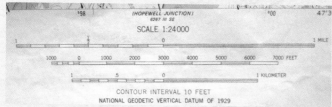

In the center at the bottom you will find the scale diagram, usually in miles, feet, and kilometers. Just below this is the Contour Interval, which is the height in feet, between each contour line.

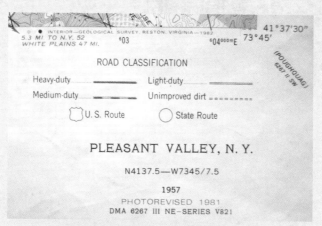

The bottom right shows the date of the map, printed in black, and any revision date, printed in purple. Often, above is a road classification diagram. Around the edges of the map are both latitude and longitude notation marks, as well as Universal Transverse Mercator (UTM) notation marks.

### Symbols and colors

The symbols give a quick visual description of things that appear on a map. An example is a small black square with a cross on top, which denotes a church. Some maps provide some of the symbols in a legend at the right bottom of the map. USGS maps use so many symbols that they provide a separate sheet called Topographical Map Symbols. If you don't want to carry this sheet with you, become familiar with the major symbols used so you can identify them on your map.

USGS maps are printed in seven colors. Color is used to more easily identify specific information or features. The following describes each color and what it represents:

**White:** An area of none or little vegetation, cleared land, desert, rocky areas.

**Green:** An area of substantial vegetation, forest, brush, orchards, etc.

**Blue:** Water such as ponds, lakes, rivers, canals. Note: A green area with small blue tufts of grass indicates a marsh or swamp.

**Brown:** Contour lines showing elevation.

**Black:** Manmade objects such as buildings, railroads, water towers, roads, and all names.

**Red:** Prominent roads and survey lines.

**Purple:** Revisions and updates added from aerial photographs (not field checked).

### Contour lines

Topographical maps have a bunch of little brown squiggly lines which are called contour lines. They represent the elevation above sea level for all land features. The difference in elevation between each contour line remains the same on a specific map. This allows you to view the topography in three dimensions, but you have to understand how to read them.

Certain rules pertain to all contour lines. If we understand the rules, then we better understand what contour lines show us.

The height, or vertical distance, between each contour line, known as the contour interval, is indicated at the bottom center of a map, below the scale. If it has a contour interval of 20 feet, then the vertical distance between each line either increases or decreases by 20 feet. Each fifth line will be thicker and will notate the actual elevation for that line.

If you continue to cross contour lines that increase in number, then you are going uphill. If the numbers decrease, then you are going downhill.

Contour lines have no beginning or end. No matter how irregularly shaped they are, they are all a closed loop. The entire line is at the exact same height and you could follow it around until you came back to where you started and never go up or down in elevation.

The closer the space between contour lines, the steeper the slope. A gentle slope is represented by the contour lines being spaced farther apart from one another. However, if the lines are spaced very close together, it indicates a very steep topography, such as a cliff.

V-shaped lines that face uphill, increased elevation, indicate a valley, ravine, etc., and always point upstream. V or U shaped lines that point downhill indicate a ridge or spur.

An hourglass shape with increasing numbered contour lines on each side indicates a saddle or pass.

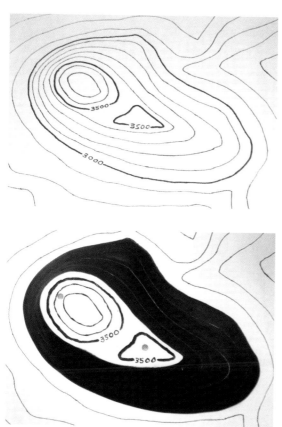

The peak of a hill or mountain is normally marked with an X or the actual elevation.

Remember that not all topography is shown on a map. If the contour interval is 20 feet and there is a decrease in height, but is less than 20 feet, then it will not appear on the map. I warn of this so you do not come to an 18-foot cliff and, because it does not appear on the map, start questioning where you are. Being the cliff is less than 20 feet (or whatever the contour interval is for that map) it won't appear on the map.

Students find contour lines difficult to comprehend at first. I often thought that if I could only take a section of a map and build a mountain depicting the various heights the contour lines represented, a student would better comprehend contour lines, as they could see a three dimensional representation of the lines. So finally, my wife and I spent a weekend, first

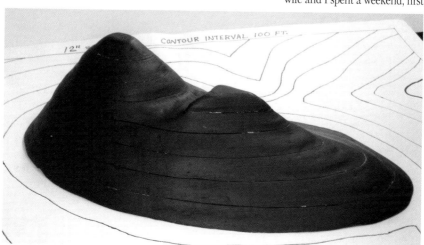

A mountain is built by adding one contour line section at a time. The result is an actual view of the mountain the contour lines represent.

hand drawing a section of a map with contour lines, and then building a mountain that could be assembled one contour line at a time. After cutting, carving and installing wooden pegs to hold it together in the proper position, we had what we needed for our students. A little paint and when our students see the mountain built, one contour line at a time, they always exclaim, "Now I get it!"

As we learned above, the scale at the center bottom of the map provides a means to measure distance on a map. Unfortunately, you may not always want to measure with a straight line; you may want to measure the distance of a road or trail. My dad taught me to use a string, which could be wound around a trail, then straighten it out and measure it on the scale at the bottom of the map. However, always looking for a better way, I started using a piece of bendable wire, usually red in color. This way I can bend it around the trail, or whatever, and it stays in the shape until I need to straighten it for measuring.

To measure distance of a curvy trail, bend a piece of wire to follow the trail, then straighten it and measure using the scale at the bottom center of the map.

## Map tools and aids

Map tools and aids can help you determine bearings and navigate with a map, as well as provide a means to determine where you are located on a map using UTM (Universal Transverse Mercator) coordinates. These are handy devices and can be carried with your maps in a survival kit.

Two real handy devices are made by the C-Thru Ruler Company. They manufacture the compass protractor which allows you to easily plot your compass headings on a map. It can also be used to determine if the degree angle on the declination diagram of a map is accurate. The protractor is a transparent circle that measures 3.5 inches in diameter, which measures in degrees (360). It can be conveniently carried in a kit, shirt pocket, with your map, in your pack or with your notebook.

The next item they make is the Land Measure Compass with Arm. This is a great land navigation tool when plotting courses on a map. The meridian lines can be lined up with those on your map, and the moveable arm swung to determine your heading in degrees. It measures five inches in diameter with a three-inch arm. Larger than the compass protractor, it can be stored in larger kits or map cases.

Many maps today are marked with UTM grid coordinates. Unlike the latitude and longitude system where you deal with minutes and seconds, the UTM system is decimal based, dealing with ones, tens, hundreds, and so on. All coordinates are measured in metric distance units of meters or kilometers. Each map using UTM can be divided into one kilometer grid squares and you read the grid values from left to right and bottom to top. To divide these one kilometer grids into smaller units, which is handy when trying to determine your specific location in a grid, a grid protractor comes in real handy.

A company that makes some of the best UTM protractors out there is MapTools. They make some full size protractors that meet the military GTA 5-2-12 requirement, as well as some small protractors that can fit in the palm of your hand. These smaller items are really great for smaller survival kits.

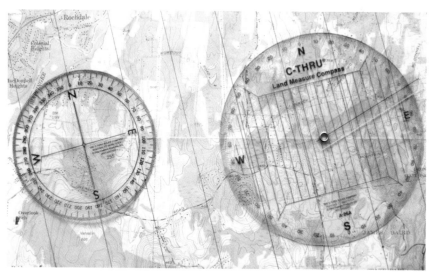

The C-Thru Compass Protractor and the Land Measure Compass with Arm help you plot compass headings and courses on a map.

Clockwise: the Military Style MGRS/UTM Grid Reader and Protractor, both the New Style and the GTA 5-2-12; the MapTools UTM Book, and the Pocket sized UTM Corner Ruler and Grid Plotter.

The first tool is equivalent to the Graphic Training Aid 5-2-12 Coordinate and Protractor used by the United States and NATO military forces around the world. However, this tool offers significant benefits over the standard issue GTA 5-2-12. It is printed on 30 mil plastic stock with a protective coating. This makes it about the thickness and stiffness of a credit card. It's 33% thicker than the standard military issue version, so it's less likely to be bent or broken when you need to use it. It also has rounded corners to keep it from wearing holes in your pockets. It offers Scales: 1:25,000 x 1km/1:250,000 x 10km, 1:50,000 x 1km/1:500,000 x 10km, 1:10,000 x 100m/1:100,000 x 1km and measures 5x5 inches.

The next tool is an improved version of the Graphic Training Aid 5-2-12 Coordinate Scale and Protractor, discussed above. By using a slot on one side of the tool for access to the map, the tool can be more compact than the traditional GTA tool. The tool features several additional map scales, including 1:24,000, which is the most common topographical map scale found within the United States, including the 7.5 minute USGS maps. The 1:100,000 scale spans 5km grid lines, making it much more usable. The overall dimensions have been reduced so that it is the size of a music CD, easily fitting into a pocket or any slot where you could store a CD. This tool is also printed on 30 mil plastic with a protective coating. It has rounded corners which keep it from wearing holes in your pockets. Scales: 1:24,000 x 1km, 1:25,000 x 1km/1:250,000 x 10km, 1:50,000 x 2 km/1:500,000 x 20km, 1:10,000 x 500m/1:100,000 x 5km. Compass Rose in both Degrees and Mils. Measures 4.5x4.5 inches.

MapTools also manufactures two really small, hand held UTM corner ruler and grid plotters. They are real handy little items and fit most anywhere. They have also published a small booklet called "UTM" which is a great starting point for beginning GPS users and folks that want to learn about UTM, MGRS, and USNG coordinates. With lots of illustrations and step by step instructions, it provides readers with the ability to convert between map locations and UTM coordinates quickly. The booklet includes a 1:24,000 scale "Pocket Sized Grid Plotter" (see above) for use with 7.5 minute USGS topographical maps. This may be a small booklet (50 pages) but provides a wealth of information and great graphics!

## Compasses

An item that should be in every survival kit, no matter how small, is a compass. A compass is the basic tool of navigation. They come in all shapes and sizes. Choose a liquid filled compass (this slows the swinging of the needle, called damping, and makes the needle stop faster).

### Button compass

With mini kits, your only choice is usually a button compass, a small liquid filled compass capsule with no frills. It is a floating dial compass, but not free-floating. It does have a pivot point on which the dial sets, which allows the dial to rotate but keeps the dial away from the sides of the capsule. This is why it is important to hold the compass level in order to get an accurate reading. Size often dictates features, and with a button compass there are no features other than the ability to determine direction.

For all of my mini kits I use a 20mm button compass that is Grade-AA (the highest grade). They are liquid filled and have a highly luminous dial, and measure 3/4 inch in diameter by 5/16 inch thick. These are great for any survival tin kit. The 20mm compass is also offered in Grade-A. Basically, the difference between Grade-AA and Grade-A is the AA should have no bubble of any size when constantly observed at 70 degrees F. A Grade-A is allowed a bubble less than 0.075 inch when constantly observed at 70 degrees F. I prefer the Grade-AA, and although only slightly more expensive, in my opinion are the best.

Button compasses are also offered in 14mm, which I have used only on occasions that warrant an even smaller size. At this size, they get a little hard to use, and at my age, to see. However they do fit applications where a miniature size is required.

A compass is one of those items for which I like to have a back-up. Floating dial compasses are also available in various configurations such as for a watch band strap, built into the top of a walking stick, and on a key chain fob. This is a handy way to carry a back-up for the main compass in your survival kit. Again, make sure it is a liquid filled compass (I was given a walking stick as a gift and it had a non-liquid filled compass on top. I am still waiting for the needle to stop swinging).

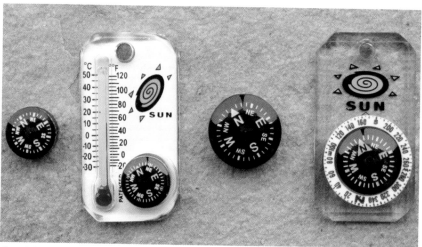

From left to right: a 14mm Button Compass, a Sun Therm-O-Compass, a 20mm Button Compass, and a Mini-Comp II, Micro Orienteering Compass.

Sun Company, Inc. uses the button compass in two items that provide an easy way to carry a back up compass. Both can be used on a key ring, or hung on the zipper pull of a jacket or rain gear, so you always have a back-up with you. The first is the Therm-O-Compass, a handy little item that provides a thermometer, a compass and a wind chill chart. The front provides the temperature in both degrees F and C and a 14mm luminous, liquid filled button compass. The back side provides a wind chill chart. You will find many uses for this little device. Hang one outside the tent so you know what the temperature is in the morning. It measures 2x1-1/8 inches and weighs only 0.3 ounce.

The next item is the Mini-Comp II, Micro Orienteering Compass. This is a great little micro orienteering compass which can also be hung off zipper pulls, placed in mini survival kits or carried in your pocket as a back up to your large compass. It is a 20mm liquid-filled button compass and has a luminous dial with a rotating bezel. It is mounted on a clear acrylic case, with an embossed inch/cm ruler. Being mounted on a small rectangular piece of acrylic, it can actually be used as a miniature base plate compass on a map! It includes a 34-inch nylon lanyard. Dimensions: 1.13 inches wide by two inches long. Weight is 1/3 ounce.

As you can see, there are various uses for a small floating dial compass. But do yourself a favor, don't rely on it as your main compass.

### Wrist compass

I have found it handy to have a compass on the wristband of my watch as a backup for quick orientation. Although not my main compass, it is always available just in case.

A nice wristwatch band compass made by Suunto is called the Clipper. This floating dial compass has a nice mounting system that allows it to be clipped on a watch band, to clothes, equipment straps, etc. (or even clipped inside a survival kit). It is liquid filled with a jeweled bearing and has directional points and a rotating/ratcheting dial. It even includes a wrist strap. I have had one on my watchband for at least ten years. It is my back-up that I always have on me.

A Suunto Clipper compass, the Clipper on a watch band and the Suunto M9 Wrist Compass each make a good backup compass.

Another wrist compass made by Suunto is the M-9 Wrist Compass, a compact, highly accurate wrist compass, and the choice of those in the know. The unbreakable black polymer housing has a sighting window for accurate bearings and sighting points on top. You do not read this compass from the top, as the bearing markings are reversed on top. You read it through the side, so that when 0 degrees appears in the side window, you are travelling north. The easy to read face has luminous markings for night use. A 2.5-degree ratchet mechanism can be used to set desired a direction. A hook and loop wrist strap is included.

### Base-plate compass

With all other kits, from medium on up, I recommend a base-plate compass (also known as an orienteering compass). These have a transparent plastic base with a compass capsule that is independent from the base. They are designed to use with a map and make traveling in a specific direction much easier than with a fixed-dial compass. Base-plate compasses are available in basic to advanced models (larger size so more frills). They range from basic orienteering to options such as sighting mirrors, adjustable declination and clinometers. Of course, if you don't have training with a compass I recommend that you get some before a survival situation occurs.

When choosing a base-plate compass, stick to the major manufactures. Some of my favorites are Suunto, Brunton (which is now owned by Silva), and Nexus (which is the brand name for Silva compasses sold in the U.S.). There are some cheaper compasses out there, but a compass is not something you want broken, or inaccurate, when you go to use it. You must be able to depend on it.

The Brunton Classic 9020G is a good basic base-plate compass. With an optic green base, the Brunton Classic has a 0-35-degree inclination scale stamped into the base to read slope and dip, and two-degree graduations, inch and millimeter scales, as well as a declination adjustment. It provides a cobalt steel needle, anti-static clear liquid dampening vial, and requires no tools to adjust declination. A highly visible non-glare white azimuth ring is imprinted in two-degree increments. It measures 3.5x2.5x0.5 inches and weighs only 1.1 ounces.

Orienteering compasses useful in survival kits include the Brunton Classic 9020G, Suunto A-10 and Suunto Leader M-3.

Another good basic base-plate compass is the Suunto Partner A-10. It features a ergonomically shaped clear base plate for easy map use, a fixed declination correction scale, and a snap-lock lanyard which enables the user to easily detach the compass from the lanyard. It measures 2.2x3.5 inches and weighs eight ounces.

The next base-plate compass is one of the top ranked compasses for orienteering and serious hiking. It is the Suunto Leader M-3DL, and it is one of my favorites for a base-plate compass without a mirror. It features an adjustable declination correction scale, a liquid filled capsule and a rotating luminous bezel. The base plate features anti-slip rubber feet, a 3x magnifier, two template holes for map marking and an attached lanyard. It measures 2.4x4.9 inches and weighs 1.6 ounces. This is a great compass for use in conjunction with a map for serious orienteering.

There are many other fine compasses out there. These are just some that I'm comfortable with, and by no means wish to downgrade those made by others. Just be careful in regard to where they are made. I have mainly stuck with the Suunto brand as they are still made in Finland and are a quality device.

Tip: If a luminous dial does not glow, shine a flashlight on it for a few moments and it should glow for several hours.

I recommend a luminous dial, when available, which is handy for using in the dark or low light conditions. If you plan to use an orienteering compass in conjunction with a topographical map, and you do not adjust your maps for declination, you should get a magnetic declination adjustment feature. Although not necessary, as you can always add or subtract the deviation at each reading, the stress of a survival situation could cause you to forget to make the mental calculation. If you are not familiar with declination, this may not sound important. However, if you were in the eastern or western most parts of the U.S., the magnetic declination can be as high as 22 degrees. If you didn't take this into consideration, you could be more than a mile off your destination at a distance of three miles.

Many orienteering compasses also have a small magnifying glass in the clear plastic base. Not only can it be used to magnify the finer features of a topographical map, but it falls into the category I call "multi-purpose use." It can be used to see a splinter for removal, or even for fire starting. The same goes for the mirror on a mirror compass, which will be discussed next. It could always be used as an improvised signal mirror, or to check those difficult areas for ticks.

### Mirror compass

Some base-plate compasses also have a sighting mirror. This provides a more accurate means to sight your compass when navigating. I prefer a mirror compass as my main compass, and carry one on each pack. These compasses are basically a base-plate compass with a hinged mirror attached at the top.

In order to explain how they are more accurate, a quick lesson in compass usage. With a normal base-plate compass, you hold the compass in front of you, about mid-chest level. In this manner, after setting your bearing, you can see that the magnetic needle is in the orienting arrow (I call this boxing the needle). You must now raise the compass in order to sight on something ahead. However, once the compass is raised, you can no longer tell if the needle is "boxed." Therefore, it is common to see users raise and lower the compass several times to ensure the needle is boxed while trying to aim ahead. The problem is that it is impossible to see if the needle is boxed while the compass is raised, and is very difficult to accurately aim the compass when it is lowered.

The mirrored compass solves this dilemma and allows accuracy while aiming. This is how a

Looking through a mirror compass, you can aim while seeing the dial through the mirror.

mirrored compass works, and why it is more accurate than a regular base-plate compass. You can hold a mirrored compass up at eye level, and adjust the hinged cover with mirror at an angle which allows you to see the orienting arrow and the magnetic needle. On some mirrored compasses, there is a line down the middle of the mirror. This line should run through the center of the center pivot point of the magnetic needle. This will ensure that you, your compass and the object you are aiming at are in a perfect straight line (limiting lateral drift).

If you want to determine an azimuth, hold the compass at eye level and, using the aiming sights, place them on a distant object, such as a tree. Rotate the graduated azimuth ring until the north end of magnetic needle (normally red) is within the north side of the orienting arrow. Without having to bring the compass down to chest level to turn the graduated azimuth ring, and with the optimized V sighting points, your accuracy has just improved over the technique for a base-plate compass, with which you must constantly raise and lower the compass to determine if the magnetic needle is in the orienting arrow. Now, if you already have an azimuth dialed in the compass, you simply raise the compass to eye level, and while viewing the magnetic needle in the mirror, turn your body until the needle is in the correct position in the orienting arrow. You can now aim on something that is straight ahead in the sites, and you know you are traveling on the desired azimuth. Again, you don't have to raise or lower the compass. As you can see, a mirrored compass provides for increased accuracy.

A Suunto MC-2DL Global provides for accurate navigation.

The best two mirrored compasses I am aware of are the Suunto MC-2DL and 2DL Global, and the Silva Ranger 515 CL & CLG. These are respected mirrored compasses and provide for accurate navigation. I prefer the Suunto model and use the standard MC-2DL, as well as the MC-2DL Global, which has a global needle system, so it works anywhere in the world. An additional sighting hole makes for superior accuracy and the luminous two-color bezel ring is very easy to see and use. A jeweled bearing, clinometer, large mirror with center line, clear base-plate with magnifying lens and a detachable snap lock lanyard round out this great compass. It measures 2.5x3.9x0.6 inches, and weighs 2.65 ounces. This is the compass I carry and use for outdoor adventures.

### Lensatic compass

The Lensatic compass is a floating-dial compass that is used primarily by the military. The floating dial is mounted on a pivot point so that it can rotate freely when the compass is held level. An arrow and the letters "E" and "W" are printed in luminous figures. There are also two scales on the disc, the outer scale for mils and the inner scale (normally in red) for degrees. The floating dial is encased in glass which has a black index line. The bezel ring is a ratchet device that clicks when turned. Each click is equal to three degrees with a total of 120 clicks when fully rotated 360 degrees. It has both forward and rear sights for aiming. It also has a hinged lens, which contains the rear sighting slot used to magnify the scales on the floating dial, and a finger loop for holding the compass in the raised position.

There is much debate on the accuracy of this type compass. Some say it is very accurate, while others indicate it is only theoretically more accurate. I will stay out of the debate and indicate that you should use what you are comfortable with, or what works for you. I do feel that, compared with base-plate compasses, this type of compass is not as versatile nor is it as easily used with a map. I carried one in the U.S. Marine Corps., and when I left, I left this type of compass behind.

If you do select a Lensatic compass, get a good one. The best is made by Cammenga, the exclusive manufacturer of the official U.S. military Lensatic compass. It is built to the demanding specification of MIL-PRF-10436N, and is battle tested against shock, water and sand. It is functional from -50 degrees F to +150 degrees F. It also has seven Tritium Micro Lights which allow for navigation in low-light conditions. It is equipped with a magnifying lens, sight wire and dial

I carried a Lensatic compass in the Marine Corps. There is much debate on the accuracy of this type compass.
Photo courtesy of Cammenga Company, LLC.

graduations in both degrees and mils to ensure accurate readings. A copper induction damping system slows the rotation of the magnet without the use of liquids. This compass is built to last with an aluminum frame and a waterproof housing.

### Back-up compass for mini kits

I always like backups to backups. Even though my mini kits usually have a 20mm button compass in them (which is a backup to my large compass), I like to back that up with something (after all, you could always lose or break the 20mm). Therefore I always carry magnetized needles for use as a make-shift compass in the field. Not the best compass, but as always, better than nothing. Many survival books show a leaf as a means to float a magnetized needle in the field.

What I like to put in mini kits is a small disc which is flat and can be used to push your magnetized needle through (I'm sure all the needles you carry in you kit are magnetized), so it floats and can be used as a compass, floating it in water. Okay, where do I get these magic discs, you ask? The grocery store. They are called foil meat trays.

After eating the meat that came on it, wash it off and punch holes in it with a hole punch. I use a 5/8-inch punch, but any size will do as long as both ends of the needle stick out.

Now you have a compass when floated in water. You can hold water in your hand for use as a transportable compass, but you can also use a titanium cup, as it is not magnetic.

## Base-plate compass nomenclature

There are various parts to a base-plate compass, and you should be familiar with them, as well as their function.

The transparent plastic base that the entire compass is mounted to is called the base plate. It often contains various tools, such as rulers, UTM grid readers, a Direction-of-Travel line or Arrow, and sometimes a magnifying glass.

The magnetic needle balances on a pivot which allows it to easily swing in any direction. The north seeking end of that needle is red.

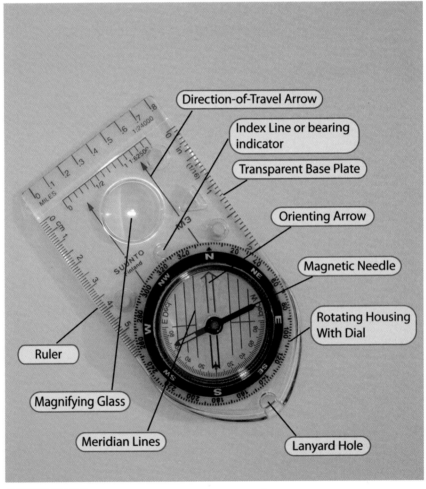

Base Plate Compass

The rotating housing with dial (also known as the rotating azimuth ring) encapsulates the magnetic needle and is filled with a damping liquid that allows the needle to quickly come to a rest and prevents freezing, allowing the needle to move in below freezing temperatures. The housing is surrounded by a numbered plastic dial marked with 360 degree markings, usually in two-degree increments.

The orienting arrow is the outline of an arrow permanently marked into the base of the rotating housing with dial. It is usually red on one end and black on the other, however, it can be another color and shape. As an example, a Suunto MC-2DL has two green lines in which to center the red end of the magnetic needle. In order to determine a bearing or direction of travel, you must exactly center the red end of the magnetic needle in the red end of the orienting arrow, which is known as "boxing" the needle.

The direction-of-travel arrow is an arrow which is permanently marked into the base-plate and points in the direction you need to travel to follow the designated bearing and reach your desired destination. On most compasses this line is in the center, however, on some compasses there can be two, both pointing forward.

The index line, or bearing indicator, allows you to set a specific bearing on the compass and sight the compass for that bearing. Some compasses use the direction-of-travel arrow to set your bearing, while others use a different indicator, such as a small triangle.

Finally, the lanyard hole allows you to hang the compass around your neck while traveling. This keeps it available to re-check your bearing or back-bearing (also known as a "reciprocal" bearing).

## Using a compass

A bearing, or azimuth, is a specific direction from one location to another, on a horizontal plane. In order to take a bearing with your compass, hold it out in front of you and keep it level. Hold the compass straight and point the direction-of-travel arrow at an object or location you want to travel to. If the arrow does not point directly at the desired object or location, don't turn the compass left or right (this is not pool so don't use body english). Instead, pivot your body left or right, taking short choppy steps. This allows you to keep the compass pointing straight ahead until it is pointing directly at the object or location you want to travel towards. You will notice that the Magnetic Needle is not "boxed" in the Orienting Arrow. This comes next.

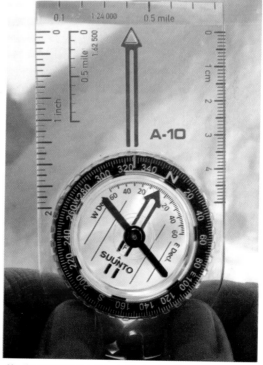

Aim the compass at a distant object or location.

Once you are pointing directly at your desired target, hold the compass steady and turn the rotating housing with dial, until the magnetic needle is precisely boxed within the orienting arrow. You can now read the bearing at the index line or bearing indicator.

As long as you keep the magnetic needle boxed in the orienting arrow, and the direction- of-travel arrow pointing directly at your target, you should be able to navigate to that point, even if going up or down hill where you lose sight of the target.

You will notice that I have not addressed magnetic declination. If you are using a compass in the field in order to navigate in a straight line, without the aid of a map, then in my opinion, magnetic declination can be ignored. However, if you are using a compass in conjunction with a map, then magnetic declination becomes an important factor. Magnetic declination will be discussed under a separate heading.

The bearing for traveling to the target location is 40 degrees.

## Back or reciprocal bearing

A "back" or "reciprocal" bearing is the opposite of your main or forward bearing. It can be used to determine your location from an observable landmark. If your main bearing is more than 180 degrees, you subtract 180 degrees from the main bearing. If it is less than 180 degrees, you add 180 degrees to the main bearing.

Let's say you have sighted on a fire tower and know that it is a bearing of 300 degrees to that tower from your position. In this example, your main bearing to the fire tower is 300 degrees (which is more than 180 degrees) so you subtract 180 degrees which results in 120 degrees. Your back or reciprocal bearing is therefore 120 degrees, and in order to travel from the fire tower to your location, you would now travel at a main bearing of 120 degrees.

If you are using a fixed dial compass, the above calculations are required to determine your back bearing. However, if you are using a base-plate compass, there is an easier way. I have always believed that the more often you turn the rotating housing with dial, the greater chance you have of setting an inaccurate bearing. Therefore, with a base-plate compass, why calculate at all.

Let's say that you are travelling at a main bearing of 280 degrees. The red end of the magnetic needle is boxed in the red end of the orienting needle (see photo 9-34). When you need to check your back bearing, simply turn around, remaining on your direct line of travel, and place the red end of the magnetic needle in the black end of the orienting arrow (see photo 9-35). The black end of the orienting needle is exactly 180 degrees from the red end. This prevents your having to turn the rotating housing from your main bearing, every time you want to check your back bearing while on the move.

## Lateral drift

When traveling using a compass, make short runs from one known point to another if at all possible. When you site your compass on a known object, it is easier to accurately travel to that point. It is more accurate than trying to travel in a straight line with a known bearing but nothing to site on.

It is easier to maintain a straight line if you can see both your starting point and the point you are traveling towards. A back bearing, as discussed above, is a good way to check that you are traveling in a straight line, and prevents lateral drift. If you can mark your starting point with a

The red end of the magnetic needle is boxed in the red end of the orienting needle. When you need to check your back bearing, simply turn around, remaining on your direct line of travel, and place the red end of the magnetic needle in the black end of the orienting arrow. The black end of the orienting needle is exactly 180 degrees from the red end.

stick in the ground or another object that you can see from a distance once you start moving, you can use it to determine if you have traveled straight forward. If you are not traveling alone, the best option is to leave a person at the starting point. As you travel from the starting point, turn around, being careful that you remain on your line of travel. Using a back bearing, determine if you are pointing directly at your starting stick, object, or person left behind. If you are, you are moving straight ahead. If you are not, lateral drift has occurred, you have drifted to the left or right of the line of travel.

If lateral drift has occurred, there is one of two things you can do. The first is return to your last known point and re-shoot your bearing, aiming on an object directly in the bearings path, and try again to travel towards that target without drifting left or right. Another way, which is not as accurate, is to shuffle left or right of the direction of travel line until your back-bearing is aimed directly at the last starting point. Then carefully turn around and continue on the original bearing.

Even though you remain on the designated bearing, if you are careless and allow lateral drift to occur you will not end up at the desired destination. Even though the original bearing keeps you in a straight line forward, lateral drift takes you on a parallel course which does not lead to where you want to be.

Keep in mind that the more often you check your back bearing, the less likely you are to drift.

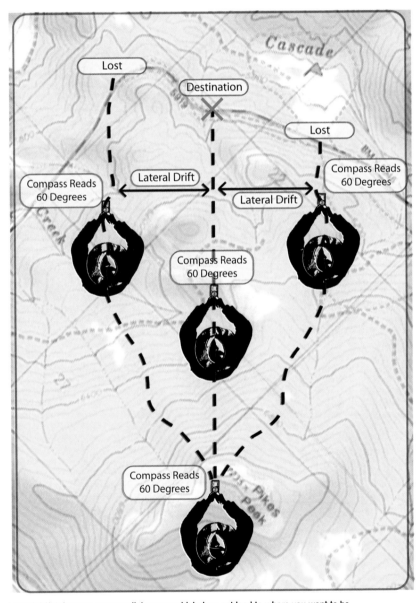

Lateral drift takes you on a parallel course which does not lead to where you want to be.

## Pacing

Before we get into practical exercises for compass use, I would first like to discuss pacing. When using a compass, it is often necessary to go a certain distance in a given direction, and you would like to have a general idea of how far you have traveled. A way to measure distance is pace counting. It takes two steps to make a pace. When walking, always start out with your left foot, and count every time your right foot hits the ground. That is one pace.

To do this, you will need a good estimate of your pace, in length. Figuring out the length of your average pace is easy. Measure a known distance of 100 feet to 500 feet (the longer the distance, the more accurate the estimate), and mark the beginning and end with a stick in the ground. Walk the known distance (in this case 100 feet) being careful to walk normally. Count your paces (every second step) from the first stick to the last, and record that number. Now walk from the last stick back to the first, again counting your paces. Compare these two numbers (they should be close if you walked normal). If they are not even close, do the exercise again. When the two numbers are close, average the two, such as 17 paces in one direction and 19 paces in the other. If you add the two together, 36 paces, and divide by two, your average pace would be 18 paces every distance of 100 feet.

If you used 100 feet and counted 18 paces (100 divided by 18), you now know your average pace is 5.5 feet (every time your second foot hits the ground). We know one mile equals 5,280 feet, so 5,280 feet divided by a 5.5 foot pace tells you that you average 960 paces per mile.

Keep in mind that your pace changes due to differences in terrain, such as going uphill (which normally shortens your pace) or going downhill (which normally lengthens your pace). Snow, tall grass, jungle, etc, will also affect your normal pace. This has to be taken into account when pacing.

So how do we record the paces we have taken? There are various ways, such as carrying a bunch of small stones in one pocket. Every time you walk one hundred paces, move a stone from one pocket to another. However, there is a better way called pace beads.

Pace beads are not a primary navigation tool, but a supplemental one. They are used to count your paces for a general idea of how far you have traveled. Note that the military distance is based on meters, and this can also be calculated. I like to use feet so I can easily determine miles traveled.

Pace beads usually have five beads at the top and nine at the bottom. If you know your pace is approximately five feet, you know that every 100 paces you travel 500 feet. So every 100 paces, pull down

Hang pace beads from your pack strap.

one of the beads from the nine-bead group. After all nine have been pulled down and after the next 100 feet, pull down a bead from the five-bead group, which means you have traveled approximately 5,000 feet (a mile is 5,280 feet). Then pull the nine-bead group back up and start over. After the next 5,000 feet, pull down another bead from the five-bead group, and you have now traveled 10,000 feet. Continue in this manner, pulling the nine-bead group back up when they are depleted. When the five-bead group is depleted, and you have traveled 25,000 feet, start over with all beads.

While pace beads only provide you with a general or approximate distance, they can help you determine approximately how far you have traveled. If your map indicates that a body of water lies two miles ahead, and you have traveled three to four miles without seeing it, you know you are probably not traveling in the right direction.

## Practice excercises for compass accuracy

Using a compass accurately takes practice. It seems that the use is pretty straight forward, but the more you practice, the more accurate you will get. The following two exercises make great practice of a navigation course. Use an open field for this exercise, until accuracy becomes the norm. Then move to a wooded area, where maintaining accuracy becomes more difficult.

### Exercise one

Place a marker between your feet at a starting point. A wooden popsicle stick painted blaze orange on one side works well. That way you cannot see your stick going out on the exercise, but can locate it once you have completed the exercise to see how accurate you were by how close you came to your starting stick.

Assign yourself a bearing, one that will get you heading in a direction ahead of your stick. It doesn't have to be straight, as an angle makes it more interesting.

Once you have the bearing set on your compass, box the needle and proceed forward and count your paces until you have travelled 100 paces. Now stop, turn around, and using a back bearing, travel another 100 paces and you should end up on your stick. It will take some practice, believe me.

### Exercise two

Start the same way you did in Exercise One. However, make sure that the bearing you use gets you heading out at an angle to the left. Travel 100 paces following your bearing and stop. Then add 120 degrees to your bearing number. Now follow that bearing for another 100 paces and stop. Now add another 120 degrees to your bearing and follow that for another 100 paces. You should end up on your beginning stick.

Once you get this exercise down, start off to the right instead of the left. At each 100 pace distance, subtract 120 degrees from you last bearing and this will take you on the same course, but in the opposite direction.

There are many other exercises you can devise for use in practicing accuracy with a compass. These are basic but build confidence. Come up with some more difficult exercises on your own. You will learn as you perform these exercise that staying on a straight line is not as easy as it would seem. You must pay attention and avoid lateral drift. The more you work with a compass, the more comfortable you will become with it, and hence, the more accurate. Try some of these exercises going up and down hill or through tall grass. Again, more difficult than you would think.

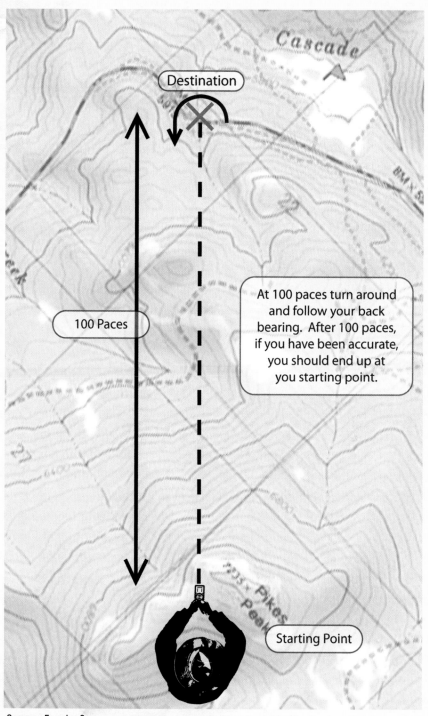

Destination

100 Paces

At 100 paces turn around and follow your back bearing. After 100 paces, if you have been accurate, you should end up at you starting point.

Starting Point

Compass Exercise One

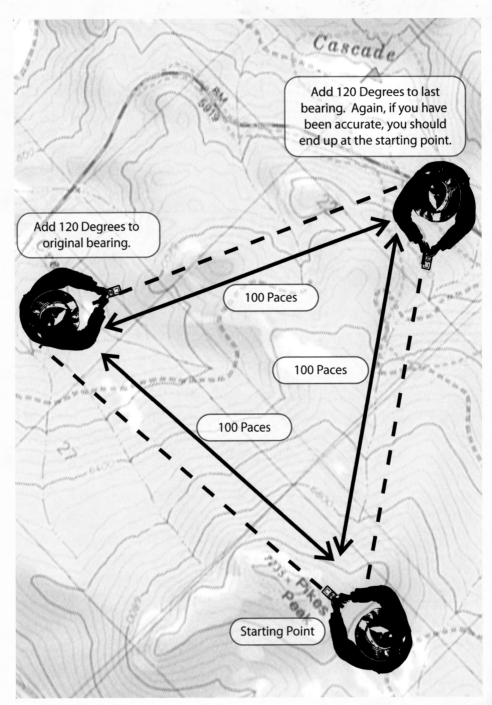

Add 120 Degrees to last bearing. Again, if you have been accurate, you should end up at the starting point.

Add 120 Degrees to original bearing.

100 Paces

100 Paces

100 Paces

Starting Point

Compass Exercise Two

## Magnetic declination

Before we get into using a compass with a map, we need to understand magnetic declination, as it pertains to the accuracy of navigation.

First of all, there are two norths, The first geographic north, also referred to as "true north." This is static, and is located about 1200 miles north of the magnetic north pole. Map makers almost always place geographic north at the top of a map. The second north is "magnetic north." The magnetic needle on your compass is attracted by the magnetism of the earth and therefore aligns with the magnetic north pole. The difference between true north and magnetic north on land maps is called magnetic declination.

Magnetic declination is the direction and amount of variation between the true north and the magnetic north. The amount and direction of declination depends upon how those poles align relative to a given point on earth. Declination is zero when the two poles align. This zero line of declination is called the "Agonic" line. If you are located west of the Agonic line, the magnetic needle on your compass will point east of true north. If you are east of the Agonic line, the magnetic needle of your compass will point west of true north. Although there is a pattern, that pattern does not follow meridians or parallels. The lines of the pattern are called isogonic lines and are like magnetic contour lines. They trace the path of constant magnetic declination.

This point is always shifting, but slowly. Therefore if your map is really old, you might need to check the current declination for your area. This can be done through the NOAA National Geophysical Data Center at www.ngdc.noaa.gov/geomagmodels/declination.jsp. This site provides an actual calculator where you can either insert your zip code, or latitude/longitude, and it will provide you with the current declination for that area, as well as the amount it changes every year.

Okay, so we covered the technical discussion in regard to magnetic declination. So why is this important to you using a map with a compass? To explain it simply, we indicated that the top of your map almost always points to true north. But your compass doesn't, it points to magnetic north. If you are in the Adirondacks in New York State the magnetic declination is approximately 14 degrees west, this means that although your map points straight up, the magnetic needle on your compass will actually point 14 degrees to the left, or west.

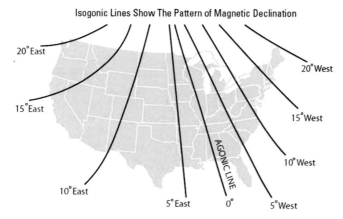

Isogonic Lines Show The Pattern of Magnetic Declination

If you are using the compass on your map and do not compensate for the declination, you will never be able to navigate accurately. How far would you actually be off? As you can see, at 10 degrees, less than the declination in the Adirondacks, you would be off almost a mile after only travelling five miles. Declination is certainly important when you combine both map and compass for navigational purposes.

| Degrees off | Distance off in feet/miles | | |
|:---:|:---:|:---:|:---:|
| | 1 mile | 2 miles | 3 miles |
| 2 | 184 ft./.03 miles | 921 ft. / .17 miles | 1843 ft. / .35 miles |
| 5 | 460 ft. / .09 miles | 2303 ft. / .44 miles | 4606 ft. / .87 miles |
| 10 | 920 ft. / .17 miles | 4601 ft. / .87 miles | 9203 ft. / 1.7 miles |
| 20 | 1833 ft. / .35 miles | 9168 ft. / 1.76 miles | 18337ft. / 3.47 miles |

This table shows the distance you will be off in both feet and miles, at various degrees, if you fail to compensate for magnetic declination when using a compass with a map. Table & Calculations by Denise McCann.

Obviously, we must compensate for declination, and there are two ways we can do that. We can adjust our compass, or we can adjust our map. Here is how we do that.

### Compass adjustment for declination

There are many little sayings and rules, such as "East is least and west is best," for remembering how to adjust a compass for declination. Most of them don't make sense to me. But, I do know that when you are east of the Agonic line, the magnetic needle points at an angle west, and so we want to make the compass point straight up for north, like the map. So if we add the degrees for the magnetic declination, the compass will be compensated for the difference.

In other words, if for the Adirondacks, you add the 14 degrees to any calculation. Now although the orienting arrow of your compass is 14 degrees to the left of the direction of travel arrow, when you box the magnetic needle you will be traveling in the correct direction in accordance with the map. It is the same for being west of the agonic line except, being west, the needle points at an angle east. So to compensate, subtract the declination and the orienting needle will now face at an angle to the right of the direction of travel arrow.

This sounds confusing at first, but there is an easier way. Just look at the declination diagram at the bottom of the map. If the magnetic declination line is to the left of true north, turn your rotating housing with dial to the left (counterclockwise) the number of degrees indicated on the diagram. If the magnetic declination line is to the right of true north, turn the rotating housing with dial to the right (clockwise) the number of degrees indicated on the diagram.

Lastly, most good base-plate compasses today have the ability to adjust for declination. Most manufacturers have a different method, which should be described in the directions for that compass, but the principle is the same. It allows you to off-set the orienting arrow to compensate for the magnetic declination. Some are done with a small screw and others need to rotate the center of the rotating housing with dial.

What you need to understand is this: when you adjust your compass, by adding or subtracting, you must do so for each and every bearing that you shoot. If you forget just once, you will be off. You will also need to adjust a different amount of declination for each map area you are in, as the declination changes form one map to another. If you adjust the actual compass using one of the manufacturers adjustments, that compass will only work correctly for an area with that specific declination. When you go to a new area with a different declination, you must re-adjust the declination adjustment on the compass.

I personally don't care to do all this work, so there is yet an easier way. It's called adjusting the map for declination. So let's look at that, as I think you will agree that it is foolproof and easier.

## Map adjustment for declination

As indicated, the vertical lines on most maps are oriented to true north, not magnetic north, and your compass is oriented to magnetic north. The difference in degrees between the two is called declination. In order to use your compass with a map, you must compensate for this difference. Instead of adjusting your compass for the difference, as described above, I find it easier to adjust the map. This can be done at home on the dining room table. This is how it's done.

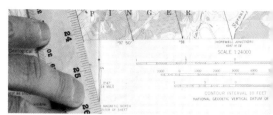

Use the declination diagram to start your first line across the map.

At the bottom of your map, you will see a declination diagram, which shows true north (with a star), magnetic north (with an "N"), and sometimes grid north (with a "GN"). All you need to do is take a long metal rule and lay it along the magnetic north line. Before using the diagram for your line, ensure the degrees are accurate using a protractor. Most maps are, but sometime the degrees are not drawn accurately. You can also use a protractor to determine the degrees indicated in the declination diagram, to ensure the degrees are accurate. This can be done using the meridian lines which run up and down on a map. The left or right sides are meridian lines as well.

Now, using a fine point pen, draw a line across the face of the map being careful that the ruler does not move. Once you have your first line, from one side of the ruler, draw a line on the other side, without moving the ruler. Now you can move the ruler, and using your previously drawn lines, draw subsequent lines. Continue in this manner, across the entire map.

The grid, or meridian lines, are now oriented to magnetic north, and these are the lines you lay your compass on for orienting your map with the compass. You no longer have to adjust your compass for declination, as the map is now adjusted. When you use your compass to obtain a bearing, instead of lining it up on a north-south meridian line, use the lines you have drawn and declination will be adjusted for automatically. Much easier than adjusting a compass, and each map will be adjusted for declination, no matter what one you use, or where you go.

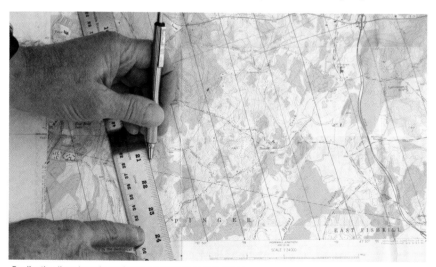

Declination lines have been drawn completely across a map.

## Using a map with a compass

The following are some techniques for using a map and a compass together. There are many techniques, but these are the basics. Using these methods, you should be able to navigate in the field in an emergency situation and hopefully find your way back to civilization. The methods discussed are based on a map being adjusted for declination, as discussed above, which is my recommendation. However, if your map is not adjusted, YOU MUST adjust your compass to compensate for the declination in the area you are operating.

### Orienting a map with a compass

I have been on many hikes on trails here in New York and have seen many people standing on a trail holding up a map and spinning around. I often ask what they are doing and they say they are trying to orient their map. Using this technique, they try to observe various lanmarks in the field that can be identified on the map. They turn around until the map is oriented so the landmarks in both the field and the map seem to line up. Well this is certainly a way to do it, but it is not very accurate. There is a better way.

The first thing you do is lay the map on a flat surface (or the flattest surface you can find on the ground). Now take your compass and make sure that the north or "0" marking on the rotating housing with dial is lined up with the index line or bearing indicator. Once this is done, lay your compass on the map, so that one side of the base-plate is oriented along one of the meridian

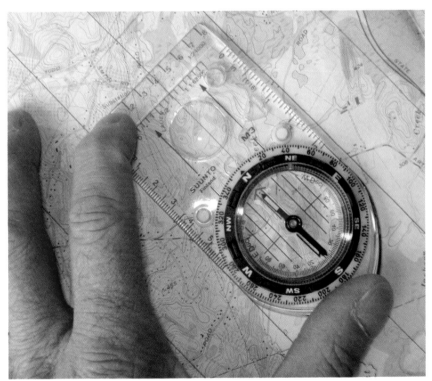

Use a compass to orient a map that has meridian lines drawn on it to compensate for declination. Align the side of the base-plate on a meridian line, facing toward the top of the map, and properly box the magnetic needle. The map is now oriented with the surrounding environment.

lines you have drawn on the map. Make sure the direction-of-travel arrow is facing towards the top of the map.

Without moving the compass or the rotating housing, carefully rotate the map until the red end of the magnetic needle is boxed in the red end of the orienting arrow. Be careful that the compass does not move off the meridian line. Once the needle is boxed, your map is oriented. You can now look at your map and identify features in the exact direction in the field that they appear on the map.

### Finding a bearing from a map

You want know on what bearing you would travel from one location on a map to another. This can be done in the field, or on your dining room table before even going out in the field.

The first thing you do is place your compass on the map so that one side of the base-plate provides a line from where you want to start to where you want to go (You can actually draw a line if you wish), making sure that the direction of travel arrow on the compass is pointing towards the point you want to travel.

Now slide the compass along that line until the meridian lines etched in the bottom of the rotating housing with dial intersect one of the meridian lines drawn on the map. Rotate the rotating housing until the meridian lines on the housing line up exactly with the meridian lines on the map, with the north end of the orienting arrow pointing towards the top of the map. The magnetic needle does not have to be boxed in the orienting arrow, and can be ignored unless the map has been oriented. Your bearing for travelling to the end goal can be read at the index line or bearing indicator on the compass.

### Locating an object observed on the map in the field

Now that we know the bearing for traveling from where we are to where we want to go, how do we locate that place? The first thing you do is dial in the bearing you want to use. If you just performed the previous exercise, the bearing should already be at the index line or bearing indicator. Using the explanation described for traveling with a compass, you should be able to navigate to the desired location.

### Locating an object observed in the field on the map

You're in the field and can see a mountain ridge off to your left. However, when you look at your map, you're not sure which ridge you are actually looking at. How do you determine where the ridge you are looking at is located on your map?

First off, you *must* know where you are located on the map. Then place your map on the ground and orient it as describe in "Orienting a map with a compass." Take your compass and, aiming as precisely as you can, point the direction-of-travel arrow directly at the top of the ridge in the field. Now rotate the rotating housing with dial until the red end of the magnetized needle is boxed in the red end of the orienting arrow. The actual bearing to the summit can be read at the index line or bearing indicator.

Being careful not to move the map that has been oriented or the rotating housing, place the compass on the map. Place one side edge of the compass base-plate on your known location, making sure that the direction of travel arrow is facing away from that location. Again, being careful not to move the map or the rotating housing, pivot your compass on your known location until the red end of the magnetized needle is boxed in the red end of the orienting arrow. Now draw an actual or imaginary line along the side of the base-plate and that line should intersect with the summit of the ridge you are looking at.

### Finding yourself on a map

Sometimes you know you are somewhere on a map but don't really know where. Using triangulation, if you can locate at least two or more identifiable landmarks, you can get a general idea of where you are. This won't give you a specific location, as most bearings will be within two or three degrees of accuracy at best, but you will have an area of possibility.

Although two landmarks will work, three or more provides a more accurate location. Keep in mind that landmarks that are approximately 90 degrees apart from your location work best, or as close as you can get to lines that will cross at almost right angles. The closer the landmarks used are to you, the greater the accuracy that will be achieved, but you don't always have a choice in landmarks.

To triangulate your position, locate landmarks. The first one is generally west of your position (let's call this peak "A"). Take a bearing on this peak that is 90 degrees from your position. Calculate the back bearing and it is 270 degrees.

Orient your map with the compass and lay your compass on the map with a bearing set at 270 degrees. Lay the side of the base-plate at the peak you shot the bearing to, and without moving the map or rotating housing, swivel the compass until the red end of the magnetic needle is boxed in the orienting arrow (making sure the direction of travel arrow is pointing from the peak back towards your general direction). Now draw a line along the side of the base-plate, from the peak back towards you. You may have to extend this line after you shoot more bearings in order for them to intersect.

Now you look southeast and choose another peak "B" and do the same as above. The bearing out is 140 degrees with a back bearing of 320 degrees. Draw a line, intersecting the first. You look off to the southwest and choose another peak "C." Do the same as before with a bearing out of 220 degrees and back bearing of 40 degrees. Draw the last line, intersecting the first two and you now have a general area where you should be located. You are in that little triangle.

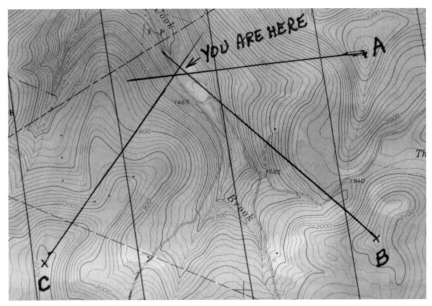

In this example of triangulation, you are in a low area and can see several prominent peaks.

## Miscellaneous navigation techniques

### Base lines

No matter how good you become with a compass, when you start navigating through swamps, thick woods, or up and down rough terrain, you are bound to lose accuracy. As you learned, a few degrees off and you will not end up where you hoped. Therefore, when studying a map, look for a long physical line that can easily be identified, such as a river, railroad tracks, power lines, a highway, trail, etc. This can be used as a base line for navigation.

A base line provides a known line that you can't miss or pass without knowing it. I live in the Hudson Valley, New York, and to the west of me is the Hudson River, which runs generally north and south. I know that as long as I head west, it would be impossible to miss the river, it is a base line. A highway, Route 9, runs parallel to the river, a few miles east of the river. If you are at the river and head east, you can't miss Route 9 without crossing it. This is another base line. If you know you are somewhere between the river and Route 9, you have a base line to the east and the west. Therefore if you head in either of those two directions, you can't miss a baseline.

### Handrails

Handrails are geographic landmarks or manmade features that can be used to ensure you are heading in a specific direction. This could be a river, mountain ridge, or power lines, railroad track, etc. They allow you to navigate, often without your map and compass, and yet keep in a general direction.

A good example was used under base lines above, in regard to having a river on one side of you and a highway on the other. To use these features as handrails as opposed to base lines, just stay between them and you can head generally north or south without worrying where you are. You will always be between the two, and if you want to leave that area, head east or west to one of the base lines.

### Off-shooting

You may want to end up at a specific bridge, crossing a stream or river, but if you are off using your compass you may miss it all together. A technique that can help you locate a specific destination, even if you are off on your navigating with the compass, is called off-shooting (also called aiming off).

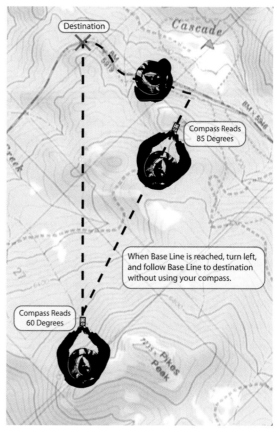

In off-shooting, use a bearing that is intentionally off to the right or left of the spot you want to travel to.

If you want to travel directly to a specific spot, let's say a bridge crossing, you must be extremely accurate or you might miss it all together. If you have a base line that you can use, in this case the stream or river that the bridge crosses, you can use that as a means of knowing you have reached the water that the bridge crosses. However, if you reach the base line and there is no bridge, do you turn left or right to get to the bridge? You won't know!

So when heading towards the known base line, use a bearing that is intentionally off to the right or left of the spot you want to travel to. If we want to travel to a location that is on a bearing of 60 degrees, instead of using 60 degrees we use 85 degrees, which will take us to the right of where we want to end up. However, because we have a base line, we know that when we reach that base line we can turn left and proceed to our desired location. You don't even have to use your compass at that point, just follow the base line to the left and you will reach your destination. This could also be done to the left of our original bearing, and when we reach the base line, turn right and proceed to your destination.

### A bearing baseline

There may be times when you just want to explore a specific area. All you need is a prominent feature that you can shoot a bearing on before you leave your position. Let's say you are in camp and want to explore the general area to the northeast of your camp. Find a prominent feature north of your position and shoot a bearing to it, then write it down and keep it, as that is your baseline.

Now while you're out exploring, you decide to head back to camp. Just pull out that bearing you wrote down and dial it into your compass. Locate the prominent feature you used to get your baseline earlier and move left or right until the red end of the magnetic needle is boxed in the red end of the orienting arrow (keep in mind that this only works if you can view the prominent feature that you used to get the original bearing). You are now on the same line you were on when you shot the original bearing. All you need to do now is calculate your back bearing and travel on that bearing back to camp.

This works even better if your camp is located on a base line like a stream or other long feature that runs perpendicular to the direction you headed out. Let's say you headed out generally north and your camp is located on a stream that runs east and west. When you figure out your back bearing later in the day, off shoot as described above, and when you get to the stream you will know which direction to turn to return to your camp.

### Boxing an object

There will be times when you are navigating when you'll come to an obstacle that you either don't want to proceed through, such as a swamp or pond, or a physical feature you want to go around, such as a cliff. But if you just walk around it, how do you stay on your designated course?

The technique to use is called boxing an object, and this is how it works. When you come to the obstacle, stop and try to determine if it is best to go around to the left or right. You may have to mark the position you stopped and explore a little in each direction (not too far, you don't want to be unable to find your way back to your marked position).

Let's say you decide to go right past the obstacle. Add 90 degrees to your original bearing, and you should now be facing 90 degrees to the right. Follow that bearing, counting paces until you have passed the obstacle.

Once you have passed the obstacle, stop and record the amount of paces you took. Then subtract 90 degrees from your bearing so you are back at your original direction of travel, 150 degrees.

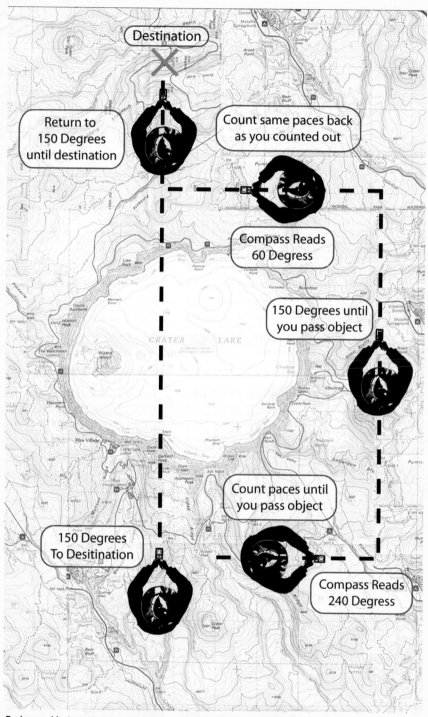

Destination

Return to
150 Degrees
until destination

Count same paces back
as you counted out

Compass Reads
60 Degress

150 Degrees until
you pass object

Count paces until
you pass object

150 Degrees
To Desitination

Compass Reads
240 Degress

Boxing an object.

You will now be facing your original direction of travel, 150 degrees, and can follow that bearing, without counting your paces, until you pass the obstacle.

Once you have passed the obstacle, stop and subtract 90 degrees from your bearing, being 60 degrees, turning left this time. Now follow that bearing, counting the same amount of paces you counted out the first time. When you reach the same amount of paces, stop.

Now add 90 degrees to your last bearing and you should be back at your original bearing of 150 degrees. If you performed these calculations carefully, and were careful with your pacing, you will be back on your original direction of travel, heading towards your destination.

## GPS (Global Positioning System)

A GPS (Global Positioning System), simply described, is an electronic device that can provide your current position in latitude and longitude. A GPS does this by communicating with at least four of the 24 orbiting satellites put in space for that reason. Some units have topographical maps downloaded into them to view on the screen and many allow you to record "way points" so you can find your way back. It is being advertised as the greatest navigation tool available. In my opinion, don't believe it. Of course it can be handy, but don't throw away your map and compass.

First, while it can tell you your position, do you know where that latitude and longitude is? If you happen to have a radio and can call your coordinates in to a rescue team, they will be able to find your exact position. If you don't have a radio, you really need a map to determine where you are located in the wilderness in which you are lost. The GPS can give you coordinates to hike out, but without a topographical map you might be directed towards an unpassable mountain ledge, or a physical barrier like water. Only a map can tell you what is ahead.

A "Caution" section in the manual for the GPS unit I use states, "It is the user's responsibility to use this product prudently. This product is intended to be used only as a travel aid and must not be used for any purpose requiring precise measurement of direction, distance, location, or topography."

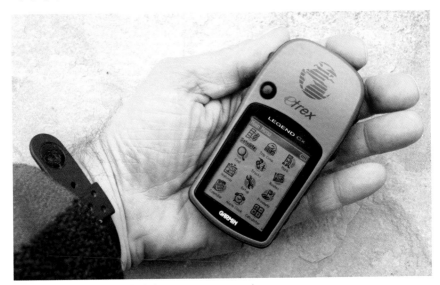

A GPS unit can be handy, but don't throw away your map and compass.

In addition, they are not easy to use, and it takes practice to become really familiar with them.

Did I mention that they run on batteries? The model I have, a Garmin eTrex Legend Cx, runs for only 22 hours in battery saver mode (less than one day), and this time is significantly reduced if you use the backlight mode (needed at night). This necessitates that I carry extra batteries if I want to use it for any length of time. I have never had a map or compass stop working because of dead batteries.

Also, it is a precision electronic instrument and can be easily broken, and although it is water resistant, it is not waterproof. You should also be aware that although they are not affected by weather or cloud cover, they don't work well, or at all, in a heavy overhead canopy. I have had problems getting a signal under heavy vegetation, and I can't always find an open field. There are some places in the Adirondacks where I also cannot get a signal for whatever reason.

I'm not trying to bash GPS units, just trying to inform you of some of their shortcomings. A GPS can be a great supplementary tool for navigation or as a compliment to a radio, but don't make it your primary or only navigation tool.

*Chapter 10*

# Food to Sustain Energy

**A** s with all aspects of survival (as you are learning), there are often strong opinions in various directions, and the need for food in a survival situation is no different. Opinions range from not needing food at all to highly technical dissertations on the advantages of various macronutrients for various situations. I am not a nutritionist and won't pretend that I am. I tend to lean towards needing less than more, and will explain my reasoning and hopefully provide you with food for thought (no pun intended... or did I...). You will ultimately make your own decision, and the more information you have, the more informed that decision will be.

Keep in mind that, in today's world, the majority of people who get lost or stranded in the wilderness are found within a few days. This book, as we have explained previously, is about those first few days. So a discussion on the long term requirements of food in a survival situation is beyond the scope of this book. So let's discuss various aspects of short term survival as it relates to food.

In a survival situation, food is not as important as shelter, water, warmth and other survival necessities we have discussed. Many people, when not in a survival situation, eat more than the body needs, and when they do that it is turned to fat. The majority of people, at least in the United States, have enough body fat to last more than a few days without eating. It may not be pleasant, and it might nag at your mind, but you can live without food for a few days.

When you eat you require water. When you have a limited supply of water to consume, you should consume less food. All food requires water for digestion, and if you eat without drinking, your body uses the water already in your system, increasing the process of dehydration. If you have plenty of water to consume, fill up on it, as it can make your stomach, at least, feel full.

Even though you can go longer than you think without food, it doesn't mean you will maintain your energy level. In a survival situation, we need energy to perform various tasks, so let's look at the energy equation.

The body changes calories from food into energy. Basically, a calorie isn't a tangible thing, but a unit of measurement. A calorie is the amount of energy necessary to raise the temperature of one gram of water by one degree Celsius. What a lot of people don't realize is that the labeling of food in the U.S. does not mean calorie when they say calorie. Are you surprised? A food calorie is actually a kilocalorie (kcal) which is actually 1,000 calories. The word 'calorie' is sometimes capitalized to show the difference, but usually is not. Therefore, for the rest of this discussion, when I say calorie, I mean kilocalorie.

There are six major nutrient groups: water, vitamins, minerals, carbohydrates, protein, and fats. Water is important and transports nutrients to our cells, carries away wastes, etc., but it does not have calories. The nutrients that provide calories to our body – carbohydrates, protein and fats – are referred to as the macronutrients.

A food that encompasses all three macronutrient groups would obviously make a good survival food. However, for a short duration survival situation, carbohydrates with their intrinsic sugars provide quick energy. Even though it dissipates quickly, it can give that boost you need. A candy bar (like a Snickers) or food bar (like a Clif bar) takes up little room in a survival kit, yet provides that necessary energy boost when other food isn't available or preparation is precluded by the weather or other circumstances.

I read over and over on survival blogs that in a survival situation, protein and fat are vital nutritional needs, and therefore you should be eating all the bugs you can find. They don't indicate how long of a survival situation, but it must be longer than a few days.

Proteins, although vital in the grand scheme of things, rob your body of water and accelerate dehydration, so if you are short on water, avoid proteins. Your body also uses more energy to process proteins, and we are trying to gain energy here, not lose it. If you have plenty of water, and are not in a hot climate, then indulge in proteins.

Fats contain the most calories, but take the longest for the body to process. For long term survival, go for the fat, but don't look for quick energy here.

Your best bet in a survival situation is to have survival food with you. Depending on the size of your kit, carry something, even if it is only a candy or food bar. Maybe supplement it with a small bag with a cup-of-soup, bouillon cubes, instant oatmeal, an emergency ration, etc. It is easier to reach into your kit and get something to provide energy than to expend energy looking for something in your surroundings. We'll discuss emergency food that can be carried in your kit later in this chapter.

## Food collection

If you need to search for food, you are already behind the curve. But if it happens, you will need to collect food available in the environment around you. Depending on where you are, you might not have the selection you desire.

There is always a lot of talk about edible plants. I don't disagree about foraging edible plants, but you need to know what you are doing. I am a firm believer in learning before needing. Do yourself a favor and spend time with a wild food expert and learn those basic edible plants that you will be able to positively identify when you need them. Many military manuals talk about the "universal edibility test" and it has been regurgitated in many survival manuals. Don't believe it. It talks about putting just a small amount in your mouth and wait to see what happens. If you do this with poison hemlock, which we have a ton of around my area, you won't have to wait long – you will be dead! Don't put anything in your mouth that you cannot 100% identify as edible. Qualified edible plant instructors are listed in the back of this book.

In regard to fishing, hunting or trapping, stay with small prey. I would rather eat several small fish than wait for the big catch. The same goes for animals. A squirrel may not look like much, but for short-term survival, we have already established that you don't need much protein and fat. Smaller animals are easier to clean and there are no leftovers. Keep in mind that in a short term survival situation, you don't have time to preserve meat. Eat what you get and move on. If this was a long term situation, I would have other advice, but this book is about the short-term.

## Bring it with you

### Emergency food and rations

With a mini kit, you won't have much room for emergency food. Carry at least some bouillon (either cubes or packets depending on the configuration of your kit). Use this as a simple soup broth, or to hide the taste of some of the things you might catch and cook. Sugar is another item that can be carried in cube or packet form. Use it in a hot drink or as an energy booster. Salt is another item that could be carried. It helps those taste buds with certain foods, and can replace salt loss due to dehydration.

A couple of tea bags (or coffee bags that are just like tea bags but hold fresh coffee, in waterproof pouches - my favorite) can be a great morale builder on a cold rainy night. Also easily carried in most kits are small foil packages of electrolyte and energy booster mixes. The first helps to replace electrolytes in the body, such as some sports drinks. The second, which I carry and use, is a dietary supplement mix including 1,000 mg vitamin C, various mineral complexes and vitamins, and antioxidants. It is called Emergen-C and not only tastes good, but can hide the taste of water that doesn't (such as water with iodine in it).

For all small and medium size kits, carry some candy or energy bars. Of course energy bars (there are hundreds to choose from) provide a maximum of calories (normally 180-260), but I haven't yet found many that taste good. One of the exceptions, at least for me, is Clif bars. They

Coffee bags, tea bags and Emergen-C Dietary Supplement mix are easily carried in a kit.

Clif bars, Snickers bars and Quaker granola bars all offer a boost of energy.

Take along some comfort food, such as instant oatmeal, tuna or Cup-a-Soup.

average 240 calories and actually taste good. My favorites are the Oatmeal Raisin Walnut and Chocolate Brownie.

Another staple for quick energy, and a favorite of many hikers, is the Snickers candy bar. With 280 calories, you get a great boost when your energy is low.

I also like granola bars; they taste good, are good for you and don't melt in the kit. I carry the Quaker Chewy Oatmeal Raisin. It only has 110 calories (about half of power bars), but is only about half the size of a Clif bar and I can carry almost two for one. Being oatmeal and raisin, they make a great breakfast bar. This is one choice that you will have to make, but carry as many as you can fit.

Sometimes, just having some small food items in a kit, can provide you with a little something to sit and relax with. I find that most of my kits allow me to carry a bag of instant oatmeal, some instant soup packages, and even a foil package of tuna, providing energy, comfort and a chance to develop a plan of action.

Emergency food should be carried in every survival kit, except maybe the most mini. A larger kit, such as a pack or vehicle kit, can include emergency rations. These provide more calories and can sustain you for a longer period of time without having to collect food. Emergency food rations are available from two main manufacturers: Survivor Industries and S.O.S. Food Lab.

Survivor Industries offers Mainstay Emergency Rations. This foil-wrapped package (waterproof) consists of six 16-ounce. bars of 400 calories each for a total of 2400 calories. I always have a couple of these in my truck and you would be surprised at how good the bars taste. The package measures six inches long by 3-1/2 inches wide and one inch thick. Mainstay Emergency Rations have a five year shelf life. They also have a new smaller package called Mainstay Energy Bars, which are the same rations, just packaged in a smaller package. It contains three servings with 400 calories each for a total of 1200 calories. I really prefer these now as you can actually carry one in a small pack or fanny pack.

S.O.S. Food Lab also offers emergency food rations. I have not tried these, but have heard that they are also good and have 2000 calories per package. These are handy because they are waterproof (until opened), need no preparation and are relatively small for a larger kit.

A second type of emergency ration is the military or civilian version MRE (Meal Ready to Eat). This is a complete food package that provides an entrée (such as beef stew, chicken and rice pilaf, chili w/macaroni, etc.), a side dish, a dessert, a cracker pack with a spread, a beverage base and condiment pack. The entrée can be eaten right out of the pouch without preparation, but they taste better if heated. The military version provides a heating device that you place in a separate pouch and add water and the entrée pouch. It automatically heats the entrée pouch. They are not included in any of the civilian versions. These rations have a shelf life of about three to five years. They are handy for large kits but are rather bulky. I find that if you carry only the entrée, they take up much less room (of course, less calories).

The last type of emergency ration I will discuss are freeze dried meals. Everyone's opinion is different, but I find that these taste the best, but are bulky. They can be folded down to take up less space, but be careful not to break the seal. The biggest drawback is the need for water to rehydrate them. In a survival situation where water is scarce, they are not the best choice.

The smaller Mainstay Energy Bars and MRE main-course entree pouches are two of many options.

Whatever your choice, carry as many emergency rations as practical in large kits. I have existed on one MRE entrée per day, plus anything I could find to eat, for eight days.

## Tools to boil water and cook

We have already discussed some pots under the water collection and purification chapter, specifically those that fit directly over the bottom of a water bottle. However, there are many types made from various materials. I personally prefer stainless steel and titanium.

A pot that you can carry that folds down very small is a foil mini loaf tin, and you can by one in any grocery store. They measure approximately 6-1/8 inches long by 3-3/4 inches wide and two inches high. I flatten them by folding in the ends and then the sides. This makes a small package and several can be carried in a relatively small space.

You can also buy larger pans for larger kits. I have taken the lasagna pans, which are large but have low sides, and folded them to fit in the back of a pack. They can be used for a fish fry or other cooking purposes in the field. Real handy items, even if only carried as a back-up to your regular pot.

### Stoves

We discussed various ways to cook over a fire in Chapter 5, but having a small stove with you makes for quick cooking, especially if the weather is bad or you are short on fuel for a fire. So let's examine some of the smaller stoves available that fit in a small survival kit.

The first, and one of my favorites for small kits, is the Esbit Folding Pocket Stove. It is compact, measuring only three by four by 3/4 inches and weighing 3-1/4 ounce. You could actually carry this stove in a shirt pocket, but let's put it in a survival kit. It has two locking positions for cooking: fully open for a large cup or pot, and angled for a small cup. In either position, it provides a stable support for cooking.

The Esbit stove runs on small solid fuel tablets which are individually sealed in airtight plastic and foil formed packets. Tablets come three per strip, and each tablet burns for about 15 minutes. You can store four tablets inside the stove when it is folded down in the carry position. I have used this stove for a small wood burning stove when the fuel tabs ran out, so it has multi-purpose usage.

Esbit has designed a new small stove called the Esbit Emergency Stove, which comes flat for easy packing. Made from pliable galvanized, hardened steel, it can be bent into a stand-up stove and can be used multiple times. After it cools, fold it flat again and put it back in your pack.

The Esbit Folding Pocket Stove provides stable support for cooking, and the fuel tabs store inside the stove when not in use.

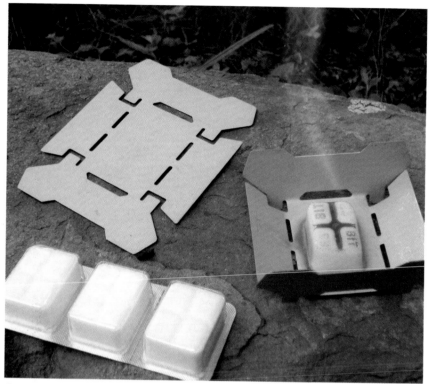

The Esbit Emergency Stove folds flat for storage and bends into a stove for use.

Folded flat it measures 4.5 by 3.5 inches. It comes with three heat tabs, and is great for flat-pack survival kits.

This next stove is new to the survival field and is really innovative. It is called the Vargo Titanium Hexagon Wood Stove, and folds to a slim, compact size for storage. The individual titanium panels are completely hinged and snap easily into place for quick set-up, providing you with a wood burning stove. The durable titanium construction can endure long term heat without damage. The conical shape focuses heat upward, directing it to your pot, for quick efficient cooking. A hinged access door can be opened or closed for air control as well as re-fueling. This stove also makes a great wind screen for use with alcohol stoves. The stove comes with a nylon carrying case. Folded flat, it measures five inches wide by 3/8-inch thick. Set-up, the stove is four inches high by five inches at the base and three inches at the top. It weighs only four ounces (4.5 ounces in case).

Because of the flat carrying size this stove fits in most small packs, and it provides a viable means to burn wood as fuel, relieving the need to carry fuel as part of your kit. I have used this stove quite a bit, and it really does focus the heat up towards the pot. I have also experimented with it as a wind screen for various alcohol stoves and it worked well.

Vargo makes a couple of titanium alcohol stoves as well. One, called the Triad, strictly burns alcohol as fuel. The other, called the Triad-XE, burns alcohol or can be reconfigured to burn fuel tabs, such as those from Esbit. I have never been big on alcohol stoves for survival, as you need to

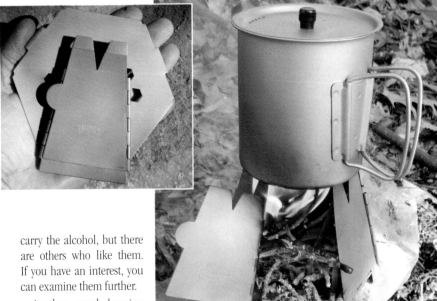

The Vargo Titanium Hexagon Wood Stove folds flat for easy storage and transport. Use it to cook or boil water over a fire made of small pieces of wood.

carry the alcohol, but there are others who like them. If you have an interest, you can examine them further.

Another wood burning stove that I have been carrying for years is the Pocket Cooker. Although a lot heavier than the Vargo Hexagon stove (two pounds), it does fold flat. If you can afford the weight, it is a good wood burner.

The newest addition to a wood burning stove for the field is called the Grill Top Stove Stand. This stove is built tough like American-made products should be, and is designed by my good friend Rob Simpson at the Canteen-Shop.com. He designed it out of necessity, with the military issue stoves becoming scarce. He decided to try and improve upon the original, and this one is made of heavy gauge stainless steel right in Cleveland, Ohio. It is compatible with all standard canteen gear, just like the originals, and works great with alcohol stoves, Trangia stoves, or wood fuel. It features a grill top design that keeps your cup above the flames to maximize heat. It can be used as a stove, grill, berry picker, strainer, small shovel, fire starting implement, and whatever else you can think of. If you have a military canteen cup, you need this Grill Top stove!

## The Pocket Cooker

I showed the Pocket Cooker in my first book, *Build the Perfect Survival Kit,* and shortly thereafter the stove was discontinued. A couple of years later, I saw it back on the market, so I called the manufacturer, Innovative Products, explaining that I would be interested in selling it. I asked why they started re-manufacturing it, and they told me somebody had written a book on survival kits and all of a sudden they were getting a bunch of calls for it, so they started making it again. I said, "That's great, can I get a case?" We have sold hundreds ever since. Even though this stove is heavy, my wife, Denise, prefers it over all others and even carries one in her day pack.

Use the Grill Top Stove Stand by burning small sticks.

### Find it in the field

If you failed to carry emergency food or rations with you, or you have run out, it will be necessary to obtain food in the field. There are various options, so let's examine some of them.

### Edible plants

The first option is edible plants. There is usually more plants available than animals, and even though plants are easier to catch than animals, like animals, they are not always available.

Many plants are seasonal. I once knew a guy that said he could not only live off edible plants, but that he had never had one run from him. Then I went to the Adirondacks with him in July and asked, "So, what are we going to eat?" He said, well, being most of the edible plants are out of season, we will eat fish. My wife and I probably eat more edible plants than most, but they are not always available (at least not the majority), and the other factor is you really need to know what you are doing.

Many plants out there are not only highly toxic, but deadly poisonous. My rule, as stated earlier in this chapter, is never put anything in your mouth that you cannot 100% identify as edible.

Foraging for wild edibles is a learned skill, and the best way to learn is with somebody who already knows. If possible, spend the money and learn from an expert in identifying edible wild food. There are many out there, but be careful. I tend to lean toward those who have more than a local knowledge, as there are plants in one area that are not in another.

One of the best experts on the west coast is Christopher Nyerges, who has not only written a book, Guide to Wild Foods and Useful Plants, and has a DVD on the subject, but takes students out on edible plant walks almost weekly. An expert on the east coast is "Wildman" Steve Brill. He is New York's best known expert on both edible and medicinal plants and has also written a very detailed book on the subject, called Identifying and Harvesting Edible and Medicinal Plants in Wild (and Not So Wild) Places.

I'm not saying these guys are the only two out there, but they are well known, have credentials and offer more than an occasional course. I have provided further information for contacting them in Chapter 12.

Last but not least, buy as many books and DVDs on the subject as you can afford. I do not believe in identifying a plant based on just one photo or diagram. Use as many sources as you can, and compare them. Make certain you have identified the plants correctly, as your life depends on it.

Various books help identify wild edibles, but the best set in my opinion was written by Samuel Thayer. He has two books, The Forager's Harvest and Nature's Garden. They both have extremely detailed information as well as color photos. Samuel Thayer goes more in depth with the various seasonal aspects of plants than most other books. He also offers a DVD actually showing him in the field explaining the particulars of wild plants.

There are other books available and I can recommend the Peterson Field Guide - Edible Wild Plants for Eastern/Central North America, as a good reference for the usability of edible plants. A couple of other books, although not specifically edible plant books, are very good at helping identify specific plants, at which time you can cross reference that plant to an edible plant book. The first is Newcomb's Wildflower Guide by Lawrence Newcomb, which provides an excellent system to identify most plants if they have a flower. The next is Botany in a Day by Thomas J. Elpel, which teaches the patterns method of plant identification. Of course there are more, and as I previously said, you can't have too many books on the subject.

I am often asked about the identification of mushrooms for edibility. I always state that even the best make mistakes, and relate a story about an expert who was a guest at a culinary school who was showing a class an edible variety of mushroom. He consumed it for the class and dropped dead. The identification of mushrooms is a fine art.

There are many poisonous mushrooms and there are edible mushrooms. If you don't know the exact difference, you can become really sick or dead. But none of this should matter to a person trying to survive. Don't eat mushrooms. What most books don't explain is that mushrooms are thermogenic. Thermogenic foods burn more calories to digest than they contain. By eating a thermogenic food, you are actually creating a calorie deficit just trying to digest them. You can literally starve yourself to death eating mushrooms (that is also why they are considered a diet food... you feel full but you gain nothing). A good Morel tastes great cut up and cooked, but, in a survival situation, do yourself a favor and find something else to eat.

Again, my best advice on edible plants is get training from a competent person. This is a skill that takes time to learn and must be ongoing. A survival situation is too late to learn, and you can never know what season a survival situation might occur. If you don't care to make this a hobby, make sure you carry emergency food or know how to trap or hunt. Edible plants may not run from you, but the wrong ones can make you very sick or kill you.

## Tools to catch fish

If ponds, streams or rivers are available, fishing is a good way to obtain food in a survival situation, but to be successful, you have to be equipped. Fishing tackle can be made in the field, but you will expend much less energy if you have the basics with you. For this reason, every survival kit should have some type of a fishing kit. Even a mini kit should have the basics for fishing.

The basic fishing tackle to carry in a mini survival kit is at least 12 assorted hooks, six swivels, and six split shot sinkers, as well as braided fishing line. Most of my survival kits have a lot more than that, but this would be the minimum. I normally carry small tackle kits in some type of small plastic vial. As we discussed in the earlier chapters, my brimmed hat has fish hooks and braided fishing line embedded, and my neck knife has a small pouch with fishing tackle and is wrapped with braided fishing line.

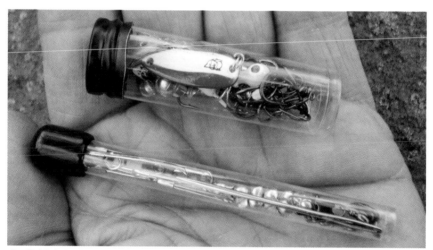

Small vials hold what you need to catch a fish.

Roll fishing line onto a sewing bobbin or a flat floss bobbin and include it in your kit.

Also carry at least 50 feet of fishing line, I prefer 12 to 20-pound test. I prefer that it be wound around something so it can be carried in a small place. For mini kits, wind the fishing line around small plastic sewing machine bobbins or on small plastic floss bobbins, depending on the configuration of the kit. I can get about 50 feet on sewing machine bobbins and 100 feet on plastic floss bobbins.

Choose a fishing line that does not have "memory" so it is not curly after being wound on the small holder. Mono-filament line has a bad habit of getting terribly tangled after wrapping it tightly around something. Some lines that I have found effective for this purpose is Spiderwire original braid and PowerPro braided microfilament line. Both are green in color (which attracted my attention), and are very strong.

Small and large tackle kits built into small Orvis tackle boxes have nice compartments to hold various tackle components.

Small balloons can be attached to your line and used as a float.

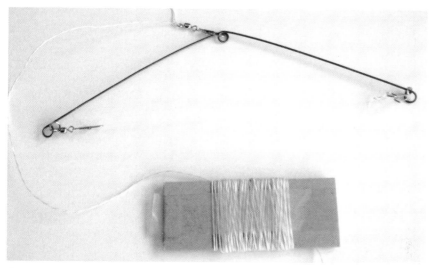

The SpeedHook comes out of the package with the fishing line already attached.

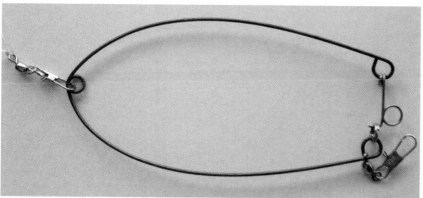

The SpeedHook is set, and when a fish pulls on the hook, it triggers and sets the hook.

As survival kits get larger, fishing kits can get larger as well. I try to carry as much tackle as possible, as in our area, fishing is a good way to eat.

Difficult items to fit into a real small tackle kit are floats. I carry several of the very small balloons, which can be inflated and attached to a line. I prefer the red, yellow and orange ones.

A commercially available item is called the SpeedHook. It is used in many military survival kits and is so effective that it is outlawed in the state of Minnesota. This device is like a mouse trap for fish. It is spring-loaded, and activates and sets the moment a fish takes the bait. No pole is required and it can be used over and over again. It can also be used as a snare to catch small animals. A handy device for any small to large kit.

Another device which can be handy for a survival fishing kit is a fishing yo-yo. They are about the diameter of a donut, and therefore only good for medium to large kits. Basically, they are an automatic reel with a stainless steel spring inside a disc. It has a line attached to it so it can be tied to an overhanging limb. This suspends it over the water. There are several feet of nylon line wrapped around the spring. You dangle the end of the line in the water after baiting the hook, and set the trigger mechanism on the side of the yo-yo. When a fish bites, the trigger is tripped, setting the hook. The reel then automatically reels in the fish. Check your local laws before practicing with them, as some states consider it "unattended fishing."

A gill net is another good supplement to any large survival kit, and required in some aviation survival kits. You can hang it in water with the bottom weighted, or string it between poles.

## Improvised fishing

If you messed up and didn't carry any fishing tackle, or lost what you had, you will have to improvise methods to catch fish. If you have any small cordage, even dental floss, you will still need hooks. They can be made from small branches, plant barbs, bones, safety pins, or any item that can be bent into the shape of a fishing hook. Improvise with whatever you can find. When I make hooks from wood, I like to fire-harden them. I am often asked how to get small hooks close enough to the coals of a fire to fire harden them. I wrap a piece of snare wire around a few at a time, and then hang them over the coals, turning to get all sides.

An important aspect of survival fishing is knowing when and where to fish. Various species feed at different times, but as a general rule, fishing is better at dusk and dawn. Watch the water and if you see fish jumping, they are feeding.

Available in either galvanized steel or plastic, the fishing yo-yo is a good option for medium to large kits.

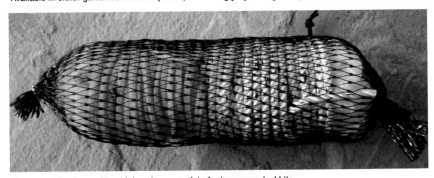

Because of its size, a gill net it is only appropriate for larger survival kits.

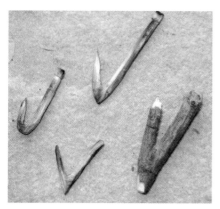 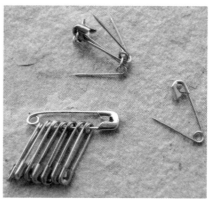

Improvised fish hooks can be carved from small branches that grow at a close angle to the main branch, and then fire hardened over coals of a fire.

Carry small safety pins for use as fish hooks. The hook at the top is a treble hook made by attaching three opened safety pins back-to-back with wire.

Gorge hooks can be carved from wood and fire hardened over coals. To use, place alongside the line then bait to hold it in this position. When a fish swallows the bait, the hook turns cross-ways and can't be pulled out.

Obviously you can't always choose where you want to fish. In shallow streams, look for shaded areas, where there is overhanging vegetation, or logs across the stream causing shaded spots. Look for undercuts of banks, pools from backwashes and behind rocks on the downside of the flow. These are areas fish might sit. On lakes and ponds, the deepest water is normally the best, as it is the coolest. However, these are also the hardest place to reach. Again, look for shaded areas. Once when in the Adirondacks, I looked across a pond with my binoculars and saw a large shaded area which appeared as though you could pull a canoe in. I headed across the pond in my canoe (which you won't always have in a survival situation) and was able to pull right under the overhanging trees. It was cool and some of the best fishing of the trip!

Concentrate on trying to catch lots of small fish instead of that one big one. Get out several lines if possible. The more you have out there the better chance you have of catching something. Use set-lines by cutting several lengths of line and tying a hook to each one. Bait the hooks and hang each from a limb overhanging the water. Hang them about a foot or two into the water. You can do this all along the water's edge, wherever there are overhanging branches. This is also a good time to use survival yo-yos discussed earlier, if you have them. This also allows you to work on your shelter or fire while the lines work for you. Check them every so often to see if you got anything.

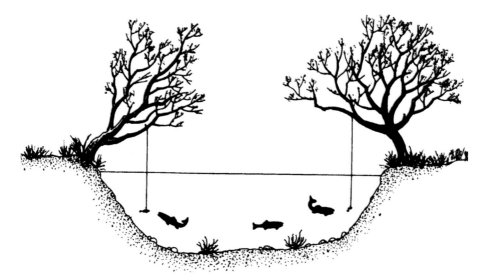

Set-lines along the shoreline, attached to overhanging branches of a tree, free you up to do other tasks.
Diagram courtesy of J. Wayne Fears.

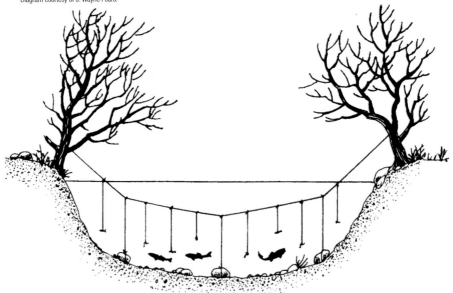

To use a trotline, weight the main line with rocks to keep it from floating up. Diagram courtesy of J. Wayne Fears.

Another method of catching fish is trotlines. A trotline is just a long cord stretched across a stream or inlet with another two- to three-foot long line hanging from it about every three feet. The lines hanging from the main line have hooks and are baited. If there is strong current, add some weight, such as a sinker, to each dangling line to keep it from floating up to the surface. You might have to weight the main line as well in a strong current.

A quick makeshift trotline can also be made by using a long sapling. Hang several baited lines off it and hang it out over the water. Secure it with weight and anchor it well. When you check it, pull the whole sapling in, remove any fish, re-bait the hooks, and place back out over the water. Again, while trotlines are working, you can be working on something else.

Keep in mind that these techniques are to be used in a survival situation. Unattended fishing is illegal in some areas, so if you want to practice this technique, make sure it is legal in your area.

If you carry a large hook in your kit, you can make a small gaff to help you pull in a fish, to ensure it doesn't get away from you. The small emergency fishing kit we make at Survival Resources provides a large hook just for this reason, along with a small nail. The hook is attached to a stick with available cordage or snare wire. The nail is not used to actually hold the hook to the stick, but to keep it from being pulled off the end of the stick, from under its attachment.

Another means to catch fish in a survival situation is by using a spear. When using a spear, keep the tip of the spear in the water. The refraction of the water's surface causes parallax, which makes a fish's position look like it is right in front of you, but is actually off in another direction. If you place your spear tip in the water, when you see it directly in front of a fish, it is actually in front of the fish.

If you make a spear with just a sharp point, you must use it in shallow water. Because there is nothing to keep the fish from falling off the end of the point, you must secure the fish to the bottom and still be able to reach down and grab it, holding it onto the point until you are over land. If the water is too deep, you won't be able to reach to the bottom to grab the fish without a snorkel.

There are various ways to make a fish spear so that something holds the fish onto the spear until you get it out of the water. There are two that I find useful. The first uses some strong thorns, such as those from a Hawthorn shrub or small tree. The Hawthorn thorns are very strong and large enough to use for this purpose. So effective are these thorns that birds have been known to get caught up in a Hawthorn bush and not be able to get out without being stabbed with one or more of the long thorns.

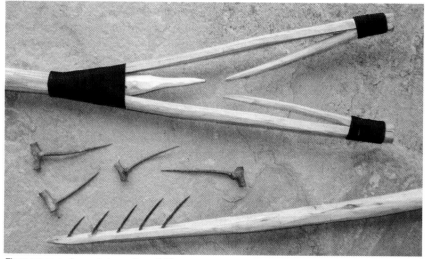

There are several ways to improvise a fishing spear.

Take a sapling about five or six feet long and whittle one end a little flat and almost pointed. Make small angled holes in that end with the holes angled back towards the end you'll be holding. Then insert thorns into the holes (this is also when a small tube of super glue from your kit comes in handy). Now, when you spear a fish, the thorns facing back hold the fish on the spear.

Another option is to split the end of a sapling and carve a wedge that has a point on one end. Use this wedge to hold the split apart, with the pointed part facing forward. You can use cordage or fishing line to tightly wrap the wedge in place. Cut off the ends of the two prongs, or if not long enough use two additional pieces of wood, and make sharp barbs that will face back towards the spear. These can also be tightly wrapped to hold them in place. Now, when you go to spear a fish, the two out-spread prongs direct the fish to the main sharp point. The two backward facing points hold the fish on the spear.

Improvised fish traps are another way to catch fish. With a weir, you place an obstruction completely or partially across a stream which funnels fish into a corral-type area and keeps them from continuing downstream. These are normally made with rocks or lots of wood. They can be time and energy consuming to make and, for short term survival, are probably not advisable.

A basket trap can be made fairly quickly using bendable limbs, such as willow, and small vines or cordage. Basically, tie a bunch of bendable branches together at one end. Spread the other ends apart and hold them there by weaving other bendable smaller branches around the opened ends, so the finished basket looks like a cone open on the wide end. Place bait in the closed pointed end and place it in the water. Hold it in place with either rocks or cordage. As the fish swim downstream, they will swim into the basket. When you pull the basket out of the water, lift it up from the wider open end so the fish does not fall out.

If you happen to find a large plastic soda bottle in the field, which often happens, you can use it to make a fish trap. Cut off the neck end, turn it around and push it back into the bottle so the small screw top opening faces the inside of the bottom. Secure it in place by making some small holes around the side using some cordage. If you are lucky enough to find two large bottles, make another type using just the top of one and all but the bottom of the other. What I like about this type, is you can take the cap off the outside bottle to empty the minnows, which are about all you will catch with this type of trap. However, the minnows are edible, or can be used for bait to catch bigger fish!

Make a fish trap using two plastic soda bottles, so the small fish caught can easily be extracted by taking the cap off the end. The small fish can be used as bait for larger fish.

## Tools to catch meat

To obtain food by catching meat you must be prepared. This means carrying something in your survival kit that will help to obtain a meat source. The first thing that can be carried, even in a mini kit, is snare wire. Snare wire can be wrapped around a sewing bobbin, which allows it to stay un-kinked. Carry as much as you can fit in a kit. Snare wire is another multi-use item; you'll be able to use it for repairs and other uses. You can also use leaders from your fishing kit to make an improvised snare.

Pre-made snares are also available, and some of the best locking snares are made by Thompson Survival Snares and available from Survival Resources.

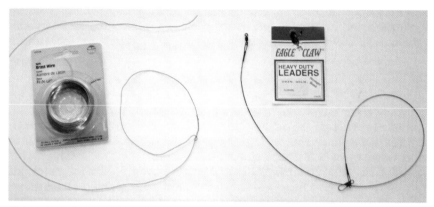

Make an improvised snare from 24-gauge grass wire or a fishing leader.

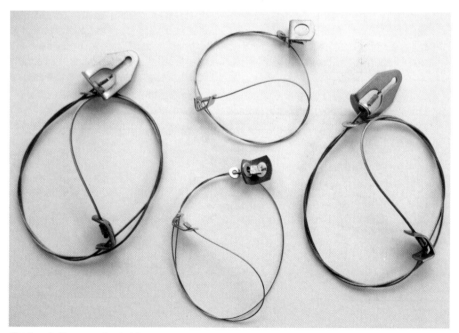

Readymade Thompson Survival Snares.

Readymade frog gigs can be carried in a kit and attached to a pole in the field. The one on the left is commercially available and the one on the right is a modified barbecue fork.

Frog gigs can be carried in a survival kit and attached to a pole in the field. Frog gigs are used to spear frogs near water. You want the pole fairly long, about six to 10 feet. Stealth is required or you lose dinner. The best way to gig is by wading around the edge of a pond or lake, but if getting wet might cause hypothermia, try to stay on shore. You won't be as successful, but you will stay dry.

Frog gigging is done best at night using a headlamp, but again, be careful as moving around at night can be dangerous. With a headlamp, scan the shore, lily pads and other objects in shallow water. Look for two little eyes reflecting back at you.

Once you see a frog, move slowly towards it, trying to keep the light from your headlamp shining in its eyes. When you get your gig about four to 12 inches from the frog, trust it forward in one swift motion. If in shallow water, try to pin it in the mud and reach down and grab it. If not, try to use the spear to throw it up onto shore and retrieve it from there. Sounds easier than it is.

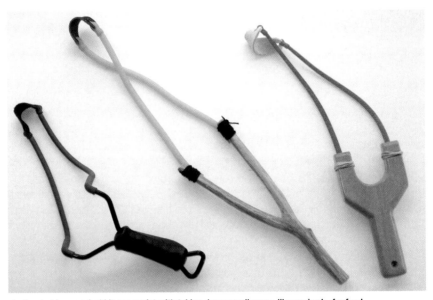

A slingshot in a survival kit can assist with taking down small game, like squirrels, for food.

Most people my age (old) remember that every small boy had a slingshot in his back pocket. In today's world, with states like New York outlawing slingshots, you don't see it so much. However, they are not toys and are still formidable weapons for small game. They can be built in the field if you carry rubber tubing, such as surgical tubing, or just the replacement rubber with pouch for a manufactured slingshot. They can definitely help put food in the pot in a survival situation.

A new type of slingshot, designed by Dave Canterbury, is called the SlingBow. It is actually a modified slingshot that allows you to shoot arrows. he basically added a whisker biscuit to the up-

The SlingBow, designed by Dave Cantervury, modifies a slingshot to shoot arrows.

rights of a slingshot. A whisker biscuit is an arrow rest designed for a compound bow, and is used to stabilize an arrow. When Dave first came up with this idea, he took the nock off the back of the arrow and glued a golf tee in the end. This allowed him to effectively hold the back of the arrow with the leather pouch on the slingshot as he pulled back on the pouch. The whisker biscuit was attached so you could fold it down and still use the slingshot with normal ammo.

In order to carry arrows in a smaller pack, Dave, and his good friend Steve "Critr" Davis, began work on an arrow that was cut in half and could then be screwed back together. They finally got the balance right and it flew straight. I asked Steve Davis if there was a means to use an arrow with a nock, so it could still be used with a bow made in the field. He told me to just add a piece of cordage through the holes in the side of the pouch and tie it off in the back. Now I could use a regular arrow with the whisker biscuit, or fold the whisker biscuit down, take off the piece of cordage and use the slingshot normally.

Another readily available item you can add to a survival kit for food gathering is a rat trap. They are very effective for catching small game in the field. Drill a hole in a corner of the back end so you can attach the trap to a tree or stake with a piece of wire, and an animal can't run off with it. Although not necessary, I prefer to paint mine OD-green, so they blend in better with my environment. In a desert environment the normal beige color might be best, but I would paint over the name, which is normally red in color.

Another handy item to carry in a kit is peanut butter. Not only is it extra food for you, it is excellent bait for rat traps and other traps in the field. After all, a squirrel is just a large rodent (so are beavers), and I catch mice in my traps at home all the time with peanut butter. You can get small packages of peanut butter commercially, as well as in some packages of MRE's. These small packages can be easily carried in your trapping kit. I use a small waterproof vial and refill it with my main peanut butter jar. I just use a small stick to get it out and apply it to a trap.

For a large survival kit or a kit kept in a vehicle, consider a larger food gathering kit. For long term, I have a kit made up in a multi-pouched bag which holds all my food gathering supplies, both fishing and meat gathering.

Add a mounting hole for wire in the rear corner of a rat trap so it won't get dragged away.

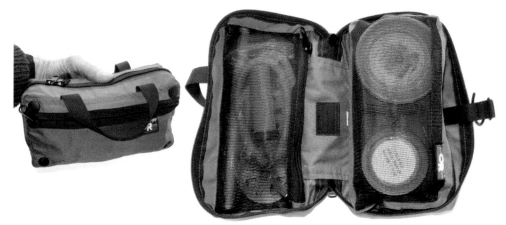

The large food gathering kit can be held in one hand. When opened, the inside is divided into separate zip pouches for holding the various components.

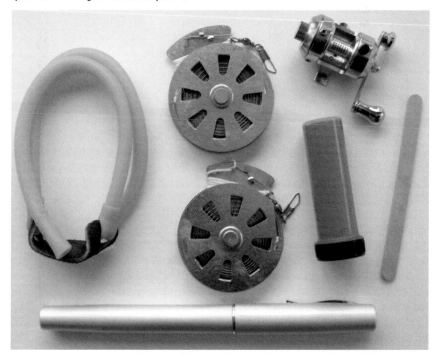

These components provide a wide range of food gathering capability.

The left inside pocket holds a replacement slingshot rubber with pouch, two galvanized survival yoyos, a small collapsible fishing pole with reel, the larger of two fishing tackle vials and a waterproof tube of peanut butter. The right side holds two rat traps, 100 feet of 24-gauge brass snare wire, and 150 yards of 20-pound test braided fishing line. The outside zippered compartment holds all of the readymade Thompson Survival Snares. Although large, this kit provides a wide range of food gathering capability.

Split a pole for a four-tine frog gig. Make a wedge with a point to hold the four tines open. Completed the four-tine frog gig with the center wedge/point, in place.

## Improvised meat gathering

The most basic improvised tool for meat gathering is the spear. However, it is not the easiest to use, especially on small game. If you decide to make a spear, DO NOT tie your knife to a pole to make a spear, as shown in so many books and movies. Use your knife to sharpen the end of the pole. That way, if you throw the spear and lose it (especially if it sticks in an animal and it runs off with it) you haven't lost your most important survival tool, outside of your brain. You still have a knife to make another spear.

When you carve a point onto the end of a spear, in order to make the point harder, fire-harden it over the coals of a fire. Don't stick the point into the coals, but hold it over, and above, the coals. Keep turning the pole so that all sides get heated and hardened. You don't want the point so close to the coals that it catches fire. You want to heat it until it turns dark brown, which must be done slowly.

If you didn't put a commercially made frog gig in your kit, you might want to make one in the field. There are various techniques to do this. I have seen people split a pole one way, then the other, so they have four in-dividual tines at the end. Then they place a small stick between the first split and then the other. This spreads the four tines out. Be sure to wrap behind the splits with cordage to keep the pole from splitting further when spreading with the sticks.

Throwing sticks are quick, easily-made weapons that will take down small game.

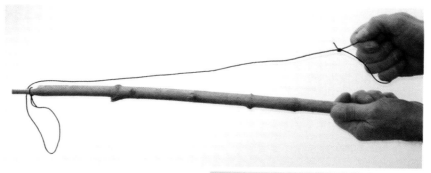

When I make a four-pronged frog gig, I split the pole twice as well. But, I then carve a quick pointed stick with square sides at the back, to use as a wedge. After wrapping behind the initial splits, I then use the pointed wedge to spread the four tines. This provides a center point on the frog gig to help hold the frog in place.

A throwing stick is another quick and easy weapon that will take down small game. It can simply be a stick of adequate weight that can be thrown at an animal, or a curved piece of wood (much like a boomerang) where you carve down the front and back side to give it a little more aerodynamics.

A noose stick can be made quickly with a small stick and some cordage. A noose stick works best on birds, such as grouse, lizards, other reptiles and snakes. I have seen them very effective to catch lizards. I was in the transition zone between the Mojave Desert and the San Bernardino Mountains in California with Lance Canterbury, Dave Canterbury's son. He had just gotten out of the Army after returning from overseas. He was catching lizards like crazy using just a noose stick.

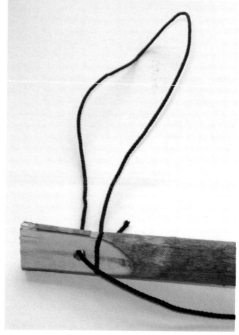

Make a noose stick with a pull for tightening the noose.

One way is to make a slipknot in one end of the cordage and tie the other end of the cordage to the end of a stick. When you slip the noose over the head, you quickly raise the stick closing the slipknot noose around the neck.

The second way is to slightly flatten one end of a stick with a knife. Then using an awl, or other means, make a small hole completely through the stick. Now tie one end of cordage to the end of the stick just behind the hole. Then place the other end of the cordage through the hole. Leaving a loop in the cordage, when you get the head of your target in the noose, you pull the end of the cordage that went through the hole. This also works well using snare wire instead of cordage, which is what I prefer for snakes.

## Traps and snares

Because of the scope of this book, it would be difficult to address traps and snares in a complete manner. However, we will discuss the basics so you have a general idea about how to make and place general traps and snares. Keep in mind that this is another one of those areas where hands-on training and practice is important in order to be proficient in the techniques discussed. Many books on survival devote a large section to traps and snares, yet few people are effective using them. I don't mean to say that these devices cannot be effective, but just because you set them out doesn't mean you will catch something.

First, let's discuss the legalities. The use of traps and snares is illegal in most situations, and should only be used for emergency survival. Be warned, each state has its own regulations. In New York State, even with a trapping license, snares cannot be used for trapping and you may not set a trap in such a manner that it causes a captured animal to be fully suspended in the air.

So if you are going to practice the making of traps or snares, take them down after you practice triggering them, so they don't catch a neighbors pet. A student once asked what would happen in a survival situation if an official of a government department regulating trapping caught them trapping. I stated that they would probably be taken to a warm place, given a phone call and possibly a warm meal. Survival situation over! In a survival situation, only you can make the decision in regard to how you will stay alive.

There are three major methods for traps and snares. They are as follows:

**Crush** – The animal is crushed when a heavy object such as a log, rock, etc. falls on it.

**Strangle** - The animal is strangled when a snare or other type noose is tightened around the neck.

**Hold** - The an animal is held in place by some type of a containers, such as a box, hole, etc.

In a survival situation I prefer the first two, crushing or strangling. With a hold trap, you never know what you might catch, and you have to be willing to kill it once you do. Just because you are trying to catch a squirrel or rabbit doesn't mean a larger animal might not get caught by the foot.

A trap or snare can be active or passive. An active trap or snare is considered active if it attracts an animal to it, such as a baited trap, or because it is activated by a trigger of some type.

A passive trap or snare is one that does not use bait to lure an animal to it, nor does not use a trigger. These traps or snares are often used for animals that have regular pathways.

The placement of traps and snares is also important. Try to disturb the area around a trap or snare as little as possible. Use well-traveled trails, and try to funnel the animal's travel into the trap or snare. You can use surrounding vegetation, logs, rocks, etc. to get the animal to move directly into the trap or snare. Make them strong and camouflage them as well as you can. Avoid removing any more bark than necessary (they don't have to be pretty, just functional), and in areas where bark has been removed, rub with dirt. If available, use gloves so that you avoid leaving your scent on the traps or snares. Keep in mind that with traps and snares, there is strength in numbers. The more you set out, the greater chance you have of catching something. Don't think that the setting of just one will yield you a meal.

### Crushing traps

I will only cover two crushing traps, one without cordage and the other with cordage. The first is the Figure Four Deadfall, which is my favorite, as you don't need cordage. This can be built with only three sticks and a knife, yet it is very effective. Basically you have an upright, with an

A Figure Four Trap crusher trap is built using two logs and two uprights, and is usually placed across a game trail.

angled stick, and a cross stick, and when put together they resemble a "4". It is held together with a series of notches that is held together from the weight of the rock, log, etc. used as the crusher.

The next crushing trap is a Paiute Deadfall. Basically it uses only two sticks, a toggle and a piece of cordage. The angled stick is held in place with a short piece of cordage tied to a toggle. When the cordage is wrapped around the upright, a trigger stick is wedged between the toggle and the crusher.

### Strangle traps

Strangle traps use a looped piece of wire or cordage tied so that it will slide closed under tension, such as when an animal tries to pass through it. This type of trap is called a snare. My preference is wire and the various types have been discussed above.

Snares should be positioned off the ground so that an animal's head will pass through the loop but the animal's body will not. This will cause the loop to tighten around the animal's neck, causing strangulation.

Place the loop at an approximate height that the animal's head will be. You can't just use any height hoping to catch just any animal. You need a general idea of what type of animal you are going after.

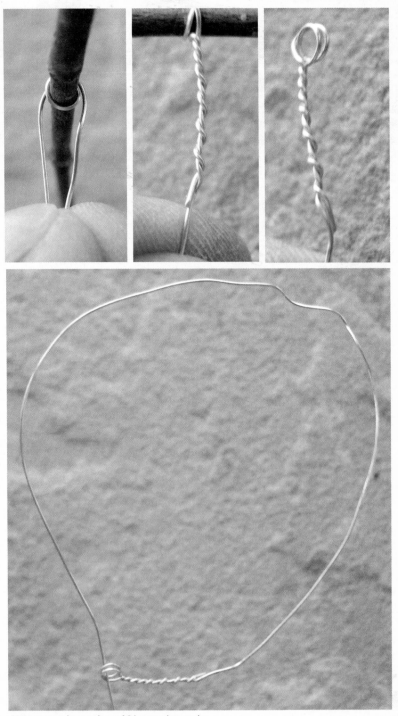

Make a snare from a piece of 24-gauge brass wire.

Prop the snare using two small uprights and two blades of grass.

First, make a looped snare. Using wire from your kit, wrap the end of a piece of wire, about one or 1.5 inches, around a very small stick twice, then spin the stick so that the end wraps around the remaining piece. Break off the stick and you now have a double loop through which you pass the other end of the wire. It is that easy.

There are various ways to prop a snare so that it stays where you want it, and this is an area where creativity comes into play. One of my favorite ways to prop a snare in position is using two blades of grass. Using a small stick as an upright on each side of the snare, use your knife and cut down on the stick making a grove, leaving the small cut piece in place. Use one piece of grass on each side, wrapping it around the snare loop, and bring it back on itself. Then slide the blade of grass into the slot you made in the upright to hold it in place. This technique allows you to use a natural source, the blade of grass, and, although it holds the loop in place, it will easily break away when the animal passes through the loop.

Wire snares can also be attached directly to logs or other obstacles that you know an animal travels over. A squirrel run can be made on a log that leans against a tree. I have often studied these in the woods and you will notice that a squirrel uses a log to get up a tree, as it is a shorter distance than going to the ground and up. A leaning log that has squirrel traffic is an ideal spot to place a bunch of snares at different angles. As the squirrel tries to navigate up the log, it will most likely pass through one of the snares.

This can also be done on a log that crosses over a stream. Squirrels and other animals use logs to get from one side to the other. Just make sure that the log is high enough from the surface of the water so that an animal caught in a snare will not hang into the water.

### Spring poles

If you are in an area where you are competing with other animals for food, use a means to raise the animal you caught in a snare, up and off the ground. These types of snares are called twitch-ups, spring poles, spring snares and branch lifts. For the purpose of this book, when I talk about the engine that raises the caught animal, I will call it a spring pole.

The engine that raises the animal doesn't have to be a branch or spring pole. It can be a large log or rock tied to a piece of cordage that goes up and over the branch of a tree, or even a seesaw type engine that has weight on one end and raises the animal when caught. If you do use a sapling as your spring pole, make sure you clean all the limbs off it, as it will spring up much faster when it is bare. Also keep in mind that, if you do not have a green sapling next to an animal run where you want to place a snare, you can cut a sapling and tie it to a larger tree next to the animal run. Tie the bottom, wide portion securely to a tree using stout cordage like parachute cord. Now bend the top portion over for your engine, just as if you had a sapling where you wanted it.

A two-pin toggle is one option to trigger a spring pole.

A rolling snare trigger is another option to trigger a spring pole.

For the spring pole to raise the animal after it is caught in the snare loop, you need some type of trigger. There are hundreds of triggers, but in order to give you an idea of the simplicity of some triggers, I will show only a few. Keep in mind – and this is important – the snare wire must always be connected to the part of the trigger that is attached to the spring pole engine. Otherwise, when the trigger disengages, the spring pole will go up but the animal won't.

The first trigger is a two-pin toggle, which just uses two carved pieces of wood that mate

Figure "H" trigger for a spring pole.

A baited spring leg trigger for a spring pole.

and are held together by the upward pressure from the engine. The snare wire and the cordage going to the engine are both secured to the top piece of the two-pin toggle. When an animal is caught in the snare, the movement disengages the two toggles and the snare is raised up by the engine. It is simple to make.

The next trigger is called a rolling snare and uses two "Y" branches. One is cut with one long side, which can be pounded securely in the ground. The other piece has one part of the Y stick slightly longer than the other. The cordage going to the engine is attached to the second Y stick, as well as the snare wire. The upward pressure of the engine holds the trigger in place. When there is movement one Y will roll off the other, disengaging the trigger and the engine will raise the animal.

The third trigger is the Figure "H". This trigger uses two uprights pounded in the ground with a notch on the top side of each one. When pounded in the ground, you face one in one direction of the animal trail, and the other notch in the opposite direction. A stick that stretches across the width of both uprights is used to attach the snare and the spring pole. When the spring pole is pulled down, you engage one side of the cross stick in one of the notches, and the opposite end in the other notch. The upward pressure of the spring pole holds the cross stick in place. The purpose of a notch in the uprights facing in opposite directions is so the snare can be triggered in either direction. If both notches were on one side, it would only be a one direction snare, and you never know what direction the animal will come from.

A two-pin toggle trigger can be used in conjunction with a spring pole. Note that the snare is positioned over the animal trail, but not the trigger. The diagram also shows a stationary snare over a trail, which should only be used if there is no concern for predators taking your catch. Diagram courtesy of J. Wayne Fears.

The last trigger I will discuss is the baited spring leg. This trigger is a little more elaborate than the previous ones, but it is one of my students' favorites and is often selected when they must go out and build a spring pole snare setup.

The baited spring leg needs a good size "Y" stick, whereby both ends of the Y must be pounded into the ground. Another piece of wood, called the bait stick, must be long enough to reach across both sides of the Y stick in the ground, and stick out one end to drape the snare over, or under (I prefer over). A third piece of wood, called the toggle stick (which both the snare and engine is connected to) is used to hold the bait stick in place. It is placed through the Y stick, with one end of the toggle placed against the Y stick, and the other end placed against the bait stick. Remember that when the toggle stick is passed under the Y stick, both the cordage attached to the spring pole and the snare wire must remain on the side you passed through from. If you have the spring pole cordage on one side and the snare wire on the other, when it triggers, the animal will be pulled against the Y stick and will not be raise up with the spring pole.

## Extreme caution advised

Whenever using any type of a spring pole engine to lift a animal, use extreme caution when setting the trigger. Keep your face and other body parts out of the line of pull. If the trigger is activated, even by accident while trying to set it up, the trigger will be pulled up at a high rate of speed. The flying trigger can poke out an eye or otherwise injure a body part. When experimenting with these things, wear safety glasses.

Many people are killed by lightning while participating in outdoor activities. Avoid the base of trees and water if lightning occurs. In an open field, insulate yourself from the ground by sitting on your pack.

©iStockphoto.com/dimabl.

*Chapter 11*

# Wilderness Hazards & Safety

**S**urvival skills keep you alive and get you back home safely. But while you are out there trying to survive, many hazards might befall you that can make your situation worse. There are also health, medical, and safety issues that might need to be addressed to ensure you return in one piece. Let's look at some of these issues.

## Environmental hazards

### Weather

Weather can present a major hazard in a survival situation. Thunderstorms can be dangerous: lightning can kill. The two major hazardous areas during a lightning storm are the base of lone standing trees, open fields and open water. If the lightning starts, keep away from both.

Storms can also cause flashfloods, which is one of the reasons you don't build a shelter in a run-off area. Storms can also make you wet, and with wind, can cause a hypothermic situation.

Extreme cold and wind chill can rob your body of heat. Extreme heat can cause heat related injuries from hyperthermia. Keep an eye on the weather. Don't let mother nature throw you a curve.

### Carbon monoxide

Carbon monoxide is a danger when you have a fire in an enclosed space. This includes a vehicle, cabin, tent or even a survival shelter. Where there is combustion, even just a candle burning, make sure you have a source of fresh air. Oftentimes in a survival situation, survivors become so concerned with keeping the cold out that they forget about ventilation.

Carbon monoxide is an odorless, tasteless, colorless gas that is known as the "silent killer." It is produced by burning material containing carbon. Carbon monoxide poisoning can cause brain damage and death. You can't see it, smell it, or taste it, but carbon monoxide can kill you.

Early symptoms of carbon monoxide poisoning, such as headaches, nausea, and fatigue, are often mistaken for the flu because the deadly gas goes undetected. However, it usually gives no warning (although if you see a small flame, like a candle, start to burn poorly, it should alert you to a lack of oxygen, which means lack of ventilation).

When you are in a small area, such as a shelter, make sure you maintain good ventilation if you have a flame present. You may not be as warm as you would like, but you will be alive in the morning.

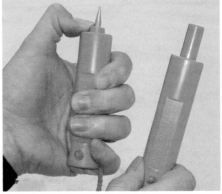

### Crossing ice

Traveling on or near ice is always dangerous. If possible, avoid it. If you must cross over it, use extreme caution. Try to check how solid it is if you can do so safely. If you must pass over ice, carry a stout pole. Use it to test the ice in front of you. If you

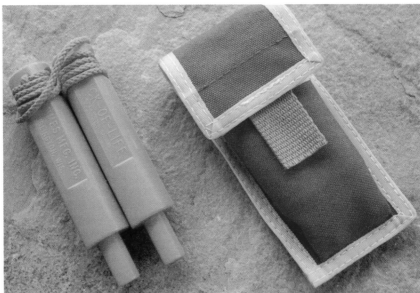

With MARSARS Ice Awls, the plastic shroud retracts into the handle to reveal the metal awls. The Ice Awls come with an attached cord and a belt pouch.

fall through, you can also use the pole as a bridge across the hole to keep you from being completely submerged in the water. You can also use a knife, or whatever you have, to dig into the ice to help pull yourself out.

If you know you will be near ice, you should carry ice awls. They were designed so, if you fall through the ice, they become a self-rescue device that allows you to pull yourself onto and across unstable ice. The ice awls have a metal pick in each handle. The awls (picks) are surrounded by plastic shrouds which retract into the handles each time the handles are pressed into the ice. They are made by MARSARS Water Rescue Systems, Inc. (www.icerescue.marsars.com), and come in a cordura belt pouch, so they are on you when you need them. I have had a pair for years and they are in my winter survival kit.

## Crossing water

Crossing water can be another hazardous activity. The first thing you should do is make sure this is what you need to do. Is it absolutely necessary? Check around (if you have a map use it) and make sure there is not a bridge over the water in the vicinity. Is there a large log which can be used for crossing? Always look for an alternative to actually getting in the water.

If you must cross, look for the best place to cross. Always assume there are hidden dangers, even if the water appears slow moving and calm. Even though water appears clear, there may be obstacles you can't see.

Begin by studying the character of the water in order to determine the best possible place to cross. If you can, try to cross between bends, and not at bends, as water flows the fastest at the outside of bends. Slow moving water is usually deeper than fast water, but can contain hazards such as weeds, mud, rocks or other hidden obstacles. Avoid areas where the bank is undercut, as

Water crossings are always potentially dangerous. Your best bet may be to find another place to safely cross.
©iStockphoto.com/Adventure_Photo.

it will make it difficult to climb back on shore. Also avoid any debris that could entangle you. The choice is not always easy, but give it some thought before you wade in.

There are various ways to cross water, but when alone, make sure you have a stout pole. Wear footwear even if you must later dry it out. You don't want a cut or broken foot, and you will need a firm footing. If you are wearing a pack, make sure you disconnect the waist strap and loosen the straps. If you fall in, you want to be able to get rid of the pack quickly so it doesn't pull you under.

As you cross, face upstream and use the pole as a third leg, leaning into the pole. This makes you a tripod and more steady. While leaning toward the pole, slowly move one foot sideways across the current, being careful not to let the current force your leg backwards. Slide the foot, don't lift it. When it is securely back down and steady, move the next foot in the same manner. Move at an angle downstream, although you are facing upstream. This way you are not fighting the current as much as if you were trying to move into it.

If you do fall into the water, try to stay on your back with your feet facing downstream. Try to keep your toes up out of the water so your feet don't get snagged on anything, and steer yourself towards a shore.

You don't want to tangle with these guys! ©iStockphoto.com/gbrundin.

## Agressive wildlife

There are many animals, snakes, etc. in the outdoors. Especially in a survival situation, be cautious of the hazards involved. Don't take chances with any animal; avoidance is the safest bet.

There is a lot of information available for dealing with bears in the outdoors, so I advise you to do some further research in regard to the subject. Some basics are, normally, if you don't bother them, they won't bother you (but there are no guarantees). Don't surprise a bear and NEVER get between a mother and her cubs. Make noise when in bear country to avoid surprising them. Talk, whistle, sing, carry a cup and spoon dangling from a pack, or even some stones in a can. Make sure they can hear you coming. Don't keep food in or near your shelter or camp, as it will attract them.

If a bear becomes aggressive (such as clicking its teeth or mouth), back away slowly, acting calm and talking in a normal voice. Try to look bigger than you are, such as raising your arms (but don't act aggressive). Back away slowly and leave the area. Never run, as a bear can run about 30 miles per hour and you can't.

If you are attacked by a grizzly, some experts suggest that you get in a fetal position, cover your head and neck and play dead. If attacked by a black bear, they say this won't work. Fight with whatever you have for as long as you can. Don't give up or, you lose.

An often encountered hazard is snakes. They are not all poisonous, but many are. If you can't identify a poisonous snake from a non-poisonous snake, it shouldn't matter in a survival situation: avoid all snakes. Keep your distance and don't play with them. Don't reach over or under things where you can't see the other side. Don't step over logs without looking on the other side. If you go after a snake for food, that is your choice. My only advice is always have control of the head, as that is the part that will bite you.

A rattlesnake is the most easily identified snake as it has a rattle, but keep in mind that just because it doesn't rattle doesn't mean it isn't a rattlesnake, as the rattle could be broken off. Avoid snakes in the wilderness whenever possible. ©iStockphoto.com/SteveMcsweeny.

## Poisonous plants

We talked earlier about poisonous edible plants and the associated dangers. But some plants can be dangerous without eating them. These plants present a hazard from contact, and three of major concern are poison ivy, poison oak and poison sumac. All three produce a allergic reaction because they contain urushiol, an oil which attaches itself to the skin with exposure. Symptoms include rashes, oozing blisters, itching and swelling.

Urushiol does not spread on its own. It spreads with your help, by scratching where it itches and then touching another part of your body. In extreme cases, immediate medical attention is needed. The best course of action, however, is total awareness of your surroundings and avoiding

Poison Ivy

**Poison Oak** ©iStockphoto.com/devdogg.

**Poison Sumac** Photo courtesy of Samuel Thayer.

contact with these plants. If you have come in contact with plants containing urushiol, as quickly as possible wash off the affected area with cold water and some sort of scrubbing soap, such as Zanfel, if available in your kit. Keep in mind, that if you have come in contact with the plants, chances are good your clothes and gear are carriers of the oil, so wash them as soon as the opportunity presents itself. If you know the plant Jewelweed, a folk remedy is to rub the juice from the stem on poison ivy rash, which reduces the itch.

## Stinging insects

What I mean by stinging insects is bees, yellow jackets, hornets, and other wasps. These flying insects can be a real problem. Many build nests in trees and look like roundish grey paper balls. However, yellow jackets also build nests in the ground. Often you won't notice them until you step on them. They are very aggressive and if their nest is threatened they will swarm out and attack.

When one of these bees, yellow jackets, hornets or other wasps stings you, it injects venom under your skin. Under normal circumstances, if a person is not allergic, the venom will only produce some burning and then some itching and reddening of the skin. If you carry After-Bite, this would be the time to use it.

However, some people are allergic to this venom, and a sting could cause anaphylaxis, also known as anaphylactic shock. Anaphylaxis is a severe allergic reaction that occurs rapidly and causes a life-threatening response involving the whole body. This reaction can lead to difficulty breathing and shock, ultimately leading to death.

If you are concerned that you are allergic, or know you are, never travel without a preloaded syringe of epinephrine, called an Epi-Pen. You usually need a prescription from your doctor to purchase these. It has also been suggested that, even though you have used an Epi-Pen, you should also take diphenhydramine, such as Benadryl. If in doubt, check with your doctor.

## Biting bugs

Various biting bugs can cause discomfort ranging from minor irritation to long term problems. Primary offenders include mosquitoes, black flies, ticks and chiggers.

Mosquitoes are little buzzing, biting insects that thrive near standing water. Some species bite at dawn and dusk, and others prefer midday. A strong breeze can help keep them at bay. Try to

Wasps build nests that hang from small bushes or trees. ©iStockphoto.com/MarvinBeatty.

wear colors than blend into the environment, as mosquitoes recognize contrast of light and dark and can find you in that manner. The mosquito is a potential carrier of diseases, such as malaria, encephalitis, yellow fever, West Nile virus and many others.

Probably the worst biting insect out in the wilds is the black fly. It is smaller than the mosquito and flourishes wherever it can breed in unpolluted moving water. They are especially thick in pristine northern locations such as Maine, Upper Michigan, and in my experience, the Adirondacks in New York. Unlike the mosquito that uses a needlelike proboscis to suck blood from its victim, a black fly gnaws a hole in your skin and sips the blood that pools there. They are abundant throughout late spring and summer, with the worst months being May and June. The bites are much more irritating than the mosquito and not only itch, but can be painful and cause sores.

Because of Lyme Disease, ticks have become a major concern. Specifically, deer ticks transmit this disease, and they are very small and difficult to see. Wear long pants and tuck them into your socks to prevent ticks from crawling up your legs. Light colored clothing makes them easier to see, and the use of DEET helps to protect your skin from them. At least once a day, check your body thoroughly (as previously indicated, they are very small), especially at your hairline, armpits, groin and behind your knees. Keep in mind that they can bite anywhere. Every kit should have a pair of fine-tipped tweezers for the removal of ticks. Studies have shown that it takes 36-48 hours for the Lyme bacteria to infect you, so be diligent and check every day. A bull's-eye shaped circular rash with a clear center around the bite can occur (but doesn't always) three to 30 days after infection. Symptoms can include flu-like symptoms, fatigue, headache, muscle and joint pain and swollen glands. Don't mess around with Lyme Disease, as it can cause some very bad long term effects. If in doubt, go to a doctor as there are several test that can determine if you have it.

Last, but not least, are chiggers. Chiggers, which are also know as harvest mites or red bugs, are essentially invisible without a magnifying glass. They produce an agonizing itchy red welt. They are so small you don't really notice the biting until about 12 - 24 hours later when you notice the rash and itching. They don't really bite you in the normal sense, but attach themselves to your skin and inject saliva with digestive enzymes that assist with breaking down your skin cells, which they drink. It is the enzymes they inject that cause the itchy rash. Chiggers can be easily brushed off and are often knocked off when you begin itching. You can also knock them off when washing or showering (something not often accomplished in a survival situation).

The best way to prevent being bitten is to carry bug repellent with a high concentration of DEET in all of your kits. A head net and a sleeping net for night can provide further protection. Wear long sleeves and keep as much of your skin covered as possible.

## Basic medical considerations

First, this is a book on basic survival skills. It was not intended to be a medical or first aid guide. As with all the skills previously discussed, reading only provides you with basic information, it does not provide you with the hands-on expertise, which particularly in the first aid area, is necessary to become proficient. I highly recommend that you participate in a course such as the Red Cross Wilderness First Aid course. This book IS NOT a substitute for a First Aid Course.

The first problem with a survival situation is you are often alone, which makes self diagnosis and treatment difficult. Secondly, the situation is often made more difficult by the lack of equipment available to assist you in dealing with the problem. Therefore, let's discuss first aid kits. They can be as small or elaborate as you are willing to carry. I find that I carry different sized medical kits based on the size of my survival kits. In a mini kit, you won't have many options. I normally just carry some butterfly bandages and a packet or two of antibiotic ointment. Not a lot to work with, but you work with what you have. As my kits get bigger, I add more items.

Cuts and burns are a primary concern. Sprains are another common occurrence. I have been fortunate never to have had a sprain, hopefully as a result of my choice to always wear high top boots.

I like to carry combine pads and rolls of gauze to stop the bleeding. I also carry a package of Steri-Strips instead of butterfly bandages in all kits above a mini. These are superior to butterfly bandages for closing large cuts. I carry antibiotic ointment to prevent infection, Benadryl in case of an allergic reaction, Imodium as an anti-diarrheal medicine, and a pain reliever. I

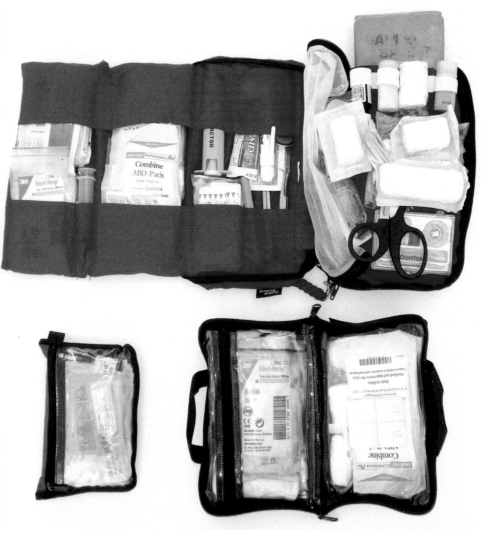

The size of the survival kit dictates what size first aid kit will be carried. Carry as much as you can afford.

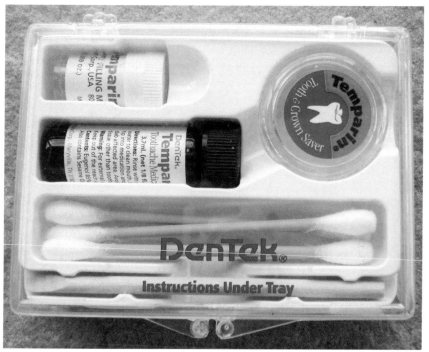

A commercially available emergency dental kit is small enough to fit in many first aid kits.

also carry tick tweezers, burn pads, an ace bandage, some blister pads and some extreme length and knuckle bandages. Of course there is more in my larger kits, but this rounds out small and medium kits.

One often neglected area is the teeth. Carry a dental repair kit in all kits that will hold one. A tooth problem in the wilderness can be a larger problem than one might imagine. Be prepared for the unexpected.

If you do not feel you are qualified to put together your own first aid kit, then buy a good one from a reputable company. I highly recommend Adventure Medical Kits, and they are well respected in the survival community. They have various sized kits designed for various concerns and various lengths of time. You can check them out at www.adventuremedicalkits.com. However, just because you buy a kit doesn't mean you should just throw it in your kit until you need it. Check it out and make sure you have the items you want. You might need to add an item or two to make it yours. Again, a first aid kit does not replace medical knowledge. Get training before you need it.

Last but not least, if a medical situation occurs, keep a positive mental attitude, and don't panic. Remember the lessons from the chapter on survival mentality.

While every effort has been made to give you a fighting chance, a survival situation might still include a medical emergency. Because of that possibility, let's cover basic first-aid for the most common outdoor injuries the lone survivor might experience. Please understand, the following information is NOT meant to replace real medical aid or training, but rather give the would be survivor a chance to stay in the fight longer until rescued.

## Hypothermia

Hypothermia is one of those threats that lies in wait, ready to ambush the survivor. Unfortunately, if the early warning signs are not heeded, you can slip into a more severe form of hypothermia that can lead to death. Caught early, hypothermia can be treated without too much difficulty. However, knowing and acting on the early warning signs is key.

Without some sort of thermometer that measures for hypothermia, you must rely on other methods of diagnosis. For mild hypothermia, use the mnemonics known as the "UMBLES."

A mild hypothermic person:

Fumbles (loss of fine motor skills)

Stumbles (loss of gross motor skills)

Tumbles (loss of gross motor skills)

Mumbles (intellectual impairment)

Grumbles (intellectual impairment)

The umbles are progressive in nature. The last two, mumbles and grumbles, show intellectual impairment which is a sign of slipping into a more severe form of hypothermia. Obviously, there are situations where you need to act quickly without measuring the level of hypothermia. Falling through the ice, taking a plunge into a cold river and getting soaked in a downpour are all situations in which you should begin to take steps to avoid hypothermia.

First, remove the threat. If you fall into freezing water, for instance, get out as quickly as possible and change into some dry clothes. Next, wrap yourself in an emergency blanket, if you have one, and get a fire going to help warm you. If possible drink warm water sweetened with the sugar from your kit. The sugar is almost more important than the water itself, as it creates a quick source of energy your body can use internally to help re-warm the core. Try and perform some sort of aerobic activity that will help generate warmth, such as running in place. The addition of using your arms is even better.

## Frostbite

In cold climates hypothermia is not the only threat. Frostbite, especially of the fingers, can almost make it impossible to survive due to the lack of feeling and inability to perform basic skills. Burning, itching, numbness, tingling or cold sensations (in the affected areas) are all signs of early frostbite. If left untreated, deep frostbite is possible. Decreased sensation, swelling, blood-filled blisters and white or yellowish skin that looks waxy are signs of deeper frostbite. Another sign is the skin turns a purplish color as it re-warms.

If you become a victim of frostbite, take off any items that may constrict blood flow, such as jewelry. Elevate the affected part above the level of the heart to help reduce swelling. Do not rub the affected areas, as it can lead to further tissue damage. Rapid re-warming of the affected area, for about 15 to 30 minutes, in hot water running about 104 degrees (but no hotter than 110 degrees) is the accepted method of treatment. Be prepared to take some sort of pain medication, as the treatment is painful. It is critical that, once you have thawed the frostbite, you do not allow it to refreeze again, as this can lead to further tissue damage.

## Trench foot

Prolonged exposure to cold wet conditions can lead to trenchfoot, a condition where the skin begins to break down. Even sweating of the feet in a cold environment can lead to trench foot. Signs include burning and tingling of the feet. Affected areas of the foot can appear gray and blotchy, and blisters and redness in the skin are also common when continuously exposed to the cold. Injured feet should be elevated and exposed to cool air. Exposure to cool air should be continued until the pain is relieved. Taking off your shoes and socks and allowing your feet to air out at least once a day is helpful to prevent trench foot.

## Snow blindness

If you expose the unprotected eye to the glare of snow, it can cause snow blindness. Always wear some type of dark glasses when out in the snow, as this can also occur on cloudy days. If nothing else, at least carry emergency sunglasses. Another thing you can use is a strip from your emergency blanket. Most people don't know you can look through these blankets. Just cut a strip and tie it around your face, and you should be able to look right through it.

If all else fails and you can find a white birch tree (paper birch can provide you with a real nice thin piece), you can make snow goggles. Cut a strip the width of your face, and cut two long slots about 1/8-inch high for your eyes. Below this in the center, make a slot for your nose. Some people cut a triangle shape to set over their nose, but this leaves your nose exposed to the sun, and sunburn. I cut a slit on each side of the nose, then carefully fold this flap up, bending the sides of this flap around the sides of my nose. This type of goggle can also be made from a piece of leather, cardboard or other material.

Make goggles from birch bark to protect your eyes from snow blindness.

## Hyperthermia

Heat cramps, heat exhaustion and heatstroke are all heat injuries associated with hyperthermia. If you begin to experience a headache, nausea, dizziness, weakness, stomach or leg cramps, thirst or are sweating profusely, you might be experiencing a heat related injury. As previously indicated in this book, if left untreated, it can lead to heat stroke and even death.

If you experience any of these signs, get out of the sun and into the shade, immediately. Loosen up your clothing. Better yet, take off your shirt and allow yourself to lose heat through convection and radiation, lay down on a cool surface to help with conductive heat loss. Elevate your legs about 12 inches off the ground. If possible, apply cool, not cold, water to your body to help promote evaporative cooling. Lie still and do not move anymore than you have to. You do not need to generate anymore heat with excessive body movement. If it's available, drink water slowly, and if available, add electrolytes.

## Dehydration

Water is essential for our bodies to function properly. All too often, we become so consumed with activity that we forget to keep hydrated, even if water is available. Usually, by the time you feel thirsty you're already dehydrated. The risk of dehydration also increases if you have diarrhea or are vomiting. The color of your urine is a good indicator to determine if you're dehydrated or not. If your urine is running yellow, chances are you're dehydrated. The darker the color, the more severe the condition of dehydration you're experiencing.

The Skin Turgor Test you can perform to evaluate your level of hydration. To perform the test, grasp the skin on the back of the hand and hold for a few seconds. Skin with normal turgor snaps back rapidly to its normal position when released. Skin with decreased turgor returns slowly to its normal position. Decreased skin turgor is a late sign in dehydration. It occurs with moderate to severe dehydration. Keep in mind, if you are old like me, your skin doesn't have the elasticity that it does when you're young, so this test might not be as accurate on older people.

The only solution to fending off dehydration is to keep hydrated. Avoid excessive activity when it is hot out. If there is no water, do not eat and avoid consuming caffeinated or alcoholic beverages as they lead to further dehydration.

## Hyponatremia

Hyponatremia is the condition where excessive water intake flushes the sodium from your blood, thus inhibiting the proper function of your body. The National Library of Medicine, National Institutes of Health, reports hyponatremia as the most common electrolyte disorder in the United States.

Many of the signs and symptoms can be confused with dehydration and heat related injuries. Fatigue, irritability, loss of appetite, muscle cramps, nausea, restlessness and, vomiting are all signs and symptoms of possible hyponatremia.

If you are experiencing any of those symptoms but your urine is clear and the turgor test shows normal, you may be exhibiting signs of hyponatremia. Immediately restrict fluid intake, rest, and attempt to consume anything you have with salt to try and replenish sodium levels.

## Open wounds

No matter how careful you may be, at some point you may experience a bleeding wound. The first thing to do is stop the bleeding by applying direct pressure and elevating the wound above the level of the heart, until the bleeding has stopped.

The preferred method is to apply direct pressure to the wound with your hand and a thick cloth pad, such as a sterile gauze, but use what you have. Hold for about five minutes, and slowly release the pressure. If the bleeding has not stopped, continue for another fifteen minutes. If the dressing you are using becomes soaked with blood, do not remove, as removing can disturb clotting of the blood, which is what you want. Just place another dressing over the first and reapply pressure. If you have an ace bandage in your first aid kit, it can be used to maintain the pressure on the dressing, freeing your hands for other purposes.

Once the bleeding has stopped, it is extremely important to keep the wound clean and free of dirt, in order to help prevent an infection. Clean the wound with mild soap and water, apply some anti-bacterial ointment and apply a clean dressing from your first-aid kit. Because you're in a dirty environment and risk infection, it is a good idea to check and clean the wound once a day (more times may be needed), reapply anti-bacterial ointment, and apply new, clean dressing.

I don't recommend suturing in the field, or even the use of super glue. Doing so runs the risk of trapping infection-causing bacteria in the wound. As previously stated, my preference is Steri-Strips.

If the wound is on an extremity and the bleeding WILL NOT STOP by the use of direct pressure and elevation *and* a threat to life is apparent, you have a final option – the tourniquet. Understand, however, once you have chosen to use a tourniquet, you have made a conscious decision and clearly understand that you risk losing your limb in order to save your life.

NEVER use a tourniquet on a neck, around the abdomen, chest, or head. Tourniquets are only used to control bleeding at the extremities, and only if you're willing to possibly lose the limb. If that choice is made, the following is the procedure.

**1.** A tourniquet should be, at minimum, two inches wide, three to four inches is better. Anything smaller can result in tissue damage at the tourniquet site.

**2.** Place the touriguet two inches above the wound site, never directly over the wound, and never directly over a joint, such as an elbow or knee. If the elbow or knee is two inches above the wound site, apply the tourniquet above the joint.

**3.** Tighten the tourniquet until the bleeding stops.

**4.** In case of an amputation, leave the tourniquet in place, DO NOT REMOVE! If the tourniquet is being used on a non-amputation, release slowly after a few minutes to see whether or not bleeding can now be controlled via direct pressure and dressing. If the bleeding persists, re-apply tourniquet.

## Antibacterial alternative

Antibacterial ointment is an important aspect of wound care. However, you may find yourself in a survival situation without some sort of antibacterial product. If it happens, you may still have an alternative in you arsenal of gear – sugar!

Sugar, like honey, is hygroscopic and, through osmosis, kills bacteria. To use, you place it directly on wound. When the sugar on the wound begins to liquefy and turns into a glazed runny substance, it is losing its hygroscopic ability along with its bacteria killing osmotic pressure. Clean thoroughly and reapply sugar. This may have to be repeated several times.

## Burns

First degree burns, such as a sunburn, can be dealt with relatively easily. Applying a cool, wet, sheet of cloth helps cool down the burn. Do not apply pressure to the cloth against the skin. Just let it sit on the surface loosely. You may also consider taking an over-the-counter pain killer to help ease the pain. Typically this type of burn will heal in about a week.

Second degree burns affect not only the epidermis (outer layer of skin), but also the dermis (underlying layer of skin). These are more serious and care should be taken in how they are treated. Many times, blisters develop with second degree burns. Aside from providing the same type of care you would with a first degree burn, it is important to not pop the blister. Blisters, as long as they remain intact, provide a sterile environment. If the blister pops on its own, as best as possible cut away the loose skin that made up the blister and clean the affected area. Apply some sort of antibacterial ointment and loosely cover the affected area to prevent dirt and bacteria from entering the wound. Because you are out in the wilderness away from help, it is important to check the wound at least once a day for possible infection. Make sure you keep the wound clean, moist and reapply the antibacterial ointment during every check for infection.

A third degree burn is very serious and the site may look charred. Cover the area to keep air out, and in this case, you will need to seek medical attention as soon as possible.

## Sprains

A sprain is overstretching of a tendon or ligament. Swelling, tenderness and discoloration are all common signs of a sprain, but may also be a sign of a broken bone. If you can still articulate your foot or wrist, chances are it's only a sprain. Of course, without proper medical evaluation one cannot be 100% sure. Nonetheless, if you feel you have an ankle sprain, do not remove your footwear unless you have lost sensation in your foot or circulation is compromised.

The acronym RICE is used when treating a sprain:

**R**- Rest the injured area.

**I**- Ice the affected area. If this is not possible, a cold wet towel is a good alternative.

**C**- Compression wrap to help stabilize.

**E**- Elevate the affected area.

You may also elect to take an over-the-counter anti-inflammatory, such as ibuprofen, to help ease the pain and help control the swelling.

## Fractures

A fracture is a broken bone. There are two types of fractures: closed or open. Basically, a closed fracture stays under the skin and an open fracture cuts through the skin causing an open wound. You should not try to set a broken bone, instead immobilize it with a splint. Splints can be made from various items from sticks to a rolled blanket. If you have a good size first aid kit, you should carry a SAM splint. The SAM splint is a flexible 4.25x36-inch sandwich of soft aluminum and closed cell polyethylene foam that, when folded in specific ways, creates a rigid yet comfortable splint used to support and immobilize injuries and fractures of the extremities and neck. The SAM splint can be folded for storage or rolled up easily to the size of an "Ace" wrap. With proper care and cleaning, it can be used over and over again.

Of course, there are many other injuries that could occur in a survival situation that we could address. However, as previously stated, this is not a book on first aid and I have merely touched on some of the more prevalent injuries you might encounter. Again, seek professional training to become proficient at dealing with these and other injuries.

## Hygiene

Staying as clean as possible in a survival situation is important! Don't neglect your hygiene, as you need to stay as healthy as you possibly can. If water is available, wash when you can. There are various types of handy wipes and that are sized so they can fit in most survival kits.

Keep your teeth as clean as possible. If you don't have a tooth brush, make one from a stick by chewing on one end until its flat and gives the appearance of a brush. Then use it to clean your teeth as best as you can.

Baking soda is a great multi-purpose item to carry in your kit. It can be used to brush your teeth, as deodorant, to powder your feet and as an antacid. I always carry a small waterproof bottle in my hygiene kit.

Your feet are another important consideration, as you will need them to get yourself out of there. Keep them as clean and dry as you can. In all but the smallest survival kit, try to keep an extra pair of socks. I have been known to vacuum-seal pairs of socks to keep in the bottom of my packs. They are there if I need them.

Keep your bathroom facilities a good distance from your camp and from any water. Carry some biodegradable toilet paper in your kit if you have room. If you need to use something in the field, make sure it isn't poisonous, or your private areas will develop a real rash and itch. If you know the Mullein plant, the leaves are very soft and can be used as a toilet paper substitute. It is known as "nature's Charmin."

## Chapter 12

# Final Thoughts & Resources

his book should not be the ending, but the beginning. As you can see, there is a lot to learn about survival, and it is now up to you to continue your education. You must practice your new learned skills until you own them, not just on a good day, but on any day! Know that you can start a fire or build a shelter in the rain, the wind, the snow, and with one hand. Don't just do it once. Do it until you can do it as an automatic reaction to a situation, which is what you'll need in a survival situation.

Continue your education as it relates to survival. Learn as much as you can from as many sources as you can. We have only touched the tip of the iceberg. There are many more skills to learn that will allow you to exist longer in a survival situation.

We have covered those skills that will get you through the first few days. But if you lose your survival kit, or a situation lasts longer, there are skills that will assist you in doing more things that will make your life more comfortable. These are known as the primitive skills. At our survival school, we start acquainting our students with these skills, along with building basic skills, in the intermediate and advanced courses. They start learning primitive fire making skills to include fire by friction, how to make cordage from plants, how to build containers using bark and wood, etc.

There is so much to learn to really become proficient at the art of survival. I am often called an expert, and I honestly don't like the term. To me, an expert is one who thinks they know it all. They have closed their mind as they feel there is no more to learn. I am, and always will be, a student of survival. I may be an advanced student, but a student none the less. I will never know it all, but will continue on my journey of learning until I leave this great earth. I would rather be considered a professional student than an expert.

Lastly, I would like to mention Mother Nature. In a survival situation, Mother Nature can furnish many of the necessities to survive. However, Mother Nature can also be a powerful force to reckon with, and all the positive things that are offered can turn against us – a double edged sword. If you want to survive in the wilderness, you must live within the bounds of Mother Nature's rules. You must attempt to live in harmony with nature. Like the tall trees in the wind, don't resist nature, but learn to bend with her. By adapting to what nature offers and living within her bounds, you increase your chances of survival. Those who resist, perish!

That said, I offer the following resources to help you to continue your education and assist you in your journey.

## Educational resources

The following list provides educational resources to help you continue your survival education. Keep in mind that learning survival skills can be dangerous and you should make a decision based on that knowledge. If you participate in a survival course, it will be at your own risk. Although the following sources have a good reputation, listing them does not mean the author or the publisher endorse them or their services. Sources are listed in alphabetical order, and not by level of expertise.

## Survival training

The following survival schools have been around for more than a few years and have a good reputation.

Aboriginal Living Skills School, LLC
P.O. Box 3064, Prescott, Arizona 86302
Phone: 928-713-1651
www.alssadventures.com
Cody Lundin: Founder, Director & Lead Instructor
Courses: Both primitive and modern survival skills.

Jack Mountain Bushcraft School
P.O. Box 77, Ashland, Maine 04732
Phone: 207-518-8804
www.jackmtn.com
Tim Smith: Founder & Owner
Courses: Wilderness survival & bushcraft skills.

Randall's Adventure & Training
School of Survival
P.O. Box 51, Blaine, TN 37709
Phone: 865-933-8436
www.jungletraining.com
Mike Perrin: Contact
Courses: Jungle & wilderness survival.

School of Self Reliance
P.O. Box 41834, Eagle Rock, California 90041
www.christophernyerges.com
Christopher Nyerges: Owner, Lead Instructor
Courses: Edible plants, wilderness survival & self-reliance.

Survival Resources
P.O. Box 307, Hyde Park, New York 12538
Phone: 845-471-2434
www.survivalresources.com
www.bepreparedtosurvive.com
John D. McCann: Founder, Chief Instructor
Courses: wilderness survival.

The Pathfinder School, LLC
4402 Shelbyville Road, Indianapolis, Indiana 46237
www.wildernessoutfittersarchery.com
Dave Canterbury: Founder, Chief Instructor
Courses: Wilderness survival, tracking, and trapping.

## Survival events

The following annual events provide survival instruction by various invited instructors that are preeminent in their field. These events are a good place to learn new skills, meet with other people of like interest, and get to know some real good instructors.

DIRTTIME - Survival & Self Reliance

This is an annual event, normally held on the west coast. It is hosted by Christopher Nyerges, Dude McLean, Alan Halcon, and John D. McCann. It provides five days of instruction on various survival (both primitive and modern) techniques, by some of the best instructors in the country. It offers three meals a day (included in the registration fee) as well as a lot of sponsor gear give-a-ways.

For more information: www.dirttime.com

Pathfinder Gathering

This annual event is offered in both the spring and fall and is hosted by Dave Canterbury in Ohio. It provides five days of instruction on various survival (both primitive and modern) techniques, by instructors from various areas in the country.

For more information: www.wildernessoutfittersarchery.com/PF-Gahtering.html

Rabbitstick - Winter Count

These events, Rabbitstick in September near Rexburg, Idaho, and Winter Count in February near Phoenix, Arizona, are the largest and oldest of the contemporary primitive skills gatherings. They are hosted by Backtracks, LLC. If you are into primitive skills, these are events for you.

For more information: www.backtracks.net/

## Edible plants

The following individuals have written books and/or made DVDs, teach edible plants full time, and are well respected in the field. Again, they are listed in alphabetical order, and not by level of expertise.

"Wildman" Steve Brill

Phone: 914-835-2153

www.wildmanstevebrill.com

Steve Brill wrote "Identifying and Harvesting Edible and Medicinal Plants in Wild (and Not So Wild) Places," and is the east coast's best known expert on edible and medicinal plants.

Christopher Nyerges

School of Self Reliance

P.O. Box 41834, Eagle Rock, California 90041

www.christophernyerges.com

Christopher wrote the "Guide to Wild Foods and Useful Plants" and has a DVD called "Useful Plants of the U.S." (as well as many other books on survival). He teaches edible and useful plants, as well as survival skills, full time. If you are on the west coast, I highly recommend attending one of Christopher's classes.

Samuel Thayer

Forager's Harvest

N8757 Breakneck Rd., Birchwood, WI 54817

Phone: 715-354-3509

www.foragersharvest.com

Samuel has written, in my humble opinion, probably two of the best books available on edible plants. "The Forager's Harvest - A Guide to Identifying and Preparing Edible Wild Plants" and "Nature's Garden - A Guide to Identifying, and Preparing Edible Wild Plants" are both full color books and provide an amazing amount of information about harvesting wild edibles. Samuel also has a DVD called "The Forager's Harvest" that covers plants from the book of the same name.

## Informational resources

The following are some informational resources that you might find interesting. Keep in mind, not all resources can be accurate in information provided. Be forewarned.

## Websites

Many websites proclaim that they have the best information available. I have checked out a lot of them and have come to the conclusion that you must be careful with the information they provide. I see the same information, some of it wrong, passed from one site to another as if it were original. Be careful and try to verify information from as many sources as you can. Don't trust information just because it is on the web. That said, there is a tremendous amount of information available, if you look, and verify.

The following sites provide survival information that is well respected.

Equipped To Survive

www.equipped.com

I have already mentioned Doug Ritter in this book, and he is the founder, publisher, and editor of equipped.com. It provides independent reviews and information on outdoor gear and survival equipment and techniques.

Survival Resources

www.survivalresources.com

www.bepreparedto survive.com

845-471-2434

A shameless plug for my own website, but we have a section called "Articles & Tips" with lots of information about survival kits, survival skills, self-reliant living, etc. And you don't have to buy anything.

The following sites provide information that, in my opinion, is not specifically related to survival skills, but may be useful.

NOAA - National Geophysical Data Center

www.ngdc.noaa.gov/geomagmodels/struts/calcDeclination

This site has a calculator that allows you to enter your location, by either zip code or latitude/longitude, and obtain the current magnetic declination for that area. Great for updating those maps you are using!

NOAA - The National Weather Service

www.weather.com

The National Weather Service from the National Oceanic and Atmospheric Administration is a great site you can go to get updated weather warnings and forecasts. Insert your state to get up-to-date warnings for your area.

USGS - U.S. Geological Survey

http://www.usgs.gov/pubprod/

Buy directly from the U.S. Geological Survey. USGS topographical maps, aerial photographs, satellite images and other publications. You can even locate and download maps.

## Forums

Keep in mind that forums are full of egos, self-anointed experts, beginners, skilled people, and just about everything in between. I have been on some that will not tolerate an opinion different from those of the favorite members or "Super Moderators" who run the forum with an iron fist. Others tolerate various opinions, but don't have any members with a high degree of skill. Also keep in mind that when you ask a question on a forum, the answer may not be a correct one. It is an opinion of a member. Forums can be great places to learn new techniques and discover new ideas, but don't consider all information valid. Check it out and verify from various sources. I have found the following forums to be friendly, helpful, and have members with talent.

Dirttime - Survival and Self Reliance

www.dirttimeforum.com

This forum is hosted by Christopher Nyerges, Alan Halcon, Dude McLean and me, John McCann. There are a lot of talented members that are willing to share information.

The Survival Forum

www.forums.equipped.org/ubbthreads.php

This forum has been around a long time and is hosted by Equipped To Survive. It doesn't seem to have the ego problems associated with some of the other survival forums. Lots of information about survival kits.

## YouTube videos

Like all things on the web, YouTube has become a place for just about everyone to post videos, and survival is no different. Be careful and be selective. Keep in mind that videos can be posted by anybody and are. There are videos out there from professionals like Ray Mears, Dave Canterbury, Steve "Critr" Davis, IAWoodsman, and many others. But there are many that are not to teach, but to "show what I am doing." I have seen excellent information, information that is copied and regurgitated, and information that is just wrong. So as usual, use caution, especially with survival skills!

# SKILLS TO
# SAVE A LIFE

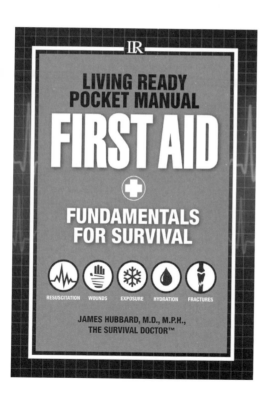

Medical emergencies are unplanned and unpredictable, but you can be prepared! Dr. James Hubbard presents first aid basics for situations like dehydration, exposure, foot injuries, fractures and sprains, and flesh wounds, and shows you how to be prepared should any of these emergencies occur. Know the steps you need to take in order to ensure a victim's survival, learn what to put inside a survival first-aid kit, and ultimately prepare for the unexpected. Should a medical emergency arise, keep this guide in hand and you'll be ready.

ISBN10: 1440333548
Retail: $12.99